# JUVENILE OFFENDERS

# JUVENILE OFFENDERS

*By*

**CLYDE B. VEDDER, Ph.D.**
*Professor of Sociology*
*Northern Illinois University*
*DeKalb, Illinois*

*With Forewords by*

**John A. Troike**
*Chairman, Youth Commission*
*State of Illinois*

*and*

**Donal E. J. MacNamara**
*Dean, New York Institute of Criminology*
*New York City*

CHARLES C THOMAS · PUBLISHER
*Springfield · Illinois · U.S.A.*

*Published and Distributed Throughout the World by*
CHARLES C THOMAS • PUBLISHER
BANNERSTONE HOUSE
301-327 East Lawrence Avenue, Springfield, Illinois, U.S.A.


Library of Congress Catalog Card Number: 62-17617



*Printed in the United States of America*

To the many dedicated colleagues in Penology, Criminology and Police Administration, who have contributed so much to our fund of knowledge.

To the many dedicated colleagues in Penology, Criminology and Police Administration: who have contributed so much to our fund of knowledge.

# FOREWORD

Of major concern to all America today is the increasing number of young people in trouble. Communities, states, and the nation as a whole have awakened to the immediate necessity of facing up to the problem with every available resource; of studying and analyzing methods; of evaluating procedures and developing new techniques.

Prevention of delinquency, measured by any standard, is still much more economical and practical than correction. The cold fact remains, however, that more and more young men and women each year are being committed to our correctional institutions as adjudicated delinquents. We are told that 3 out of every 100 youngsters between the ages of 10 and 17 will go before the court and be adjudged delinquents this year, and that one out of every nine young people in this vulnerable age group has a delinquency record.

Countless books have been written on the subject of delinquency, and scores of "experts" have come forth with programs and theories for the solution of the problem. Although nearly all are in agreement that there is no simple panacea for a problem with so many ramifications, still many praiseworthy ideas have been presented, and many practical procedures have been suggested. It is hoped that the quest for answers to the complex problems of delinquency prevention, correction, and complete rehabilitation will be a never ending one, and that persons with workable solutions will continue to share them.

*Juvenile Offenders* should prove a valuable resource not only to students but to practitioners in correctional work, in probation, parole, and law enforcement. In this very thorough treatment of the subject, special emphasis is placed upon the role of the court, and on programs which have been effectively tested and demonstrated.

The book is the product of a practical man, who believes in taking a down-to-earth approach to the problem. No mere theorist, Dr. Vedder is a realist who combines a rich academic background with many years of grassroots experience in community work and in juvenile institutions. He has prepared an outstanding document which is concerned with the *real, genuine* delinquent as distinguished from the neglected, abandoned, or poverty-stricken boy or girl.

Dr. Vedder points up the need for juvenile courts to concentrate on this "real delinquent," rather than dissipating their services by attempting to process emotionally and economically handicapped youth who might be better served by other agencies. At the same time, he makes it clear that such other agencies are not normally equipped to treat the needs of the youth with criminal inclinations.

*Juvenile Offenders* is destined to become a significant reference book for all those who would know more about current findings in this field, and a guidebook for those seeking practical solutions to the problem.

JOHN A. TROIKE
*Chairman*
*Youth Commission*
*State of Illinois*

# FOREWORD

It is not the function of an introductory comment such as this to discuss exhaustively either the general problem of juvenile delinquency or any one or a number of its constituent elements—nor yet to summarize, synopsize or evaluate the author's approach. Rather I think it is appropriate in an introduction to raise questions, stimulate thought, posit controversial opinions, and so direct the reader-student to seek answers, explanations and enlightenment both in the text and in independent study. I shall therefore, although I recognize all too clearly the importance and seriousness of the problem of juvenile sociopathy in our twentieth century America, play "devil's advocate" for our modern youth, including the delinquents, and posit ten interesting premises which all who deal with this inordinately complex and difficult area of social pathology might do well to keep in mind—even though they may not accept as factual some or all of the premises or the reasoning which supports them.

*Premise 1*—Neither human nature nor the characteristics, drives and conduct of boys and girls have changed significantly through the centuries . . . modern youth is no worse and no better than the youngsters of any preceding generation. As one who has approached behavioral phenomena in their historical framework, I have learned that each generation has suspected (or alleged) that the succeeding generations somehow had lost, rejected or discarded the sterling virtues of their ancestors and were proceeding toward perdition at an accelerated rate. I have a thick folder of quotations, some hundreds and others thousands of years old, which with no change whatsoever could be inserted into one of the "I view with alarm. . ." diatribes about the juveniles of today. Castigating the young is not seldom a product of the envy and misunderstanding of those who resent the loss of their youthful zest and virility—or who perhaps suffered unfortunately an unhappy adolescence.

*Premise 2*—While crime statistics in general are inadequate, delinquency statistics are frequently so distorted, manipulated and misinterpreted—and so fraught with "built-in" error—as to be almost useless. Statistical tables which lump together murder and truancy, swiping apples with armed robbery, rape with adolescent sex experimentation, and malicious assaults and property destruction with normal juvenile horseplay are at best suspect. When one then confuses the number or percentage of juveniles arrested with the number or percentage of persons who may have committed the specific offense studied (and forgets that the juvenile offender is far more susceptible to arrest than is the more experienced adult criminal in the same category)—or when one ignores, as some statistics compilers do, the many differences in the age limitations and the prohibited acts which might lead to categorization as a delinquent in the various jurisdictions—or when one fails to take into account Parkinson's principle that the work-load expands to fill the time of the staff available and so study the ratio between statistical increases in delinquency and increases in staff of juvenile courts and police juvenile bureaus—then indeed does the problem of juvenile delinquency assume mammoth proportions.

*Premise 3*—Adjudications of delinquency in juvenile courts are quite frequently made on "evidence" which would be either inadmissible or insufficient to support a finding of guilt in the trial of an adult charged with the same offense. The juvenile, neither entitled to nor supplied with a defense attorney, is thus often labelled a delinquent (and despite the fiction that such adjudication is not a conviction and that the record is confidential, the finding very often redounds to his future disadvantage) when there is neither a "preponderance of evidence" nor absence of "reasonable doubt"—and not unfrequently for a "crime" that would be no offense whatsoever if committed by one a few days or a few months older than this victim of society's solicitude for the welfare of the young.

*Premise 4*—Much so-called juvenile delinquency is in reality a healthy, normal response on the part of the juvenile to the negative circumstances which impinge upon him. Thus more frequently than not the runaway is escaping from intolerable home conditions which society is either unable or unwilling to correct; the truant is reacting to the boring, brutal or incompetent teacher—or to enforced attendance in a curriculum unsuited to his abilities, interests or needs; the young Negro, Puerto Rican, or Mexican, joining his peers in an anti-social gang, is reacting defensively to the ill-concealed hostility, often expressed in actual physical assaults, as well as the socio-economic discrimination of the dominant majority; and the girl or boy exploring extra-maritally the mysteries of sex is rejecting consciously or unconsciously the prurient-puritanical shibboleth, unique to our anti-sexual America, that an interest in the human body, made in the image and likeness of God, and in its physiological functioning is somehow dirty and delinquent.

*Premise 5*—Much juvenile delinquency is merely conduct imitative of adult behavior patterns, accepted as normal in our society but prohibited to those who have not as yet attained an age which differs from jurisdiction to jurisdiction. How one who has studied our divorce rate or the well-publicized adulteries of many Hollywood celebrities favorably regarded by large masses of our adult population—or who has assessed the billions expended annually on alcoholic beverages and gambling, legal and illegal—or who has evaluated the level of public and business morality (tax evasions, bribery, padded expense accounts, violations of the anti-trust laws, unkept campaign promises, etc.)—and who admits honestly that such conduct is not only seldom condemned or punished but is actually very often rewarded—can categorize youthful imitation of such accepted conduct patterns as delinquent and punishable—and seek the rehabilitation of the juvenile rather than of society—is to me one of criminology's minor mysteries.

*Premise 6*—Adults frequently label delinquent juvenile conduct which is qualitatively undifferentiated from the accepted conduct patterns of the older generation at a similar age level. We who danced the Charleston, Black Bottom and Bunny Hug fulminate with ill grace against the Twist, Madison and Rock'n'Roll; we who wore yellow oil-skins (inscribed with risque mottoes) and patent leather hair-styles (cemented to the scalp with vaseline) should find little fault with blue jeans and the duck-tail coiffure; and those of us who yodelled "Ta-Ra-Ra-Boom-De-Ay," "Blue Bananas," and other classics have little cause to look askance at the "meaningless" lyrics of the modern adolescent's hit parade. To translate our lack of appreciation for and disapproval of these peculiarities of the young into a charge that these differential preferences are symptoms of delinquency and degeneracy (and to demand that school and police officials enforce our "dated" tastes) requires both a degree of self-righteousness and a lack of self-knowledge wholly inappropriate to objective observers of social phenomena.

*Premise 7*—Youngsters from minority groups and from the socially and economically under-priviledged classes are disproportionately represented in our delinquency statistics. The invisible or hidden delinquencies of the more favored juveniles in suburbia, our colleges and prep schools seldom result in formal police or court records; and the differential tolerance patterns which not only permit but encourage riots and property destruction by, for example, college boy mobs while condemning similar aggressive outbursts by the less-advantaged serve to reinforce the already paranoid hostility of the latter toward a society which accepts so negative a differential.

*Premise 8*—Neither our juvenile institutions nor our extra-institutional preventive and/or rehabilitative programs—nor the more punitive and repressive campaigns favored by the neanderthal sub-stratum in some of our communities—can claim much success in coping with the juvenile problem. With few exceptions our reform schools prepare their alumni for successful post-graduate careers in our penitentiaries while our out-patient facilities succeed only rarely in adjusting or conforming their clientele to what is in so many cases an abnormal environment. Few institutions, police or probation services are provided with sufficient funds, professional staff, and public understanding and support to carry on other than a holding operation—while astronomical sums are appropriated for programs of questionable importance and necessity, the agencies concerned with the juvenile problem must usually make do with wholly inadequate budgetary allottments. Compounding this problem is the rejection by many agencies and workers in the field of approaches which give promise of somewhat greater success than our present abortive efforts. Medical research has abundantly demonstrated that early diagnosis is basic to a favorable prognosis—yet the behavioral research of the Gluecks, of Wilkins, Kvaraceus and others, which has indicated that by the use of intelligently interpreted experience tables, predictive devices can be constructed which will differentiate at an early age the potential true delinquent (from the normal youngster who may occasionally offend adventitiously) and permit social interposition to interrupt his well-outlined progress toward a criminal career, has been attacked and rejected without adequate study. The energies expended in decrying and resisting the utilization of these early diagnostic-predictive techniques might better, especially in view of our admitted minimal success with traditional approaches, be employed in applying, testing, evaluating and improving the suggested scales or in developing new and better early diagnostic devices.

*Premise 9*—We have imposed consistently more restrictive limitations on our youngsters while at the same time exposing them to increasingly more attractive temptations inconsistent with the imposed restrictions—and we have subjected them to a longer and more terrifying experience of threatened mass annihilation than has been the lot of any previous generation. No longer can the youngster unhappy at home, or unsuccessful in school, or bursting with a lust for adventure and independence escape the bonds by running away, getting a job, going to sea, joining the army—but he can find substitute escapes in alcohol and narcotics. Compulsory education, child-labor, and similar elemosynary legislation protects the young from abuse and exploitation—but too rigid an application of such laws has contributed in no small part to the magnification of the delinquency problem.

*Premise 10*—Sparing the rod does not spoil the child. If there is one thing I have learned in dealing with the more serious delinquents it is that they have been subjected either by their parents or those in authority who stood in loco parentis to far more than their fair share of physical abuse—and they have almost to a man denied their needed allotment of affection, sympathy and understanding. A return to corporal punishment in our homes, schools and institutions as has been advocated by many "arm-chair" criminologists will not only fail to stem the tide of delinquency but will insure an even more hostile and maladjusted generation—we might as reasonably campaign for a regression to the days of the pitch-cap, the rack, and the ingenious, but non-rehabilitative, medieval tortures.

There are few students of juvenile sociopathy so well-equipped as Dr. Vedder to discuss these controversial premises and to introduce both the student and the practitioner to the many complexities of this seemingly insoluble social problem. A thoroughly sound academic criminologist, humane, sympathetic and understanding, he is at the same time practical and realistic. With a scientific objectivity that admits of neither cynicism nor sentimentality, he balances a paternal concern for the maladjusted and misunderstood juvenile, at war with "a world he never made," with a mature recognition of the right to security of the law-abiding members of our society. He recognizes full well the need for an individualized approach to the potential or overt delinquent but does not ignore the more generalized responsibility of the police and the courts to enforce the penal laws, maintain public order, and protect life and property. And finally he is all too aware of the extensive gap which yawns between what we have been saying we would like to do (or in some cases claiming we are doing) and what is actually being done in preventing delinquency and in rehabilitating delinquents.

Donal E. J. MacNamara
*Dean, New York Institute of Criminology*

# PREFACE

THE CHIEF AIM of this book was to produce a shortened, yet an up-to-date version of the author's *The Juvenile Offender.* Present-day trends seem to indicate a preference for brevity and compactness in texts concerned with the field of Criminology and Juvenile Delinquency.

Because the author is so indebted to the writers and their publishers who permitted the inclusion of articles in *The Juvenile Offender,* an attempt was made to preserve the more pertinent contributions in this text by *summarizing* their thought as succinctly as possible. Many of these former contributors were so-called "practical men" as distinguished from academicians, and their insightful observations that characteristically are not exploited in the classroom are again made available to the student of today. Mere passage of time has not necessarily dimmed the validity of their observations.

The author is particularly indebted to Random House, Inc., who so graciously relinquished copyright privileges, that this abbreviated version of *The Juvenile Offender* might once again appear in print. In addition, large segments of the author's remarks in *The Juvenile Offender* appear almost verbatim in this new effort. This cooperation from Random House, Inc., is deeply appreciated.

Since *The Juvenile Offender* first appeared in 1954, there seems to be no discernible slackening in the incidence of juvenile delinquency and criminality. In the 1960 report from the Federal Bureau of Investigation, over half of the major crimes—burglary, automobile theft, larceny—were committed by those under twenty-one years of age.

As a result of the absolute and relative increase of youthful criminality, public interest and concern is noted in all levels of government—local, state and federal. The need for a Federal Program to control and prevent juvenile delinquency was recognized on May 11, 1961 when President John F. Kennedy established the President's Committee on Juvenile Delinquency and Youth Crime, naming the Attorney General as Chairman and the Secretary of Labor and the Secretary of Health, Education and Welfare as the other two members. To assist in this task the committee has the services of a Citizens Advisory Council composed of twenty-one members representing both public and voluntary organizations.

In transmitting his message, the President stated that "Juvenile delinquency and youth offenses diminish the strength and vitality of our Nation; they present serious problems to all the communities affected; and they leave indelible impressions upon people involved which often causes continuing problems." Through the authorization of ten million dollars for each of three fiscal years ending June 30, 1964, Congress has now made it possible for the Federal Government to become a partner with the States and local communities in finding solutions to the spread of delinquency.

Juvenile delinquency and criminality continues to be a frustrating social problem. It is hoped that this condensed text of juvenile delinquency will appeal to the busy practitioner in probation, parole and law enforcement; the layman, the teacher and the University student.

C.B.V.

# CONTENTS

# CONTENTS

# JUVENILE OFFENDERS

1

# THE JUVENILE OFFENDER

EVERY YEAR TENS of thousands of American boys and girls get into trouble. Most boys and girls, with little or no outside help, conform to society's rules and grow into good citizens; but others, too many of them, continue to pursue the practices that lead to delinquent careers. They could be the professional criminals of tomorrow.

There is no need to dwell upon the current deep concern over "juvenile delinquents," as these young people have come to be known. Sometimes this concern expresses itself in such questions as these: Why does one boy steal a car and another refuse to commit any depredation? Why does one child become a thief and another in the same family a "pillar of the community?" Why does a son of a criminal father follow in his footsteps while his brother does not? Questions of this order that seek explorations of specific individuals' behavior are exceedingly difficult to answer without careful *psychological* study. Questions of another type—why, for example, are the delinquency rates of this group or that relatively high or low? How do certain cultural and social conditions stimulate delinquent behavior? Why are rates going up or down or even sideways? What is wise and realistic policy in coping with juvenile delinquency and criminality?—which demand *sociological* answers. Some of these answers are developed in the pages that follow.

## THE MEANING OF DELINQUENCY

A very difficult problem in studying juvenile delinquency is deciding upon an exact definition of the term itself. No two authorities agree on this matter. In a broad sense, juvenile delinquency refers to the anti-social acts of children and of young people under a given age. Such acts are either specifically forbidden by law or may be lawfully interpreted as constituting delinquency or as requiring some form of official action. According to one authority, delinquency actually has many different meanings. There are *legal* delinquents (those committing antisocial acts as defined by law), *detected* delinquents (those exhibiting antisocial behavior), *agency* delinquents (those detected who reach an agency), *alleged* delinquents (those apprehended, brought to court), and *adjudged* delinquents (those found guilty).[1]

Juvenile delinquency is not a disease or a clinical entity. It is a descriptive term referring to a huge area of asocial and antisocial behavior. In most juvenile research, the term "juvenile delinquent" denotes a child who has been *officially* acted upon by the courts, the *adjudged* delinquent.

The age which the term "juvenile" covers varies in different states, with the upper limit ranging from the ages of sixteen to twenty-one, with the majority of states considering individuals as juvenile if they are under eighteen and over six. A Massachusetts law defines a juvenile delinquent as "a child between seven and seventeen who violates any city ordinance or town by-law or commits an offense not punishable by death." Under this law nearly every child within this age group range is, or will be, a delinquent-by-definition.

Professor Charles W. Coulter points out that a child who runs his bicycle on a stretch of sidewalk in a New Hampshire community becomes delinquent or an eight year old girl who lights a firecracker to celebrate the Fourth of July likewise is considered delinquent, hence the term "delinquency" is vague and the definition stuffy and cockeyed.[2] Bloch and Flynn prefer the British common law definition of delinquency as "any act, that if committed by an adult, would be considered criminal." In the United States, there are too many purely moral judgments as "wilful disobedience," "incorrigibility," "stubbornness," "associating with vicious persons," and similar terms upon which there can be no general agreement. Community attitudes and policies of referral are often acted upon selectively by sex, age, and offense. As a rule, the community only reacts if the behavior is dramatic or bizarre.[3]

Sophia M. Robison avers that "delinquency" is an umbrella term for a wide variety of socially disapproved behavior varying with time, place, and administrative attitudes, as well as extra-legal definitions put out by "experts" (parents, teachers, phychiatrists, social workers, preachers, and judges) that are often inconsistent and sometimes mutually exclusive. Delinquency is *any* behavior which a given community at a given time considers in conflict with its best interest whether or not the offender has been brought into court.[4] Ruth S. Cavan has indicated how little use laws are in defining juvenile delinquency. Children are delinquent if they break any law designed to control adult behavior, but the child gets into trouble with police and courts under indefinite parts of the law. Illinois law includes in its definition of delinquency, a child who is incorrigible or growing up in idleness, who wanders about the streets in the nighttime without being on lawful business, or is guilty of indecent or lascivious conduct. In New Mexico, a child is a delinquent who "habitually" refuses to obey his parents, or who is "habitually" wayward, disobedient or uncontrolled. How often may a child perform an act before it is considered "habitual?" Exactly when does misbehavior become delinquent behavior? Are there gradations in delinquency? If delinquent behavior has "gradations does good behavior have gradations? [5]

While the term "juvenile delinquency" has probably been in use less than one hundred years, juvenile misconduct has been the concern of society since records have been kept. Teeters and Reinemann illustrate this by a quotation allegedly attributed to Socrates:

> The children now love luxury. They have bad manners, contempt for authority, they show disrespect for elders and love chatter in place of exercise. They no longer rise when their elders enter the room. They contradict their parents, chatter before company, gobble up dainties at the table, and tyrannize over their teachers.[6]

Judging from the past, the delinquent seems destined to be in evidence in the distant future, as connoted in the term "Der Goettlich Schelm" or the "eternal delinquent."[7]

The legal status of juvenile delinquency was created to remove the child from the classification of criminal and convict, to provide specialized courts so he would not lose citizenship rights, not be barred from military service or from holding public office.

The "delinquency status" was originally designed to be protective, but the public now attaches stigma to juvenile delinquency as it does to criminality. The innocent word "juvenile" connotes badness and to reformatory inmates, the term is synonymous with disobedience, defiance, toughness and troublemaking. What is significant is the frequency and persistence of the misbehavior and its seriousness. The attitude toward delinquency is more important than a definition of delinquency, about which there appears to be little consensus.[8]

Of course, real delinquents do exist. Moreover, it should not be forgotten that it will take more than semantic magic to solve the problem of juvenile delinquency. There *are* genuine delinquents. Realistic sociologists may not agree with the pious and frequently not insincere expression that "there is no such thing as a bad boy," only an emotionally disturbed child or an unhappy one. But when a boy strikes and permanently injures an old man merely because he wants to steal some cigarettes from his shop, or when a boy attacks and injures a young girl merely to satisfy his own selfish desires—such a boy is "bad"—or perhaps there needs to be a new interpretation for "badness."

The complexity of "delinquency" is further emphasized by the fact that it may mean one thing morally, something else legally, something different practically, and another thing statistically. It seems impossible to define the term so that it will satisfy all interests.

According to Peter Lejins, there are two basic types of delinquent behavior: the *conformist* delinquent (the child learns delinquent behavior from other members of his own primary group), and the *non-conformist* delinquent (the child is a rebel against his law-abiding primary group). These delinquent behavior systems appear relatively seldom in pure form, since the majority of actual cases is usually located somewhere between.[9]

There is great variety of offenses among the various states that encompass juvenile delinquency. Sussman lists such offenses by their order of frequency as they occur in the various state statutes:

1. Violates any law or ordinance.
2. Habitually truant.

3. (Knowingly) associates with thieves, vicious or immoral persons.
4. Incorrigible.
5. Beyond control of parent or guardian.
6. Growing up in idleness or crime.
7. So deports self as to injure or endanger self or others.
8. Absents self from home and without consent.
9. Immoral or indecent conduct.
10. (Habitually) uses vile, obscene or vulgar language.
11. (Knowingly) enters, visits house of ill repute.
12. Patronizes, visits policy shop or gaming place.
13. (Habitually) wanders about railroad yards or track.
14. Jumps train or enters car or engine without authority.
15. Patronizes saloon or dram house where intoxicating liquor is sold.
16. Wanders streets at night, not on lawful business.
17. Patronizes public pool room or bucket shop places.
18. Immoral conduct around school.
19. Engages in illegal occupation.
20. In occupation or situation dangerous or injurious to self or others.
21. Smokes cigarettes, or use tobacco in any form.
22. Frequents place whose existence violates law.
23. Is found in place for permitting which adult may be punished.
24. Addicted to drugs.
25. Disorderly.
26. Begging.
27. Uses intoxicating liquor.
28. Makes indecent proposal.
29. Loiters, sleeps in alleys, vagrant.
30. Runs away from state or charity institution.
31. Operates motor vehicle dangerously while under influence of liquor.
32. Found on premises occupied or used for illegal purposes.
33. Attempts to marry without consent, in violation of law.
34. Given to sexual irregularities.

The intent of this exhaustive list is to protect minors, yet at same time delimits the rights of minors, making illegal activities as in items 5, 15, 17, 20, 21, 27, which are permitted to adults. Thus juvenile delinquency as a legal status combines characteristics of social protection and restriction.[10]

Important as may be the information concerning the delinquents who come under the official custody of society, an adequate picture of juvenile delinquency is still unavailable. The recorded delinquency cases are only a known fraction of those actually existing. The majority of delinquents solve their own problems without the ministrations of the court, the clinic, or the psychiatrist.

Delinquency varies from place to place, time to time, season to season and year to year. What is considered delinquency in one state is not delinquency in another state. Although the fundamental difference between adult crime and juvenile delinquency appears to be chronological, it must be noted that many trivial or "immoral" acts that are forbidden to delinquents are not forbidden to adults, such as smoking, drinking and the like. Juvenile offenders have only one thing in common—they got into conflict with the law.

## THE NATURE AND CAUSE OF DELINQUENCY

Many approaches have been explored in an effort to secure information revealing the nature and causes of juvenile delinquency. Among these are the *legalistic* approach (the juvenile treated as an adult offender, based on the assumption that age is a correlative of increasing responsibility), the *individual* approach (a case study method), the *group* approach (a study of gangs and other youth groups, with implications for the delinquent or studies of delinquency in relation to social situations), the *cultural* approach (the effects of culture conflicts and culture contacts on the delinquent), and the *ecological* approach (the study of spatial and temporal factors as they are related to the physical setting).

The approach, however, generally followed over the years has been *"hit-or-miss."* Authorities continue to attack with panaceas the problems of juvenile misbehavior which persist despite the rush to construct various recreational facilities with the hope that these will alleviate the situation. Failure of one approach after another continues to breed more failure. Youth still comes before the bar of justice.

There seem to be nearly as many "causes" of juvenile delinquency as there are individuals who have studied the problem. Delinquency has been attributed to bad companions, adolescent instability, mental conflicts, extreme social suggestibility, early sex experience, love of adventure, motion pictures, school problems, poor recreation, excessive street life, vocational dissatisfaction, sudden impulses, bad habits, obsessive ideation, poor physical structure, ill health, or premature puberty. Yet most children have experienced one or more of these "causes" and have never become officially delinquent.

As Lejins has indicated, searching for "causes" is apt to be disappointing as far as juvenile delinquency is concerned. A lifetime is not long enough to familiarize oneself with the writing available on the subject of juvenile delinquency and criminality. The great mass of research on this subject appears to be in a state of confusion.[11]

Most delinquents who come before the courts are underprivileged children from impoverished, overcrowded homes in deteriorated neighborhoods, where they run in gangs from whom they learn to steal and to rob. Does one conclude from this that poverty, slums, and bad companions are the causes of delinquency? If this is so, then why is everyone who is poor and who lives in slum areas not delinquent? Many delinquents are undernourished and are undersized; they have physical defects or they are mentally deficient. Is delinquency then caused by a physical condition or mental deficiency? Again, if this is true, how do you account for the many healthy, bright delinquents—the college graduates who are in the penitentiaries? One hears about the pernicious influence upon children's behavior of the radio, the motion pictures, and comic book crime thrillers. Still, a multitude of children are exposed to such items of popular culture every day, yet they never commit a delinquent act that gets them into trouble. A large proportion of delinquents come from miserable homes, broken homes, homes in which discord is rife. Can it be that the cause of delinquency is bad home environment? Then why does one child become a thief and another in the same family become a useful citizen? These questions, of strategic importance in the study of the causation of delinquency, are raised by Edith K. Lesser in a provocative discussion.[12]

To understand the delinquent fully it is imperative that information be secured concerning his physical structure, his intellectual abilities, his family background, his family relationships, his school, his neighborhood, his playmates, his interests and his activities. Even more important is the knowledge of how he feels and thinks about these things, because ultimately reformation must come from within.

Jerome E. Bates indicates that those of psychiatric orientation are critical of efforts to fix the etiology of delinquency in such social factors as "the broken home," "habits of thought," "incompetent or indifferent parents," "evil associates" and "inadequate supervision." Millions of persons experience these social situations and do not become criminals. Important questions to ask would be: "Why did the defendant commit the act?" "What personal needs and urges in him were satisfied by its commission? Experiences, particularly those which were charged with painful emotion and have since been repressed are of especial importance in understanding motivations of delinquency.[13]

According to David Abrahamsen, M.D. delinquency and crime are a product of the person's tendencies and the situation of the moment, interacting with his mental resistance. Letting "C" stand for crime, "T" for tendencies, "S" for situation, and "R" for resistance, the following formula is derived:

$$C = \frac{T + S}{R}$$

"T" represents not only aggressive tendencies but also aggressive inclinations of an indirect nature, as projections, protest reactions, or excessive motor activity.[14]

Leontine R. Young directs attention to the fact that juvenile delinquents *are* children who far too many in authority apparently have forgotten. Behind the delinquency, behind the mask is a hurt and miserable child, twisted by violence, stunned by hate and blinded by fear. As adults, our concern is not for the child but for his behavior. We ask of him conformity, but do not inquire into his unhappiness and proceed on the naive premise that a delinquent child is simply "bad" because he wants to be, because he enjoys being that way. The commonly accepted theory that only by punishment and more punishment can "bad" children be made "good" should be questioned. Unless children are respected as individuals not much respect for adults may be anticipated.[15]

Hertha Terrasch, a physician, states that some form of delinquent behavior in children might be almost an expression of normalcy. Few adults would expect a child to be 100 per cent obedient, abiding by every rule and always doing what is expected of him. Every child has a delinquency potential, caused by strong selfish impulses which demand satisfaction and which are frustrated by social codes. The delinquent child is often the victim of the unhappy marriage of his parents.[16]

The legalistic point of view, as represented by Paul W. Tappan, states that despite all the idyllic euphemisms to the contrary that embellish the literature on rehabilitative therapy, the official delinquent implies involvement with the police, detention, court handling, correctional treatment, and a role and stigma that are ineradicably injurious. The child is not a delinquent unless the court has found him so.[17]

According to Martin H. Neumeyer, juvenile delinquency should be viewed as a social problem. Juvenile delinquency and adult crime are old problems which have increased in extent and intensity during recent years. Juvenile delinquency is sufficiently widespread to require concerted social action on the national, state and local basis.[18]

Delinquency results, one writer stresses, when there is a relative absence in the individual of internalized norms and rule governing behavior in conformity with the norms of the social system to which legal penalties are attached. Delinquency may be seen as a functional consequence of the type of relationship established between the personal and social controls.[19]

In a more recent article, Reiss together with Albert Lewis Rhodes examine the social class structure of our society and point out the implications for theories of delinquency. It seems clear that there is no simple relationship between ascribed social status and delinquency. Both the status structure of an area and the extent to which delinquency occurs as a cultural tradition affect the delinquency life-chances of a boy at each ascribed status level. While the life-chances of low ascribed status boys becoming delinquent are greater than those of high status ones, a low status boy in a predominantly high status area with a low rate of delinquency has almost no chance of being classified a juvenile court delinquent. In this latter situation, the delinquency life-chances of a high status boy are greater than for low status boys. The delinquency life-chances of boys in any status group tend to be greatest in the lower status areas and in high delinquency rate areas. Reiss and Rhodes present the following conclusions:[20]

(1) There is more frequent and serious delinquent deviation in the lower than in the middle stratum when the self-reports of delinquent deviation by boys are examined.
(2) The career oriented delinquent is found only among lower class boys.
(3) Peer oriented delinquency is the most common form of delinquent organization at both status levels.
(4) The major type of lower status boy is a conforming non-achiever while the conforming achiever is the major type in the middle class.
(5) Conformers are more likely to be isolates than are non-conformers; the lone delinquent is infrequent in a population of boys.

Another insightful "explanation" of juvenile delinquency is suggested by David Matza and Gresham M. Sykes in that a number of supposedly delinquent values are closely akin to those embodied in the leisure activities of the dominant society.

> Current explanations of juvenile delinquency can be divided roughly into two major types. On the one hand, juvenile delinquency is seen as a product of personality disturbances or emotional conflicts within the individual; on the other hand, delinquency is viewed as a result of relatively normal personalities exposed to a "disturbed" social environment, particularly in the form of a deviant sub-culture in which the individual learns to be delinquent as others learn to conform to law.

> This image of delinquents and the larger society as antagonists can be misleading. Many delinquents . . . are essentially in agreement with the larger society, at least with regard to the evaluation of delinquent behavior as "wrong."
>
> Rather than standing in opposition to conventional ideas of good conduct, the delinquent is likely to adhere to the dominant norms in belief but render them ineffective in practice by holding various attitudes and perceptions which serve to neutralize the norms as checks on behavior. "Techniques of neutralization" such as the denial of responsibility or the definition of injury as rightful revenge, free the individual from a large measure of social control.[21]

It is generally agreed that no child is *born* a delinquent. Delinquency is acquired through the learning process and is a form of social behavior. The alleged delinquency of youth is often the reflection of his adult surroundings . . . perhaps better said, the sum total of the transmitted patterns from these surroundings, and the influence of response-tendencies that help shape his personality. Juvenile delinquency may not be the real issue under discussion; it may well be adult personal and social disorganization.

J. Edgar Hoover stated in *This Week* magazine on October 26, 1958 that "delinquency is now a world-wide disease . . . self-indulgence and principle of pleasure before duty are on a vast and growing scale . . . there has been enough talk already, now it is time for action." In the editorial section of the National Probation and Parole *News,* May, 1957, Hoover espoused a newer attitude toward juvenile criminality when he stated:

> Are we to stand idly by while fierce young hoodlums, too often and too long, harbored under the glossy misnomer of juvenile delinquents, roam our streets and desecrate our communities? If we do, America might witness a resurgence of the brutal criminality and mobsterism of a past era. Gangstyle ferocity, once the evil domain of hardened adult criminals, now centers chiefly in cliques of teen-age brigands. No longer can we tolerate the "tender years" alibi for youthful lawbreakers.

Since juvenile delinquency is increasing both relatively and absolutely, year after year, it is suggested that the scope of delinquency be narrowed to the more serious violations. Terms laden with moral freight, such as "incorrigibility," "stubbornness," "associating with evil persons," "waywardness," and the like, as well as the lesser types of juvenile misbehavior of "running away" and "truancy" might well be stricken from our legal definitions of delinquency. Such minor infractions could be handled by social agencies, leaving the juvenile courts to process the felonies committed by youth. Within this narrower band of felonious juvenile misconduct, the chances that control, possibly prevention, of such juvenile criminality would be materially enhanced.

## REFERENCES

1. Carr, Lowell J.: *Delinquency Control,* New York, Harper and Brothers, 1950, pp. 89–92.
2. Coulter, Charles W.: *Federal Probation,* Vol. XII, September, 1948, p. 14.
3. Bloch, Herbert A. and Flynn, Frank T.: *Delinquency: The Juvenile Offender in America Today,* New York, Random House, Inc., 1956, p. 7.
4. Robison, Sophia M.: *Juvenile Delinquency: Its Nature and Control,* New York, Holt, Rinehart and Winston, Inc., 1960, pp. 3, 11.
5. Cavan, Ruth S.: Presidential Address, Midwest Sociological Society, Omaha, Nebraska, April 28, 1961.
6. Teeters, Negley K. and Reinemann, John Otto,: *The Challenge of Delinquency,* New York, Prentice-Hall, Inc., 1950, p. 29.
7. Illing, Hans: Book Review, *Der Goettiche Schelm, The Journal of Criminal Law, Criminology and Police Science,* Vol. 46, November-December, 1955, p. 543.
8. Diekhoff, Mrs. Vera J.: *What P.T.A. Members Should Know About Juvenile Delinquency,* Pamphlet, National Congress of Parents and Teachers, 700 No. Rush St., Chicago, Illinois, 1957, pp. 8-11.
9. Lejins, Peter: Pragmatic Etiology of Delinquent Behavior, *Social Forces,* Vol. 29, March, 1951, pp. 317–320.
10. Sussman, Frederick: *Law of Juvenile Delinquency* (2nd Ed., rev.) New York, Oceana, 1959, p. 21.
11. Lejins, Peter: *op. cit.,* p. 318.
12. Lesser, Edith K.: Understanding Juvenile Delinquency, *Federal Probation,* Vol. XIII, September, 1949, pp. 56–58.
13. Bates, Jerome E.: Abrahamsen's Theory of the Etiology of Criminal Acts, *The Journal of Criminal Law and Criminology,* Vol. XL, December, 1949, pp. 471–475.
14. Abrahamsen, David: *The Psychology of Crime,* New York, Columbia University Press, 1960, p. 37.

15. Young, Leontine R.: We Call Them Delinquents, *Federal Probation,* Vol. XV, December, 1951, pp. 9–13.
16. Tarrasch, M.D., Hertha: Delinquency, is Normal Behavior, *Focus,* Vol. 29, July, 1950, pp. 97–101.
17. Tappan, Paul W.: *Juvenile Delinquency,* New York, McGraw-Hill Book Company, Inc., 1949, p. 4.
18. Neumeyer, Martin H.: *Juvenile Delinquency in Modern Society,* Princeton, New Jersey, D. Van Nostrand Company, Inc., 1961, p. 4.
19. Reiss, Jr., Albert J.: Delinquency as the Failure of Personal and Social Controls, *American Sociological Review,* Vol. XVI, April, 1951, p. 196.
20. Reiss, Jr., Albert J. and Rhodes, Albert Lewis: The Distribution of Juvenile Delinquency in the Social Class Structure, *American Sociological Review,* Vol. 26, October, 1961, pp. 720, 732.
21. Matza, David and Sykes, Gresham M.: Juvenile Delinquency and Subterranean Values, *American Sociological Review,* Vol. 26, October, 1961, pp. 712–713. Also Gresham M. Sykes and David Matza, Techniques of Neutralization, *American Sociological Review,* Vol. 22, December, 1957, pp. 664–670.

2

# THE EXTENT OF JUVENILE DELINQUENCY

NOWHERE DOES the failure of crime control show up more clearly than among our youth. Even before World War II, national statistics indicated that some two million boys and girls below the age of twenty-one came to the attention of the police annually. Youths play a top-heavy part in the traditional crimes that feed the headlines and for which arrests are made. They frequently commit the familiar crimes against property, often with attendant violence, and their inexperience and lack of judgment make them relatively easy to apprehend.

According to Katherine B. Oettinger, Chief of the Children's Bureau, juvenile delinquency appears among the top three concerns of the American public. Only defense and peace rank higher. An increase in delinquency is hardly surprising in the wake of World War II and a period of rapid growth and development. There has been a ten year steady climb in the rate of juvenile delinquency and the general public have become alarmed. Over twenty bills concerned with some aspect of juvenile delinquency were introduced into the 86th Congress during 1959.[1]

The most reliable and comprehensive statistics on crime in the United States are published by the FBI in *Uniform Crime Reports*. Beginning in 1930, crime reports were solicited from police departments throughout this nation based on uniform classifications and procedures developed by the Committee on Uniform Crime Records, and International Association of Chiefs of Police. In that year, the FBI, on request of the above organization, assumed the role as the national clearing house.

The primary objective of the *Uniform Crime Reports* is to produce a reliable program of nation-wide criminal statistics for administrative and operational use of law enforcement agencies, provide meaningful data for other professionals with related interests in the crime problem and inform the average citizen of general crime conditions. A crime index is made up of seven selected offenses which are most apt to be known to police agencies: criminal homicide, forcible rape, robbery, aggravated assault, burglary, larceny and auto theft. These offenses are called "Index Crimes" (formerly Part I crimes). "Other Crimes" include those less likely to be known to the police, such as drunkenness, traffic violations, forgery and counter-feiting, prostitution, sex offenses, disorderly conduct, vagrancy, gambling, driving while intoxicated, parking violations, liquor law violations, carrying and possessing concealed weapons and formerly called Part II crimes.[2]

Most persons think of criminality in terms of Index Crimes which is the best available measure of the extent of general criminality. Hence, Index Crimes committed by juveniles is the best available measure of the extent of juvenile criminality.[3]

During the calendar year 1960, crime reports were received from 7700 law enforcement agencies representing 96 per cent of the total population of the United States. Not all crimes come to the attention of the police. With 1,861,300 serious offenses reported in 1960, crime continued its upward surge, up 14 per cent over 1959. The first year of the 1960's recorded an all-time high, with 98 per cent more crime than in 1950. According to the *Uniform Crime Reports,* about every fifteen seconds, hour after hour and day after day, a crime of serious proportions—robbery, assault, burglary, rape, kidnaping, manslaughter, murder—is committed in the United States. Crime has increased, both relatively and absolutely, since the inception of the Uniform Crime Reports. More public agitation and increased police activity is a partial explanation of this phenomena.

According to the FBI, one person in every six arrested in 1946 had not reached the age of twenty-one. These minors made up half of all the arrests for auto theft, a third of all arrests for robbery, burglary and larceny; one in four was arrested for statutory and forcible rape, and one in eight for murder. In 1960, one person in less than five arrested had not reached the age of twenty-one. During 1960, these minors accounted for more than three-fourths of all the arrests for auto theft, nearly one half of the arrests for robbery, about two-thirds of the arrests for burglary.

Convicted adolescents constitute a large group in the prison population. New York State just before World War II, the youths between the ages of sixteen and twenty-one formed over 35 per cent of all admissions to prisons, reformatories, and institutions for defective delinquents. Crime as a habit evidently is generally acquired in youth. J. Edgar Hoover, head of the FBI, informed the Boy Scout convention at the New York World's Fair in 1939, that criminals out-numbered the 1,200,000 Scouts in the United States nearly four to one.

Since 1926, the United States Children's Bureau has been gathering data on cases from reports from juvenile courts which voluntarily submit them. These courts are largely located in the north-east-central geographic division of the United States. Scattered throughout the country there are about 3,000 courts which handle juvenile cases; and in the past quarter-century only about one-sixth of these have made reports. According to Sophia M. Robison—in some years, almost one-fourth of these reporting courts are located in one state—Connecticut.[4]

In 1954, the Children's Bureau report had data for only 586 courts out of over 3,000 juvenile courts, covered only 29 per cent of the child population, and omitted the states of New York and Massachusetts.

One survey made by a large metropolitan area revealed that six public agencies knew about twice as many delinquents as did the juvenile courts of that area. One Manhattan judge stated that hundreds of juvenile violators are not adjudicated only because they lacked institutional facilities, hence New York statistics may measure the public's unwillingness or inability to provide facilities. Anyway, delinquents are always other people's children.[5]

The Children's Bureau is constantly trying to improve its juvenile court statistics and in 1955 initiated a plan for collecting data from a national sample of 502 juvenile courts. The United States was divided into about 2,000 primary sampling units, which were then grouped into 230 strata, each consisting of a set of units as much alike as possible in such characteristics as regional location, population density, rate of growth, per cent of nonwhite population, principle industry, etc. From each stratum, a single primary sample unit was selected at random. This resulted in 230 sampling units in which there were 502 courts. The Bureau anticipates that all 502 courts will volunteer to participate. Once the sample plan is fully working, the Bureau will collect reliable information not only on the number of juvenile court cases but also on certain characteristics of children referred to court.[6]

There are many sources of error in the statistics of juvenile delinquency, such as deliberate suppression, failure to complain by the victim, differences in the application of legal processes within the same jurisdiction and outright duplicity. Due to the overcrowding of prisons in one state, the legislature changed some felonies to misdemeanors so some offenders could be sent elsewhere, and the public were informed of a sharp decrease in some types of felonies. One community cut juvenile delinquency rates 50 per cent by starting a "youth bureau" in the police department, and hence enabled to handle many cases unofficially, with only the flagrant violators processed by the police department *per se*. Actually, juvenile delinquency rates had increased 33 per cent, but the public were pleased with this "miraculous cure." Even if statistics were honest, they still indicate little or nothing, since the official public policy, nature of community standards, and the numerous variables make comparison difficult if not impossible.

The expression "the figures speak for themselves" does not apply to juvenile delinquency statistics or even suggest an hypothesis. Delinquency is so ambiguously defined that it is impossible to measure or categorize. Juvenile courts handle cases they are best equipped to handle, hence the attitude of the juvenile court judge, the philosophy of the court staff, especially in the "intake" department, the public temper, the number of community agencies determine the amount of juvenile delinquency.

Juvenile delinquency becomes for the most part, hidden delinquency. A Boston study revealed that in 1946, of some 6,416 infractions of the law by juveniles, only 95 were brought to official action. Over 600 of these infractions were considered to be serious, but only 68 of them were prosecuted.[8]

It has been generally "understood" that while all boys are delinquent at times, only the poor boys are hauled into court or committed to the reformatory. Much delinquent behavior is overlooked and many middle-class and upper class boys and girls have committed misdemeanors that could have brought them to the juvenile court. Short and Nye compared the misconduct of high-school students with the correctional-school students and found that the latter committed far more offenses and more serious offenses, than did the high school sample. To illustrate, about half the high-school students had truanted, but almost 100 per cent of the correctional school group has skipped school. Five per cent of the high-school boys contrasted with 90 per cent of the correctional-school boys had stolen things worth fifty dollars or more.[9] Discrimination against the "under-privileged" youngster may be less a fact than is realized at the present time.

According to Ronald H. Beattie, juvenile delinquency is usually defined to include a much broader area of deviate behavior than is included in adult crime. Juvenile delinquency statistics are much more incomplete and uncertain than adult criminal statistics, because a different type of behavior is included in the delinquency area and because there is more informality and discretion used in handling delinquent juveniles. No satisfactory agreement has yet been reached, even among law enforcement people, as to exactly what constitutes a juvenile arrest. There is a tremendous variation in what is reported, and it would appear at times that some communities have many times more juvenile delinquency than others merely because the definition of an arrest differs. The sources of local data for both juveniles and adults are the same at the police level, but the juvenile court laws that establish procedures to be followed in handling juvenile cases are state laws.[10]

In an effort to decrease the rising incidence of juvenile delinquency, considerable effort has been expended to identify potential delinquents by utilizing various prediction techniques, so that preventive services could be offered children before delinquent patterns became established. The best known is the Glueck Social Prediction Tables, in which a score of probable delinquency is assigned to each child on the basis of five factors in family life:

father's discipline, mother's supervision, father's affection for son, mother's affection, cohesiveness of the family. Other prediction techniques in this area that are frequently used are the KD Proneness Scale and the KD Proneness Check List, developed by Dr. William Kvaraceus; and the Minnesota Multiphasic Personality Inventory (MMPI), consisting of 550 statements which the respondent checks to indicate whether they apply to him. Results from these three instruments have not been encouraging.

The New York City Youth Board is making a study to test out whether the Glueck scale has predictive as well as post-dictive value. The claim of 90 per cent accuracy to date is open to serious question, both substantive and statistical. So far, the method is more accurate for predicting those who will not become delinquent than those who will, because the majority do not become delinquent. The problem common to all three prediction instruments demonstrates the vast difference between saying which *kinds* of children are most likely to become delinquent and saying which *children* will do so. The detected delinquent act may be part of a passing phase or become a continuous pattern. A good many of the so-called non-delinquents resemble the known delinquents in having indulged in delinquent behavior—and presumably in related traits. As Kvaraceus, among others, has commented, delinquent and non-delinquent behavior form a continuum rather than a dichotomy, and the cutting point is very hard to establish. The greatest problem shared by these predictive devices is that they over-predict, incorrectly labeling as pre-delinquent many children who do not merit that stigma.[11]

## AGE AND SEX

The age factor is a significant element in juvenile delinquency and criminality. The *Uniform Crime Reports,* which gives the arrests of all age groups, shows that the ages seventeen to twenty-one predominate in the frequency of arrests. Arrests of persons under eighteen more than doubled since 1950, while the population of youths, ages ten to seventeen, increased by less than one-half. For a number of years, crime has been increasing about four times faster than the rate of population increase.

In 1960, there were 215,868 arrests made of those under fifteen years of age. In that same year, two boys, fourteen and fifteen, were sentenced to twenty-five year terms in the State Penitentiary at Stateville, Illinois. The Criminal Code of Illinois, Section 571, stated that a person under the age of ten is incapable of committing a crime. Under the new, revised Criminal Code, the former age of ten has now been extended upward to age thirteen, the lowest age under which a child can not be charged with crime. The Chicago *Sun-Times* reported on April 23, 1961 that the youngest murder trial defendant in Illinois was Howard Lang, twelve, when he stabbed, and beat to death seven-year-old Lonnie F. in 1947 and was sentenced to twenty-two years in prison. Later, the Supreme Court of Illinois remanded his case on the ground he was unable to understand that he could be given a prison term when he pleaded guilty. Later, he was found "not guilty," but in another trial for beating a thirteen-year-old witness, was given a one-year sentence.

The Miami *Herald* on February 19, 1952 reported that there were 256 youths, ranging in ages from eight to eighteen, who were serving time in the State Prison at Raiford, Florida. Included in this sample were three boys, age fourteen, who were considered too "incorrigible" for the state correctional school. In the October 15, 1951 issue of *Time* appeared a report that police of an eastern city had arrested a six-year-old boy found playing on the floor of a meat market with sausages for a train. His gang had lowered him from the skylight, but the rope had broken. On the way to the station house, he remarked to the arresting officers: "this ain't the same auto you had last time when you arrested me." In one community in Ohio, police apprehended a thief having a record of twenty-eight previous offenses. He was caught with a younger brother in a river hideout. The culprit's age was seven.

Age, as a variable may contribute to situations that appear almost facetious. In Illinois, at one time the age limit of juvenile delinquency for boys was raised to eighteen because case loads of probation officers in the southern Illinois counties were too low. Subsequently, the age limit was reduced back to seventeen because the facilities in Cook County were becoming too overcrowded. The first change was the right thing for the wrong reason; the second change, the wrong thing for the right reason. In one Illinois hospital, the father was not permitted to visit his new-born baby unless accompanied by his parents, since he was only fifteen.

Even *one* year can make a great difference in the sentence for identical crimes. Robert L. Noble, Jr. reports a case where a young defendant robbed a United States postoffice using a gun. When captured, he stated his age was seventeen. Later, a certified copy of his official birth certificate indicated that he was actually eighteen years of age, and, if so, could not be considered as a juvenile within the meaning of the law and the Federal Juvenile Delinquency Act. In view of the fact that so much hinged on the birthday (twenty-five year sentence against a possible minority commitment of three years, seven months and twenty-seven days), every effort was made to determine the correct date of birth. Fortunately, the youth's original contention was substantiated.[12]

The law itself recognizes but one kind of age—the chronological age; ignoring the mental, emotional, biological and endocrinological ages. This is not a realistic policy, for some younger boys and girls are mature and sophisticated and far from childlike in their attitudes and actions. Many a boy or girl may be legally a child, but physically, emotionally, and even intellectually, an adult in attitudes and actions. Many eighteen year old boys are big, strong and dangerous and cannot be trusted in insecure custodial facilities. Some girls of that age are even more problematic than the boys.

Sex factors are significant in juvenile delinquency, as the sex ratio is about five boys to one girl. The girls tend to be concentrated in the same age periods as the boys, except there are fewer cases of girl delinquents in the pre-adolescent period. The sex ratio of those committing offenses has varied from time to time, and the ratio of males to females in police records is considerably greater than the ratio of boys and girls in juvenile court records.

The ratio of boys' and girls' cases handled by juvenile courts, according to Neumeyer, have ranged from four to one, to about five to one, but the ratios vary by types of offenses, types of courts handling cases, their procedures in dealing with individual cases and to some extent the kinds of areas in which the courts are located. Boys seem more inclined to steal, to commit offenses against the person; while girls are more inclined to stay away from school, run away from home, be ungovernable, and commit sex offenses. In nearly all classes of offenses, the total number of offenses by boys exceeds those of the girls.[13]

Under the law and as a basic tenet in the legalistic approach, age is assumed to be a correlative of increasing responsibility, but chronological age frequently fails as a reliable criterion of guilt. An eighteen-year-old boy has sexual relations with a fourteen-year-old girl of considerable experience, yet the boy is charged with statutory rape, and has a record which will last a life-time, while the guilty aggressor, the girl, may go free. Frequently, it is a question of "who raped whom," and one reason why statutory rape is no longer included in the Index Crimes of the *Uniform Crime Reports*.

According to Hertha Tarrasch, sex misbehavior is the leading problem in handling girls as far as clinics and social agencies are concerned. Agencies seem less afraid to deal with other antisocial tendencies, therefore more rehabilitation work is being done with boys than with girls. Everyone seems to regard adolescent girls with their sex problems as a special group, yet sex misbehavior is just as much a compensatory mechanism for anxiety and insecurity as are stealing, lying, bedwetting, or day-dreaming. While the delinquent boy fears he may be called a "sissy," or some term suggesting the lack of masculinity, for the girl, the important question is: "Am I attractive enough to please boys?" The sex-delinquent girl usually feels unable to compete with other girls, and gives in to sexual demands to prove she is adequate and able to compete successfully.[14]

While early sexual demoralization is not uncommon in the careers of the delinquents, *official* charges of sexual misbehavior do not appear with high frequency in the public records, except in the case of female offenders. In the Glueck study, only 3.6 per cent of the cases studied, all male, had been officially charged with sex offenses as compared with 59 per cent who had records of burglary and 58.4 per cent charged with larceny. The low incidence of sex offenses in this study is attributable in large part to the fact that most delinquencies committed by girls are sexual in nature, whereas those delinquencies committed by boys and young men are mostly nonsexual.

The relatively small number of cases brought before the courts for sex offenses is primarily a reflection of current court practice and community attitudes rather than an accurate index of the extent of sexual irregularity. The courts are apt to be indulgent of the male offender in respect to sexual lapses but severe in the handling of girls who have actual or suspected records of sexual freedom.

## MINORITY GROUPS

Adult attitudes of the larger community toward minority groups, particularly racial groups, add to the difficulties in dealing with juveniles. The tendency towards relatively high juvenile delinquency rates in certain minority groups may be explained by a number of conditions, including low economic status, bad housing, overcrowding, restricted employment opportunities, racial proscriptions, and intensified conflict between the older and newer generations.

In the years between 1880 and 1920, many authorities were concerned with the "criminality" of the immigrant or the children of the foreign-born. Since the passage of legislation in the early 1920's, which materially reduced the influx of immigrants, it must be recognized that most non-native Americans are past the middle years and their children are nearly all born in the United States. Studies conducted on the relationship between immigration and delinquency will rapidly become obsolete as first-generation, even second generation immigrants tend to disappear from the scene.

The number of children of foreign-born parents reported delinquent has dropped since the curtailment of immigration in 1922. Until this time, native-born children of immigrant parents, growing up in areas of cultural conflict, made a substantial contribution to the number of recorded juvenile delinquents. In 1930, about two-fifths of the girls and one-half of the boys were of foreign-born parentage. Today, the vast majority of offenders of both sexes, over 70 per cent are native-born of native-born parents.

Decrease in delinquency appears to occur in direct proportion to the assimilation of minority groups. The new marginal groups are those rural workers coming to such large industrial areas as Detroit, Chicago, and Los Angeles. On the labor market, the Negro might be considered the "new immigrant."

Negro convictions and imprisonment seem to be three to five times that of the white population when population proportions are equated. Negro children, because, in part, of the functions of bias, become delinquent officially at an earlier age than do white children. Negro rates of delinquency have mounted to quite large proportions during the last two decades. It is easier to arrest, convict, and incarcerate Negro children than white children. Frequently, Negro children are charged with offenses that would not be imputed to white children.

The social factors underlying Negro criminality are well stated by Davie as they affect and are affected by juvenile delinquency. He shows that in the cases handled by the juvenile courts Negro children appear more than three times as often as an analysis of the phenomenon would predict on a general population basis. In the distribution of offenses for which white and Negro children are brought before the courts, Negroes are more often guilty of stealing than of any other crime. A study of the disposition of these cases indicates that Negro boys are less likely to be dismissed for their offense than white boys and their commitment to an institution is more likely to occur. Cultural inferiority, economic pressure, and racial antagonisms play as important a part in Negro child delinquency as they do in adult crime.[15]

According to Wattenberg and Balistrieri, Negro youth guilty of car theft are relatively few. In a study of Detroit police records of 1,179 boys, it was found that during the period of ten to seventeen years of age, automobile thefts were proportionately three times as frequent among white boys as among Negroes. Police officials said that colored youngsters were almost sure to be challenged by parking-lot attendants and thus were barred from some opportunity to take cars. Also, squad-car crews are more prone to investigate credentials of Negro young people driving automobiles.[16]

According to Sidney Axelrad, the courts commit on a differential basis, in favor of the white group. At the time of the gathering of the case material for the study, Axelrad was a member of the Medical and Research Department, New York Training School for Boys, and found that Negro children are committed to a state institution as delinquents, younger, with fewer court appearances, less previous institutionalization, and for fewer and less serious offenses than white children. In contrast to the white delinquents, the Negro children came from homes where there was more death or deprivation of a parent, desertion, neglect, rejection, separation, and sexual promiscuity. Contrasted to the Negro delinquents, the white delinquents came from families where there was deficient discipline, language handicap, ethnic difference, and religious difference. Negro children came from more unstable homes and from homes with a different kind of family pathology than the white delinquents.[17]

Delinquency rates appear to be in part a function of ethnic and racial discrimination. In the December 13, 1954 issue of *Time,* a sheriff in a southern state posing as an expert in racial anthropology, challenged the right of five children to attend the local school, although officially listed as white children. His statement, "I don't like the shape of that one's nose" was sufficient "evidence" to cause withdrawal of the children from school. When the editor of the community paper tried to help this family, KKK crosses appeared on her lawn, her dog was poisoned, and KKK was smeared on the office windows. The family claimed Irish-Indian ancestry, but the sheriff opined that "there must have been a smoked Irishman in the woodpile."

The arrests by race of the offenders in 2,446 cities with populations over 2500, as reported in the *Uniform Crime Reports*[18] for 1960, revealed that of the 3,498,929 persons arrested during the year, the racial composition was as follows: White 2,320,635; Negro 1,064,814; Indian 71,662; Chinese 2,066; Japanese 5,570; and all others 34,179.

As Professor Neumeyer points out, only a few studies have been made of ethnic and racial differentiation in law violation. Some minority groups make up a greater percentage of the delinquent group than their proportion of the general population. Economic status, racial discrimination, amount of education, housing and other variables among subcultural groups may explain why Negro and Latin-American children seem to have higher rates of delinquency than do the children of the majority whites. As Negro population proportionately increases in a given area, the delinquency rate tends to decrease. The most populated Negro areas have the lowest delinquency rates, whereas in areas where Negroes are in the minority, the rates tend to be higher.[19]

## RURAL-URBAN DIFFERENCES

It is generally believed that cities have higher rates of delinquency than rural areas. Proportionately, more children are committed to correctional institutions as the density of the population increases. Various studies have tended to show rural delinquency to be somewhat less than urban delinquency per unit of population.

According to the *Uniform Crime Reports,* urban crime has had an upward climb. In most instances it was found that the larger cities had the highest crime rates. Although the chief concentration of offenses, both adult and juvenile, are in the larger urban centers, the next highest rates seem to fall in those rural areas converging about these urban areas. The more industrialized the rural areas the greater is the tendency to commit delinquent acts.

As for criminal behavior at both juvenile and adult levels, indications are that rural areas have lower rates than the urban areas for most offense classifications. On the basis of available data, it is estimated that the urban arrest rate for criminal offenses in general is about three times higher than the rural rate. It should be remembered, in considering this statistical contrast, however, that the rural reporting is not as complete as urban reporting. According to the FBI, in some instances it appeared that the reports used in preparing rural data may have been limited to cases in which arrests were made.[20] Although delinquency is still closely associated with urban life, rural trends toward delinquency appear to be increasing and are likely to continue to do so because of rapid modern industrial and social change.

Rural children as a whole fare worse in health than do city children. Selective Service experience of World War II found this to be true of educational and cultural advantages also. Apparently, fresh air, sunshine, and green meadows are not sufficient to guarantee health or to reduce delinquent behavior. As one rural girl phrased it, "Out here there's nothin' to do, and what there is to do, ain't decent."

It is difficult to make general estimates concerning the volume of juvenile offenses and the general trends since the beginning of this century. The FBI is fully aware that reports of crime submitted to them cannot be checked for accuracy or honesty and state in the *Uniform Crime Reports* that since the accuracy of the data depends upon the degree of sincere effort exerted by each contributor to meet the necessary standards of reporting. For this reason, the FBI is not in a position to vouch for the validity of the reports received.[21]

Some studies appear to bolster the opinion that the volume of delinquency for both sexes is increasing steadily. It seems that rural-urban differences are not as great in regard to crime and delinquency as in years past. As the processes of communication, mobility, and urbanization proceed, it is reasonable to assume that the gap in reported delinquency between urban and rural areas will continually diminish. From the available evidence it seems reasonable to conclude that little decrease in the extent and volume of delinquency can confidently be anticipated, but rather it might be expected that there will continue a gradual upward rise in the years that lie immediately ahead.

## REFERENCES


1. Bradbury, Dorothy E.: *The Children's Bureau and Juvenile Delinquency,* Children's Bureau Publication No. 1, Washington, D. C. 1960, (Foreword), p. iii.
2. Pittman, David J. and Handy, William F.: Uniform Crime Reporting: Suggested Improvements, *Sociology and Social Research,* Vol. 46, January, 1962, pp. 135–143.
3. Wilson, O. W.: How to Measure the Extent of Juvenile Delinquency, *The Journal of Criminal Law and Criminology,* Vol XL, November-December, 1950, pp. 637–650.
4. Robison, Sophia M.: Wanted-An Index of Crime and Delinquency, *Proceedings,* American Prison Association, 1945, pp. 203–213.
5. Short, Jr., James F. and Nye, F. Ivan.: Extent of Unrecorded Juvenile

Delinquency. Tentative Conclusions, *The Journal of Criminal Law, Criminology and Police Science,* Vol. 49, November-December, 1958, pp. 296–309.

6. Perlman, I. Richard.: Reporting Juvenile Delinquency, *National Probation and Parole Association Journal,* Vol. 3, July, 1957, p. 245.
7. Short, Jr., James F., and Nye, F. Ivan.: *op. cit.,* p. 308.
8. Murphy, Fred J., Shirley, Mary M. and Witmer, Helen L.: The Incidence of Hidden Delinquency, *American Journal of Orthopsychiatry,* Vol. 16, 1946, pp. 686–696.
9. Short, Jr., James F. and Nye, F. Ivan.: *op. cit.,* p. 303.
10. Beattie, Ronald H.: Criminal Statistics in the United States-1960, *The Journal of Criminal Law, Criminology and Police Science,* Vol. 51, May-June, 1960, pp. 49–65.
11. Herzog, Elizabeth: Identifying Potential Delinquents, *Children's Bureau* Publication No. 5, Washington, D. C. 1960, pp. 1–5.
12. Noble, Jr., Robert L.: What a Difference One Year Makes, *Federal Probation,* Vol. XIII, June, 1949, p. 49.
13. Neumeyer, Martin H.: *Juvenile Delinquency in Modern Society,* Princeton, New Jersey, D. Van Nostrand Company, Inc., 1961, pp. 40–41.
14. Tarrasch, M.D., Hertha: Delinquency is Normal Behavior, *Focus,* Vol. 29, July, 1950, p. 99.
15. Davie, Maurice R.: *Negroes in American Society,* New York, McGraw-Hill Book Company, 1949, p. 258.
16. Wattenberg, William W. and Balistrieri, James: Automobile Theft: A 'Favored-Group' Delinquency, *The American Journal of Sociology,* Vol. LVII, May, 1952, pp. 575–579.
17. Axelrad, Sidney: Negro and White Male Institutionalized Delinquents, *The American Journal of Sociology,* Vol. LVII, May, 1952, pp. 569–574.
18. *Uniform Crime Reports* for 1960, Table 20. Report released July 24, 1961, p. 95.
19. Neumeyer, Martin H.: *op. cit.,* p. 43.
20. *Uniform Crime Reports, op. cit.,* p. 16.
21. *Ibid.,* p. 28.

# 3

## ECONOMIC CONDITIONS AND FAMILIAL FACTORS

MORE THAN ANY other factor influencing delinquency, the economic conditions of the nation and changes in these conditions seem to exert the greatest power. The business cycles react profoundly upon delinquency trends. These economic swings are especially important as they directly affect the economic conditions of families and communities.

Thus it is that juvenile delinquency tends to follow the business cycle—up in prosperity, down in depressions. Less crime is committed by young persons during depression periods in part because families devise "fun" at home. There is less money for outside recreation and more parental supervision, since adults are less likely to work on "grave-yard" and "swing" shifts at the factory. Moreover, there seems to be a greater reluctance on the part of the complainants to press charges against children committing offenses during poor times. Tradespeople, especially, are more lenient in overlooking delinquent acts because they realize that the child who steals food may be hungry. Budget slicing of police personnel also means fewer chances of detection and apprehension of delinquency behavior. Therefore, Carr, writing about the 1930's, states that the reduction of delinquency during a depression may be due to: (1) changed attitudes, (2) decreased deviation pressures, and (3) increased out-of-court facilities.[1]

The contributions of poverty cannot be ignored in juvenile delinquency. Many child offenses against private property can be traced to economic causes, but usually causes other than sheer hunger or economic misery. To go through life forced to submit to an apparent substandard level of living is a dim prospect for most youths and sometimes will not be tolerated at any cost. Yet, in 1949, ten million families struggled to live on an income of less than $2000 per year, eight million individuals and families had an income of less than $1000 and five million persons who were able to work could earn no wages whatsoever.[2] In 1955, nearly one fourth of all families in the United States lived on a yearly income of less than $2500.

William A. Bonger (1876-1940), a widely known Dutch criminologist, conceived of crime as a social phenomenon, caused chiefly by adverse economic conditions. These, in turn, he believed, are the result of the pressures and abuses of the capitalistic system, which frequently lead individuals, particularly those belonging to the poorer classes, to delinquency and crime. The present economic system is based upon exchange and exchange isolates individuals by weakening the bond that unites them. The two parties interested think only of their own advantage even to the detriment of the other party.[3]

It is improbable that poverty is ever a direct cause of juvenile delinquency. Many of the most exemplary children come from the poorest homes. Temporary financial reverses, temporary unemployment seem to have no statistically demonstrable effect—good or bad. Only where both parents work out and the child is left unsupervised, especially at night, does the delinquency pattern develop.[4]

"Poverty" is not a monopoly of the lower classes. Members of the lower, even middle-middle categories often find themselves in straightened economic plights. However, the attitudes toward juvenile misbehavior are less lenient as one moves up the social scale. In this connection, the findings of Allison Davis and Robert J. Havighurst are significant, that middle-class families tend to rear their children more rigidly than do lower-class families and that differences in socio-economic status are more important in rearing than those of race. The rearing practices of middle-class Negro mothers tended to approximate the tightness of control by middle-class white mothers as opposed to the relative permissiveness of the lower socio-economic groups of mothers in both races.[5]

The *New York Times* reported in February 4, 1957 that one per cent of the New York families produced 75 per cent of the delinquency that was *officially* recorded. These families made up the "hard core" of the economically dispossessed, and virtually all were on welfare. Most truants are from poor families, too poor to go to school. Children confined in state industrial schools are for the most part from poverty-stricken homes.

Due to the press of economic circumstances, many juveniles attempt to assist their parents by taking various jobs in street trades or domestic service. One of the romantic stereotypes of life's success myth in the United States is the "little business man" newsboy who rarely becomes a business man. Actually, he runs afoul of the law more frequently than the nonworking child. It has been said that about 50 per cent of the inmates of Sing Sing prison once sold newspapers.

Street trades include street vendors, errand and delivery boys, as well as newsboys; the domestic service jobs include waitresses and housemaids. In the United States over 250,000 children under sixteen years old are employed in street trades and in domestic service. Domestic service constitutes an occupation of high moral risk for girls, not solely because of unprincipled male employers but also due to the cheaper types of commercialized recreation centers these workers characteristically frequent during their leisure hours. Domestic service has been termed an "occupational slum" since it is neither a profession, trade, nor a business. When working children are compared with nonworking children, from three to ten times as many children employed in the street trades and in domestic service become delinquent each year.

Contrary to public opinion, most children in the street trades tend to come from good homes which appear in the background of 65 per cent of the street vendors and bootblacks, 78 per cent of the messenger boys, and 78 per cent of the delivery and errand boys, according to Carr.

According to Wattenberg and Balistrieri, in their study of automobile theft, crime and delinquency may be culturally defined rather than culturally determined; it is not the fact of criminality but the form of it which varies with socioeconomic level. Thus we have burglars and embezzlers, holdup men and blackmarketeers, prostitutes and fashionable mistresses. The antisocial conduct of the "lower classes" often offends middle-class legal norms and may lead to prison terms and criminal records. The antisocial deeds of "respectable" folk appear less reprehensible and are more often "covered up." All this casts doubt on many research data by implying that we have not been measuring the extent of delinquency but only of the varieties we do not like. Among adults, "white-collar" offenses are difficult to establish. It is not unwarranted to assume that among juveniles there is much hidden misconduct analogous to adult "white-collar" crime.[6]

Automobile theft was found to be a "favored-group" delinquency, a "white-collar" juvenile delinquency. If a boy's friends got pleasure from riding in automobiles, he would oblige by "borrowing" a car. Similarly, an adult may find he can get along well in business by violating price controls or by bribing public officials. Boys who steal automobiles tend to come from neighborhoods rated "above average" by the police and not from areas rated as "slums."

The automobile-theft group came from racially homogeneous neighborhoods, tend to live in single-family homes, to come from homes not showing need of repairs, and to have only one parent employed. The Houston *Chronicle,* March 5, 1956 reported that ten Houston juveniles stole 4,500 hub caps in eighteen months, mostly Oldsmobile hub caps. All of the offenders lived with their parents in an upper-middle class subdivision. Many of the parents were professional people. One of the youths caught remarked: "What's the fuss about. Stealing hub caps is just a part of growing up."

Most of the studies made on the relationship between crime and economic factors have been concerned with adult crime rather than juvenile delinquency. As far as the *official* recorded juvenile delinquency is concerned, economic conditions, with the changes in society that these bring—about, seem to exert the greatest influence on juvenile delinquency trends.

## INFLUENCE OF HOME AND FAMILY

It is generally recognized that juvenile delinquent behavior is influenced by the physical condition of the dwelling, the slum type of neighborhood, the housing shortage. Mental attitudes are affected by physical surroundings, and the care and love of the parent for the child may be subjected to a severe strain due to conditions of bad housing. A "good home" is not a matter of wall paper, pretty rooms, solid furniture, or even cleanliness. Occasionally, welfare workers react in negative fashion to lower-class living conditions and when the report is read, the reader has a more accurate picture of the social investigator than of the home and the family that was interviewed.

Since most of our knowledge of behavior stems from family living, it is important to determine where the distortion took place, whether it is remediable, whether it is possible to treat an individual *invacuo:* i.e., without reference to past experience in a family constellation.[7]

As Carr has pointed out, every culture contains certain norms for home life. In the United States "normal" home life has been said to be characterized by seven fairly definite criteria: (1) structural completeness; (2) racial homogeneity, (3) economic security; (4) cultural conformity; (5) moral conformity; (6) physical and psychological normality, and (7) functional adequacy (emotional security).[8]

Some family homes seem to violate many of Carr's criteria. The January 30, 1956 issue of *Time* reported the following case. For killing a police officer H. was electrocuted at McAlester, Oklahoma. When H. was sixteen months old, his Uncle was electrocuted in Texas for murder of a prison guard. His mother shot her second husband to death, but was acquitted. When she shot her third husband, she received a five year sentence. His brother is now serving a ten year sentence for burglary, and another Uncle is serving life as an habitual criminal. His girl friend is in a West Virginia prison for car theft. His father pleaded with the Governor, but was escorted there from Paris, Texas by police because he is awaiting trial for burglary.

Despite adverse family conditions, delinquency and crime are social, not biological conditions, and many such family members manage to overcome these initial handicaps. At one time, considerable effort was made to trace the "bad" effects of heredity, and "bad" families as the Jukes, Kallikaks, Nams and Zeros to mention but a few, were used as the horrible examples of disorganized if not criminal family patterns. These were compared with a so-called "good" family, the Edwards family. But some of the "researchers" failed to disclose the fact that some of Jonathan Edwards' ancestors did have criminal records; his maternal grandmother was divorced on the ground of adultery, his grand aunt murdered her own son, his grand uncle murdered his own sister.[9]

Not all families residing in "delinquent areas" are derelict in their duty toward their children and there are "good boys" in delinquent areas. The outstanding characteristic of the family profile is the great personal interest in the children and supervision over them. The mothers knew the boy's friends and knew their whereabouts at all times, and insisted on having this knowledge. Nearly 80 per cent of the boys in one survey held remunerative jobs. These were the "insulated boys" and only a handful had delinquent friends.[10]

In some families, training and discipline are lax and juvenile delinquency has been defined as "the result of parents trying to train children without starting at the bottom." Such families may be embarrassed by mischievous pranks, which nevertheless may be potentially serious. The Arizona *Republic* (Phoenix), December 31, 1955 reported an instance of family embarrassment by a juvenile member. One youngster threw a note from the family automobile when leaving the Yuma, Arizona border inspection station, which read: "I am being kidnapt in a blue '53 Buick bearing Iowa license 1716107." Arizona law forces rolled into action and caught the car thirty-two miles East at Wellton. In the Buick were four children, mother and grandparents. All children denied writing the note, but a handwriting test betrayed the twelve year-old boy.

It cannot be overemphasized that a child's family is the most important influence in shaping his personality and character. In this profound primary group the child acquires his basic ideals and a sense of right and wrong. Here he first experiences social interaction and becomes conscious of standards, goals, values, and the formulation of judgments. Here he is a member of the cell-unit of society, the first stage upon which he learns to imitate his elders as he begins his awakening into a fuller knowledge of the world about him. Undoubtedly, the preeminent requisite for the prevention of delinquency is a stable and secure family.

The stable and secure family should address itself to the ten basic needs of children that have been listed by The National Association for Mental Health, Inc. of New York.[11] They are as follows:

1. *Acceptance:*
   Every child needs to believe his parents like him for himself; that they like him all the time and not only when he acts according to their ideas of the way a child should act; that they always accept him, though they may not always approve of the things he does.
2. *Control:*
   Every child needs to know there are limits to what he is permitted to do and that his parents will hold him to those limits; he must be taught self-control to avoid hurting himself and others when he feels jealous or angry.
3. *Faith:*
   Every child needs a set of moral standards to live by, a belief in human values, kindness, courage, honesty, generosity and justice.
4. *Guidance:*
   Every child needs to have friendly help in learning how to behave toward persons and things; grown-ups around him show by example how to get along with others.
5. *Independence:*
   Every child needs to know his parents have confidence in him and will help him develop his ability to do good things for himself and others.
6. *Love:*
   Every child needs to know his parents love him, want him and enjoy him; that he matters to someone and that there are people around him who care what happens to him.
7. *Praise:*
   Every child needs approval. Children, like adults, need a pat on the back for something good they have accomplished. It is small but important to the child.
8. *Protection:*
   Every child needs to know his parents want him safe from

harm; that they will help him when he faces a strange or frightening situation.

9. *Recognition:*
   Every child needs to be recognized for what he is inside and outside the home. Consider him in planning a new home, buying furniture, a new car or going on a vacation.
10. *Security:*
    Every child needs to know his home is a place of safety; that his parents will be at hand in time of need, and that he does belong to, and is an important member of the family.

There are ten well-known symptoms of juvenile delinquency which could be checked in the family setting such as: (1) Flagrant disobedience, (2) Truancy, (3) Cruelty to animals, (4) Possession of articles not purchased, (5) Unexplained cuts, scratches and bruises, (6) Unexplained late hours, (7) Untidy appearance, improper dress as (Boys—uncut hair) and (Girls—skin-tight clothing) (8) Friends who are not brought to the home, (9) Possession of weapons, and (10) Evidence of alcohol, drugs, or needle marks on the arms. It has been suggested that if the family recognizes only one of these symptoms, *look into it,* and if three are recognized, *look out!*

Delinquency and delinquent recidivism are often viewed as a consequence of a defective home life, with accompanying inadequate religious and moral education. Many cases of delinquency are directly attributed to the failure of this primary group, the family, to provide the child with appropriate nondelinquent social roles and to exercise social control over the child, so that these roles are accepted by him.

A few of the problems of youth caused by defective home life are listed by Jessie F. Binford.[12]

> The brother and sister, only ten and twelve years of age, who finally decided that he, being a boy, would run away, but that she would have to commit suicide to escape from the quarreling of their parents which they could no longer endure.
>
> The twelve-year-old girl kept out of school, in the house all the time and denied medical care, subject, her mother said to "spells" which were "from Heaven and God-inspired."

> The fifteen-year-old boy, an illegitimate child, left alone so much at night that he roams the streets, steals, and has told the children in his school that he has a "G.I." knife hidden at home with which he is going to kill the next man his mother brings home to live with them.

One of the most persistent problems of probation work with juveniles is the lack of a normal home environment. In a great many cases inquiries reveal that the young delinquent is either unwanted at home or has no real home. It is essential to find him someone who will love him and whom he himself will love in return. There are several possibilities. First of all it is worth seeking around for any relatives. Sometimes it appears that there is a married sister, an uncle, a "granny" somewhere. They may be quite concerned, but unable to do much. Occasionally they are able to offer a real home, but they may be unsuited to help the youngster, and because of the possibility of disappointment, the probation officer should make a reconnaissance first.[13]

The Gluecks in their well-known study *Unraveling Juvenile Delinquency,* observed that delinquents as a group were to a greater measure the victims not only of less stable households but also of broken homes. To a much greater extent than nondelinquents, they had substitute parents—that is, foster or step-parents—or lived with relatives. In the affectional relations between the parents and the boys, the delinquents were much more the victims of the indifference or actual hostility of their fathers and mothers and were, in turn, less devoted to their parents than the non-delinquents. Both the mothers and fathers of the delinquents were less consistent and less kindly in their disciplinary practices. Delinquent children, that is to say, grew up in a family atmosphere not marked by the obedience to legitimate authority.

The Gluecks stress "five highly decisive factors" in family life that may result in delinquent behavior. If the father's discipline is too harsh, if the mother permits the boy to roam the streets, if the father dislikes his son, if the mother is indifferent or hostile, and if the family is not integrated, the mother away from home, the father a heavy drinker who ignores his family, the child is headed for trouble, nine out of ten times, regardless of his intelligence, color, or family income.[14]

It is generally recognized that broken homes constitute an underlying cause of juvenile delinquency, but the concept "broken home" does not have an adequate definition or a universal connotation. Broken homes are usually classed as those disrupted by divorce, separation, desertion, or death. The number of broken homes is not known and available statistical data on "broken homes" are by no means reliable. Moreover, a home may be broken by death, divorce, or otherwise, without inducing delinquent behavior. Most of the actual delinquents continue to come from homes that are not "broken" at all. The Wickersham Commission made a study of the parental situation of 40,503 children appearing in ninety-three different courts during 1919. Results of the study showed that 64 per cent of the children lived with both parents and only 36 per cent came from broken homes. Later studies have borne out these findings. Broken homes are not nearly so serious as a causal factor in producing juvenile delinquency as disorganized homes.

Illegitimacy may also induce deviant behavior, especially when the child is aware of his "fatherless" status. The stigma attached to this situation, rooted in traditional mores and reinforced by many adults in the name of "morality" all too often becomes a part of the child's own deep concerns. And this situation is further aggravated by legal conditions. The term "illegitimate" is stamped on the birth certificates of such babies in Iowa, Minnesota, New Jersey, Ohio, and West Virginia. In Illinois, Montana, and New Mexico the words "father's name unknown" are written on the certificate.

Although the information concerning sibling relationships and numbers of the family is inconclusive, it is known that the delinquent ratio is higher for the girls who have only brothers than it is for girls who have only sisters. The order of birth may have some significance; but, contrary to the popular belief, the Gluecks report in the study referred to above, that lone children, first, and last children, are least apt to become delinquent. The inbetweens are more inclined to show danger signs—such as temper tantrums, profanity, obscenity, and, in 33 per cent of the cases, overt acts of delinquency—before they are eight years old. However, unlike the "rotten apple in the barrel," the delinquency of one sibling does not tend to spread to the other brothers and sisters.

The value of family life is so firmly established in our culture that numerous reformatory delinquents frequently attempt to construct some facsimile of it. Large groups of girls divide themselves into extended "families" and assume fictitious family names, headed by a "father," or "grandfather." Included in these groups may be both whites and Negroes. This system is sometimes highly organized; for example, in one female reformatory two separate "clans" existed and carried on a family feud akin to the historic feuds of the southern mountaineers. Perhaps these delinquents are seeking, in their own way, a stable family life which they never had.

Joseph G. Wilson, a physician, is of the opinion that this organized house-playing by delinquent girls is simply a continuation into the age of puberty of the ordinary house-playing of little girls from five to ten years of age. These little girls had toy furniture, kitchen, parlors, bedrooms, and dolls, and called each other husband and wife, uncle and aunt, brother and sister. Now as they grow into puberty and early adolescence they seek to find the substitutes for the real objects of love and affection which they would have had if they were outside the walls in a normal family environment.[15]

Not infrequently a delinquent may have modeled himself after some family member who also may be delinquent. Though some children cry out in court, "I would rather die than go home," others have strong attachments to unworthy parents or to depraved relatives and crave to return to their "care." Frazier tells the story of one boy who committed burglary with an uncle. The uncle stole a watch and chain; the boy grabbed a raincoat and shoes. The uncle escaped the police; the boy was apprehended. The boy, however, accepted his punishment and did not betray his uncle.[16]

## PARENTAL RESPONSIBILITY AND PUNISHMENT

Many individuals in responsible positions tend to blame the parents for juvenile delinquency, and suggest getting tough with parents. The "man-in-the-street" likewise blames parents for their neglect and lack of home training. Statements like "parents who fail to provide moral training and discipline must be held accountable and are to blame for juvenile delinquents" are fairly common throughout the literature on juvenile delinquency.

The increasing number of divorces, many of which involve the welfare and future of children, may become an important factor in juvenile delinquency. These children are deprived of a normal home, their loyalties are confused; they become the vehicle through which each parent so often vents his enmity against the other; they are subjected to the emotional strain of divided custodial rights.[17] However, evidence to date suggests that there is litttle causal relationship between delinquent behavior and the home broken by desertion, divorce or death.

Incompetent parents and their irresponsible actions may cause guilt feelings in their children that may lead to delinquent behavior. Ernst G. Beier relates an example established in a group therapy session, in which the subject felt responsible for his mother's death. She had asked the boy to go to a nearby store to buy her a quart of liquor and because he refused, she decided to go to the store herself, despite her intoxicated condition. She never returned, and the next morning, her body was found in a snow bank, frozen to death.[18]

The probation officer is often faced with the adjustment problem of his charge and the family beset with neurotic problems. The neurotic delinquent almost invariably comes from a family where other members, particularly the parents, are neurotic, and where there are numberless opportunities for stirring up the feeling of hopelessness and revolt.[19]

Boys need emotional identification with the father, otherwise they may admire the strongest, toughest hoodlum in the block. If the girl is unhappy at home due to rejection by her parents, she may become the willing victim of the pedophiliac or child molester. The child molester is apt to be from her own family or family friends. If the child is happy at home, she will probably tell Mother about "Uncle Bob's" advances, but if she is unhappy, this experience may continue for years.

Some parents are immature and incapable of mature leadership by precept and example. The children in such families may "raise" the parents. In some instances, the wife has transferred her child-dependency from her parents to her husband, or the husband prefers to be mothered, rather than being "wifed." Some parents apparently wish they could be as childish as their children. In an article which appeared in *Life,* January 27, 1958, it was pointed out that kids know that any grown-up who gets down on all fours and makes mudpies is either a spy or a fool. What children want is to be taken out to the grown-up world . . . . of cigars, restaurants with linen napkins, automobiles and tall people. Children know the child's world, they need no help, but many parents are too busy being "Teen-Age Pals."

In 1945, a parental responsibility law was enacted in California, that when a minor is brought before the juvenile court, his parent, guardian or custodian must show cause why a criminal complaint should not be filed against him for contributing to child delinquency. Both court officials and social workers consider this impractical and ineffectual. The child in court has usually long presented a problem in his home that his parents have been unable to solve. In Wilmington, California recently, some parents were sent to jail because their sons violated the curfew law and the judge remarked that "if these defendants spend a few days in jail now, their children may spend less time there in the future."

The judge is often faced with the problem of handling parents who appear to have contributed to the child's delinquency. The subject of parental responsibility and retraining of parents is beyond his province, and it is doubtful that a "tongue-lashing" does any good. Judge Hunt, juvenile court judge of Bartow, Florida has stated that "most talk is useless." Some parents take no responsibility and sending parents to jail also fails. The best soultions seems to be, "try and see it from the parents' point of view."

Occasionally, the juvenile court has to take charge when the parents prove incapable of doing the job. In a Phoenix, Arizona case, the boy, at age eight, disrobed a little girl, aged five, tied her up, put her in a garbage can, and pressed the lid down tight. When the deputies questioned the boy, the father told him to answer no questions. A week later, the boy grabbed a nine-year-old girl, dragged her off a bicycle, shouting he would take her in the bushes and rape her. The parents stated they would straighten the boy out.[20]

Because of the continuing increase in juvenile crime and delinquency, it has been increasingly popular to blame delinquency on the parents due to their neglect, incompetence, or indifference. Fixing the blame on mothers and fathers falls utterly short because it deliberately excludes some of the most fundamental social factors which strike far beyond the parents' control of the situation and are directly or indirectly contributing to the increase of child crime.[21]

Some parents are inadequate in rearing their children, despite the fact they are sincere in their effort. Some parents cannot even think of names for their progeny. One inmate thought that prison might be preferable to returning to his family in the deep South. There he had a wife and so many children that he'd run out of names. The last two were officially baptized Coca-Cola and Pepsi-Cola. "Couldn't think of no more," he explained.[22]

The handy little slogan, "It's not the children who are delinquent, it's the parents," is probably the all-time favorite of every columnist, editorial writer and lecturer at community meetings who specializes in pointing the finger of shame at the obvious. This is merely mouthing a platitude, as though it could solve a serious problem. Fixing the blame on parents automatically with the intent to correct the difficulties would only lead to more corruption and strain within the family. Had this fallacious approach been utilized, Saint Monica might have been imprisoned for the misdeeds of her ne'er-do-well son, the future St. Augustine.

Because, directly or indirectly, relatives and parents are frequently abettors of juvenile misbehavior, many of the specialists working in the field would punish parents as well as children who are apprehended. Some social workers believe that juvenile delinquency is primarily parental delinquency. They propose that the parents be jailed or fined and forced to attend lectures on how to rear children. It has become almost a fad to ascribe the children's misbehavior to parental neglect or indifference. Judge Paul W. Alexander of the Domestic Relations and Juvenile Court, Toledo,

Ohio, pursued a parent-punishment policy for over ten years. During this time he sentenced ninety-one parents to prison terms totaling over eighty years. From this experience, he later concluded, however, that to punish parents accomplishes nothing for the children themselves.

Judge Alexander found five different categories of delinquent parents: (1) *Runaway Parents,* who leave their children without supervision, (2) *Vicious Parents,* who expose their children to vice, (3) *Aiders and Abettors* who directly encourage delinquency in their children, (4) *Triangular Parents* involved in extra-marital love affairs, and (5) *Inadequate Parents* (more important than all others combined) who have failed to give their children adequate moral and ethical teaching, training and supervision.[23]

Passing laws cracking down on parents is like the Mann Act legislation tactics and about as ineffectual. Coulter suggests that only as the value of congenial home relations is re-emphasized, only as parents are made aware of the significance of the personal relations within the home can we hope for improvement of the delinquency situation in our society. Discussion centers could be set up for parents in every city and hamlet in every state in the Union, looking to the building of more wholesome family relations. This would be an adult education venture with the physician, psychiatrist, clergyman, social worker, nurse, probation officer, and socially-minded citizen participating. Our problem of delinquency is basically a problem of educating, directing, training, advising with and safe-guarding parents and of impressing upon them their continued responsibility.[24]

Based on the alleged "growing sociological theory that a child takes the criminal path because his parents, unwittingly or not, have shoved him that way," some courts continue to punish parents by sending them to jail. One mother was jailed for thirty days and fined $25.00 because her boy was found drinking in the streets. It may well be asked: will the mother, after thirty days in jail, be a better mother? Will her son respect her more and have confidence in her? Does the jail offer training in parenthood? Will the parent-child relationship be improved? Or is not such an attitude toward parents another community rationalization in an effort to wash its hands of its social responsibility? The problem child in court has probably long been the problem child in his home.

## FOSTER HOMES

As Teeters and Reinemann point out, the idea of placing children in foster homes was not new to the United States. Foster home care resulted from the breakdown of the feudal system in England. Dependent children were indentured, based on the previous system of apprenticeship, which made some person or family responsible for the care of a destitute child. Hence the first organized efforts to use foster homes was limited largely to the care of destitute, abandoned and dependent children.

In Philadelphia, as early as 1800, the Magdalen Society was organized to care for young girls who "in an unguarded hour have been robbed of their innocence and sunk into wretchedness and guilt." The nobleminded men—not women—who founded this rescue society envisaged placing these "little Magdalens" in foster homes. These girls were placed in a "respectable and religious family" in order to "inure their minds to habits of industry." Many girls were helped by this method.

In 1853, the Children's Aid Society of New York began to take children out of almshouses and place them in foster homes. The first Society for the Prevention of Cruelty to Children was begun in 1875 in New York City; here again, children from homes where cruelty and abuse were practiced were farmed out in foster homes. Interestingly enough, the New York Society for Prevention of Cruelty to Animals in 1874 had been confronted with a case of cruelty to a child, hence agitation began for a Society to Protect children. The movement spread rapidly, some cities dealt exclusively with children, while others worked with both animals and children. The Colorado Bureau of Child and Animal Protection states that "the protection of children and animals are combined because of their helplessness; because all life is the same, differing only in degree of development and expression." [25]

The Children's Aid Society from 1853 to 1879 placed some 48,000 children in western and southern states. These placements were completely informal and were subject to abuses, which were gradually corrected by more careful investigation of prospective homes, employment of staff to visit the home and children, and keep good records.

Over a half century ago, the first White House Conference on Child Care (1908) recommended that every child should have a normal home—or its nearest substitute. Where efforts to preserve the natural home were not successful or seemingly possible, it was urged that children be placed in foster homes in preference to placing them in institutions.

Legally viewed, foster-home care refers to care of a child by adults not related to the child by blood or marriage or by legal adoption. It is a provision for dependent and neglected children, for children awaiting adoption, for those who are physically or mentally handicapped, or children who are delinquent. Although foster-home care has been practiced fairly extensively for many decades, the use of this procedure in the case of juvenile delinquents is of quite recent origin and is relatively restricted.

Herbert D. Williams evaluates some basic considerations in use of foster homes.[26] While it is a truism to say that the best place for a child is in his own home, there always will be some older adolescent delinquents who cannot be contained in a regular foster family boarding home. They are the aggressive, gang-minded, excitement-seeking, chronic run-away types of individuals.

Approximately 85 per cent of normal children who have been labeled as delinquent make a satisfactory adjustment in foster homes and cease to be delinquents. Apparently the type of offense committed has little bearing on the rate of success or failure. The one significant factor that increased the rate of failure was the presence of abnormal mentality or personality. The normal, successful placement for the older group, between thirteen and eighteen, is "only slightly less successful" than for those under thirteen.

In general, foster homes work best for those who have a need for affection, individualized attention, who require closer and more intimate relationships with adults, and whose personal habits and attitudes are not such as to make them too conspicuous in a community. Children who do not respond to casework treatment are not ready for foster home placement, nor are those with strong aggressions against parent persons.

Leontine R. Young suggests that placement should be made from the child's viewpoint. For the child, placement can be a shocking and bewildering calamity, the reasons for which he usually does not understand. Some caseworkers move juveniles around like a bundle of laundry. One child expressed it by saying, "the social workers are the bat and I'm just the ball they sock from one place to another." No child is capable of selecting a foster home, but only the child can make the decision of whether or not he will genuinely accept it.[27]

When the juvenile court judge commits a delinquent to a foster home, he has the responsibility of explaining where the place is, what kind of a home it is, the visiting hours and other helpful details. Presenting the pleasant features and opportunities of the place to which the child is committed allays the fears of the juvenile and others interested. Commitments should be explained as being made for the improvement of the juvenile, instead of for punishment.[28]

In the absence of long-tried experience and of conclusive information about foster-home care of delinquents, various opinions are expressed concerning the wisdom and efficacy of this procedure. For example, it has been argued, on the basis of some studies, that foster home prospects should be first offenders only, that is, should not include recidivists, and should be young in years, preferably under ten years. Experience with older children in foster homes, many of whom represent "failures" in the sense that delinquent behavior persists, suggests, at least, that these offenders tend to define the foster home itself as a "punishment" much as they regard assignment to an institution for delinquents. Certainly further investigation is needed in this area, but it must be agreed that a crucial element in correction is always to be found in the offender's own attitudes and sentiments.

## REFERENCES

1. Carr, Lowell J.: *Delinquency Control,* New York Harper & Brothers, 1941, p. 57.

2. Cited in Teeters, Negley K. and Reinemann, John Otto: *The Challenge of Delinquency,* New York, Prentice-Hall 1950, p. 128.
3. Vedder, Clyde B., Koenig, Samuel and Clark, Robert E.: *Criminology: Book of Readings,* New York, The Dryden Press, 1953, p. 158.
4. Coulter, Charles W.: Family Disorganization as a Causal Factor in Delinquency and Crime, *Federal Probation,* Vol. XII, September, 1948, p. 16.
5. Cited by Shulman, Harry M.: Intelligence and Delinquency, *The Journal of Criminal Law and Criminology,* Vol. XLI, April, 1951, pp. 763–781.
6. Wattenberg, William W. and Balistrieri, James: Automobile Theft: A 'Favored-group' Delinquency, *The American Journal of Sociology,* Vol. LVII, May, 1952, pp. 575–579.
7. Crystal, David: Family Casework in Probation, *Federal Probation,* Vol. XIII, December, 1949, p. 47.
8. Carr, Lowell J.: *op. cit.,* p. 110.
9. Sutherland, Edwin H. and Cressey, Donald R.: *Principles of Criminology,* (Fifth Edition), Philadelphia, J. B. Lippincott Company, 1955, p. 99.
10. Reckless, Walter C., Dinitz, Simon and Murray, Ellen: The 'Good' Boy in a High Delinquency Area, *Journal of Criminal Law, Criminology, and Police Science,* Vol. 48, May-June, 1957, pp. 23–24. Also Reckless, Walter C., Dinitz, Simon and Kay, Barbara: The Self Component in Potential Delinquency and Potential Non-Delinquency, *American Sociological Review,* Vol. 22, October, 1957, p. 569.
11. Quoted in Chicago Police Department Pamphlet, Parents Rights, Responsibilities, Regulations, *Youth Division,* January, 1961, pp. 2–3, 5.
12. Binford, Jessie F.: Postwar Problems of Youth, *Federal Probation,* Vol. XI, October-December, 1947, p. 7.
13. Glover, Elizabeth R.: Probation: The Art of Introducing The Probationer to a Better Way of Life, *Federal Probation,* Vol. XV, September, 1951, pp. 8–12.
14. Glueck, Sheldon and Eleanor: *Unraveling Juvenile Delinquency,* New York, The Commonwealth Fund, 1951, p. 133.
15. Wilson, M.D., Joseph G.: *Are Prisons Necessary?* Philadelphia, Dorrance & Company, 1950, p. 209.
16. Frazier, E. Franklin: *The Negro Family in the United States,* Chicago, University of Chicago Press, 1939, p. 271.
17. Binford, Jessie F.: *op. cit.,* p. 9.
18. Beier, Ernst G.: Experimental Therapy with a Gang, *Focus,* Vol. 30, July, 1951, pp. 97–102.
19. Lippman, M.D., Hyman S.: The Role of the Probation Officer in the Treatment of Delinquency in Children, *Federal Probation,* Vol. XII, June, 1948, pp. 36–39.

20. Arizona *Republic* (Phoenix), October, 1957, p. 12.
21. Lessner, Milton: Controlling War-Time Juvenile Delinquency, *Journal of Criminal Law and Criminology,* Vol, XXXV, November-December, 1944, pp. 242–248.
22. Dressler, David: *Parole Chief,* New York, The Viking Press, 1951, p. 107.
23. Alexander, Paul W.: What's This About Punishing Parents, *Federal Probation,* Vol. XII, March, 1948, pp. 23–29.
24. Coulter, Charles W.: *op. cit.,* p. 17.
25. Teeters, Negley K. and Reinemann, John Otto: *op cit.,* pp. 75–76.
26. Williams, Herbert D.: Foster Homes for Juvenile Delinquents, *Federal Probation,* Vol. XIII, September, 1949, pp. 46–51.
27. Young, Leontine R.: Placement From the Child's Viewpoint, *Social Casework,* June, 1950, pp. 250–255.
28. Beckham, Walter H.: Helpful Practices in Juvenile Court Hearings, *Federal Probation,* Vol. XIII, June, 1949, pp. 10–14.

# 4

# COMMUNITY INSTITUTIONS

IN THEIR FULLEST sense, "institutions" incorporate attitudes and reciprocal behavior patterns of groups of individuals, guided by established culture standards, and designed to fulfill specific human objectives and needs. The belief in public education, for example, profoundly rooted in American tradition and mores, has found expression in such specific institutions as the public school and the state university. One important function of these organizations is to implant common standards and forms of behavior.

Despite the general trend towards standardized behavior in this society, strong tensions arise in the community because of differences in value standards and modes of operation of the several institutions governing our lives. Inconsistencies within and between community institutions help to aggravate social problems, such as crime and juvenile delinquency. The roots of juvenile delinquency do not lie only in the homes, the schools, and the churches of the nation. Because of the discrepancies between what juveniles are taught by these agencies and what they find existing in fact in our city life and government, many children have lost respect for integrity and authority.

## THE SCHOOL AND DELINQUENCY

While the home is the first and most important influence in shaping the personality and character of the child, other environmental forces, such as the school, help to determine them also. The school is perhaps the most strategic community agency in the effort to prevent delinquency, since it reaches practically all children at a relatively early period of their growth.

An important group of youngsters who need attention are the problem cases in the schools—the children who have not yet necessarily become delinquent but who are showing symptoms of emotional strain and maladjustment. Many teachers are utterly unaware of the psychiatric significance of many types of behavior, hence much goes undetected. So in every community, urban and rural, there is a considerable percentage of problem cases. The estimates vary but a conservative figure would be from 2 to 5 per cent of the school population at any given time.[1]

One reason that this potential advantage of the school is not exploited fully is found in the intellectual diversity of the students combined with a fairly standardized program. The public school, it has been claimed, does a fair job with the pupil of average intelligence, a poor job with superior children, and practically no job with the dull group. Thousands of boys and girls quit school because they are offered little opportunity to learn anything which their limited mentality can grasp. Another complicating factor is the situation in which school administrators frequently lack the insight to deal effectively with disciplinary problems.

In some communities, the public school situation is a matter of great concern. In one school there had been a new principal almost every year for eight years. Teachers were being regularly transferred in and out of the district. School assemblies and extra-curricular activities common to schools in the better sections were lacking. Children are handicapped in unstable and restricted school situations.[2]

Of basic importance, however, in any school program is the realization that the school is working with growing personalities who enter the classroom with attitudes already shaped by the home and neighborhood environment. Children come into contact with their teachers and learning routines with likes and dislikes, fears and anxieties, unsatisfied cravings and unfulfilled desires. If schools fail to recognize these background conditions and to take them into account in their educational activities, some children will rebel against school itself and may take the first step toward delinquency.

According to Bloch and Flynn,[3] by the time the child reaches the school, his basic personality traits have already been formed, and many of the incipient and active tendencies to delinquency and waywardness have been well established. The school's primary function is educational and it is limited to certain procedures which may have little value in overcoming behavioral difficulties of a child.

Children who are frustrated in school and become delinquent show consistent records of truancy, retardation, and antipathy toward school. The reasons for such strong antipathy are inability to learn, resentment of restriction and routine, and lack of interest, in that order. Delinquents seem to show a marked distaste for subject matter that demands strict logical reasoning, persistency of effort, and good memory such as is required in arithmetic, social studies, foreign languages, science, and commercial subjects.

Bloch and Flynn conclude that the school contributes to delinquency by accentuating delinquent trends in children who are already predelinquent, actively delinquent, or emotionally disturbed. It has not been determined to what degree the school situation creates frustrations that render socially and economically deprived children susceptible to delinquency.

Increasingly, the public schools have come to acknowledge these facts and are slowly broadening the scope of their interest and responsibility. Both the school and the juvenile court recognize the fact that delinquency frequently can be prevented by redirecting the child's antisocial and destructive impulses. With the growing awareness of the need for such attention to be given the child, educators have increasingly stressed the need to provide individualized services for problem children.

Destructive impulses pose a serious problem for school authorities from the grade school to the University level. In some metropolitan school systems, the three new "R's" seem to be Rowdyism, Riot and Revolt. According to *Time,* March 1954, some teachers are unable to cope with vandalism because school officials won't back them up. Teachers are beaten up who won't graduate or promote students and few teachers report to the police lest reprisals occur. In a Harlem high school, five fires were set in one week.

Frederic Wertham, M.D. relates how older boys steal lunch money from younger boys, and threaten to cut their eyes out if they squeal. A thirteen-year-old boy stabbed his teacher eight times, in the back, and in the face when she fell to the floor, and he came from an excellent home.[4]

One book-trained juvenile "pulled" 220 thefts while on summer vacation. According to the Florida *Times-Union* (Jacksonville), July 21, 1955, this offender, a fourteen-year-old boy, stated he intended to be the best crook in the business. He was an able gymnast and tumbler at his junior high school and found his agility most helpful in running from the police. His motto: "Always be polite to policemen."

A Freshman matriculating at M.I.T. possessed an enviable record. He had a place on the super-honor roll at his high school, was president of the student council, a cadet colonel in the R.O.-T.C. and held the American Legion's high-school award for his class, and was an active member of his Presbyterian church choir. According to *Time,* December 24, 1956, this student successfully engineered a bank robbery in Illinois to finance a free-spending semester, was finally apprehended in Oklahoma City. His explanation: "I'm a mixed-up character . . . one of those teen-agers who know how so many of our age feel. There's the Army, war clouds, decisions about school and future occupation and we think we're taking them in stride; then one does something like I did, and we realize we're really mixed up."

In the April 8, 1952, issue, Life chronicled the "panty raid" which occurred at the University of Michigan. Male students marched on the women's dorms and soon depleted the stock of lingerie. The coeds bravely retaliated by pouring water on the men, but opening a few back doors and windows at the same time. The Dean explained: "No human being, has ever attempted to shift the vernal equinox."

The Easter Holiday vacation from school seems to be a "critical" time for student misbehavior. The Gainesville *Daily Sun* (Florida) April 7, 1953 reported more than 15,000 students "invaded" Fort Lauderdale and celebrated by hurling coconuts through hotel lobbies and car windows, and tossing a dead six-foot hammerhead shark into the municipal swimming pool. In Balboa Beach, California, another tribal gathering place, 35,000 youth swarmed in to swim, fight, drink and woo.

In a similar student "pilgrimage" to Fort Lauderdale in 1960, a student major in Journalism at Northern Illinois University observed celebrating students falling into four categories: (1) sight-see'rs, a minority; (2) lovers, monopolized the beach, wouldn't move even when the tide came in; (3) sun-bathers, with their books, learning while burning, and (4) the nameless beer-drinkers, who stood in line to get into the taverns. One caravan from Connecticut arrived in a shiny, black hearse with the words: "This is really living," or "Don't laugh lady, you may be next." It was a week of the "uninhibited." [5]

A different type of student misbehavior, cheating on examinations, was reported in *Newsweek,* May 20, 1957 and seems to be persistent in all grade levels including Universities. According to polls taken by the students themselves, nearly one half reported they were guilty of cheating. It is called the "Good Neighbor Policy" at the University of Southern California, "The Wandering Eye" at Georgia Tech, and "Collaborating" at the University of Washington. The accepted attitude is "Do it unless you get caught."

As a force in preventing delinquency, the school has many limitations. Teachers do not necessarily agree on what constitutes "delinquency." Teachers, for obvious reasons, are primarily concerned with deviant behavior in the *classroom.* Many teachers emphasize actions that unsettle classroom decorum, while mental hygienists are more interested in such behavior symptoms as extreme shyness and suspiciousness. Most teachers undoubtedly recognize the recalcitrant, unyielding and perverse child, the bully, the promiser who never delivers, the constant eraser of written work, the pencil chewer, the devotee of obscene words, phrases or pictures written or drawn on the walls or sidewalks. The teachers' reactions to such behavior and their informed and understanding treatment of children who engage in these symptomatic acts are of vital importance in the prevention of delinquency.

One of the familiar dilemmas of the teacher is "Which is more important, the boy or the book, the child or the curriculum?" About 25 per cent of high school graduates continue on to college and the curriculum is usually dedicated to college requirements to retain favorable secondary school ratings. Schools transmit knowledge, not behavior patterns; their function is to pass on "the cultural heritage of the race." The traditional conflict posed between the child and the curriculum is eloquently described in the following often quoted report by Naomi John White in "I Taught All." [6]

> I have taught in high school for ten years. During that time I have given assignments, among others, to a murderer, an evangelist, a pugilist, a thief, and an imbecile.
>
> The murderer was a quiet little boy who sat on the front seat and regarded me with pale blue eyes; the evangelist, easily the most popular boy in school, had the lead in the junior play; the pugilist lounged by the window and let loose at intervals a raucous laugh that startled even the geraniums; the thief was a gay-hearted Lothario with a song on his lips; and the imbecile, a softeyed little animal seeking the shadows.
>
> The murderer awaits death in the state penitentiary; the evangelist has lain a year now in the village churchyard; the pugilist lost an eye in a brawl in Hongkong; the thief, by standing on tiptoe, can see the windows of my room from the county jail, and the once gentle-eyed little imbecile beats his head against a padded wall in the state asylum.
>
> All of these pupils once sat in my room, sat and looked at me gravely across worn brown desks. I must have been a great help to those pupils—I taught them the rhyming scheme of the Elizabethan sonnet and how to diagram a complex sentence.

A witty but somewhat exaggerated picture of the conflicting roles of the teacher has been given by the journalist, Robert Quillen, creator of the newspaper character, Aunt Het, who describes the plight of the small town school teacher:[7]

> The only difference between teachers and the Christian martyrs is the date and the lack of a bonfire . . . . . . they are hired to teach and they do it. They teach the younguns that can learn and entertain the ones that fell on their heads when they was little . . . . . . and make geniuses out of children that couldn't have no sense with the parents they've got . . . . . . and when they ain't doing nothin else, they're supposed to be setting a good example.

The character of school work likewise must be considered in the effects it induces in children. What is the effect, for example of subjecting the child to laborious exercises far removed from the central experiences of his life? Reading about "innocent little lambs" (unreal creatures, at best), fairies, trips to the country, or the volume of rainfall in Tibet, for example, may have only negative impact on children raised in city streets. To these pupils delinquency offers thrills and excitement in contrast to uninteresting and confining school work.

Some juvenile students are such trouble-makers they must be sent to "Special Schools." At a Greenwich Village School in New York, the boys line up for a pre-class contraband check-up which prohibits knives, cigarettes, matches and combs with teeth broken out (face slashers). In Westchester County, New York, one truant phoned in anonymously that a bomb was going to explode, so all classes were suspended for the rest of the day, so his own absence was covered up as well. Today's youth are more exuberant, virile, volatile, self-centered, surfeited with modern privileges and gadgets and impatient of the hurdle between any wish and its gratification.[8]

It is expecting too much of schools, of course, to assume that they can overcome the influences of undesirable homes and community conditions. Yet a more developed preventive program in the school surely is one important weapon in the fight against delinquency and juvenile criminality. Most delinquent children come directly from the American public school room, where they have presumably been indoctrinated with the standards of a law-abiding society. The fact that this indoctrination is often ineffective presents a challenge to the schools and to the communities of which they are a part.

## TRUANCY

For many maladjusted and potentially delinquent children, school seems to be just another frustrating and unhappy experience. The school sometimes intensifies feelings of frustration and inadequacy, often generated in the family and play groups. And many pupils caught in these circumstances seek an outlet for their frustrations in truancy and delinquent behavior. Truancy has been called the "kindergarten of crime," for often enough the young truant, under the influence of older boys and girls, learns techniques of stealing and other forbidden activities during his stolen hours. An adequately conceived preventive program in the school could aid considerably, perhaps, in lowering the juvenile delinquency rate. The frequency of truancy and dishonesty in children in the schools before their first contact with the law suggests that an efficient visiting teacher or counselor program might have prevented some later delinquencies.

Arthur C. Johnson[9] lists the "reasons" why many boys ran away from school.

(1) "The teacher tried to make me wear better clothes like the other children. I finally told her to go to hell and walked out. I swore then that I would have better clothes if I had to steal them and I did."

(2) "I had a stutter. I was put in a class with a lot of screwballs. My pals kidded me and I quit."

(3) "My mother was going nuts and I was worried about her. One day the teacher called me crazy too. I never went to school regular after that."

(4) "I just couldn't recite in class. The teacher nagged at me and to avoid trouble I left school."

(5) "I was put in a class with a lot of dumb clucks. It was too much for me and I quit."

(6) "One day I got to school late and was told that if I couldn't get there on time, not to come at all, just to spoil the class record. I took them at their word."

Equally obvious end-prdoucts of poorly considered school "influences," are to be found in any reformatory or prison. Although many individuals accept the occasional trouble-maker as an inescapable headache for the school, the school is frequently an even greater headache for the child.

In the study of Sidney Axelrad's Negro and white male institutionalized delinquents,[10] it was found that white delinquents were more prone to be committed for truancy than the Negro delinquents, 38 per cent as against 18 per cent. This should not be understood to mean that the white children were less adjusted than the Negro. Almost all the delinquents were school problems. It is probable that the community, or at least the school system, considers truancy in the white child as something about which it is willing to be active. Seemingly, it did not care so much in the case of the Negro child.

The magnitude of the nonattendance problem is worthy of serious consideration. In urban areas of the United States roughly 12 per cent of all pupils are absent from school on a given day. Most non-attendance is not truancy. Only about 13 per cent of all school absences have nonmedical causes.[11]

Kahn distinguishes between various categories of children not attending school. The *lawful absentee* is the child whose excuse is acceptable according to the criteria of a given school system. The *unlawful absentee* is the child without an explanation, or the child whose explanation is unacceptable. The *truant* is the juvenile who has been absent without the knowledge and permission of the parents. It is a fair estimate that not over 15 per cent, and probably closer to 10 per cent of all school absences represent truancy.

While school systems have collected large volumes of statistics on nonattendance, these statistics reflect not efforts to understand the phenomenon, but rather, what has been called "statistics anxiety."[12] How many children who are ill (and may spread infection) attend school daily because they fear to spoil the class attendance standing? Those who create the attendance-rate pressures ignore the fact that the vast majority of eligible children do attend school regularly.

Kahn summarizes the major considerations for those in child-helping services as: (1) many truants never become serious delinquents. (2) More truants than nontruants are potential delinquents. (3) The major importance of truancy is that it identifies a child who may be in trouble. Only as we see truancy as an early danger sign, marking a challenge to the child-helping services, can we move in attendance work from the medieval ages of statistics anxiety and punishment to the modern maturity of promoting personality health and development.[13]

Acording to John Otto Reinemann,[14] in practically all juvenile court laws the term "delinquency" is defined so as to include truancy, thus establishing the jurisdiction of the juvenile court in such cases. Any effective program of controlling truancy is predicated upon a close co-operation between the board of education and the juvenile court and a clear understanding about the limits of their respective functions. It has proved of great value to have a representative of the school authorities attending all juvenile court hearings.

As John R. Ellingston[15] points out, the defiance of law and authority involved in truancy usually means the child has reached a major crisis in his life. Probably the school, perhaps the family, the home, or community has become intolerable and he runs away from it. This calls not for strong-armed attendance officers, nicknamed "talent scouts for the reform schools," but for teachers trained in case work. While public opinion has forced the abolition of corporal punishment in most schools, one still hears the occasional pedagogue or righteous citizen demanding to have the whip restored "to put the fear of God into the children of America."

From a vantage point of twenty years equally divided between public and prison educational work, Arthur C. Johnson summarizes the truancy problem and the best solution in case incarceration becomes necessary. Out of every one hundred boys of school age, about eighty are average, healthy, normal youngsters. Being slow mentally, ten have to be "pushed." Highstrung and rebellious against restraint, the remaining ten become behavior problems and "must be sat on." It is with this ten per cent that the school fails. The expression, "I may as well have the game as the name," sums up the whole distorted outlook. Continued, it may lead to delinquency and crime.

Truancy is clearly associated with later criminal records. In a group of 634 consecutive prison commitments, 258 were recidivists of whom 78 per cent had truancy as the first entry in their crime ledger. Of the 376 first offenders, 61 per cent had the same start. On their own admission, 67 per cent of the remainder had been off-the-record truants. This is a serious indictment of our schools.

The public school becomes such an anathema to some juvenile delinquents that they fail to realize that a reformatory is basically a school. For the rehabilitation of children who have failed to adjust in public schools, the first step with each boy is to "get under his skin," not "in his hair." Men and women who can attract boys becoming hardened to life and suspicious of motive must be brought into the work.

The job is to establish emotional control, create habits of humility in thought, consideration in action, responsibility in performance—all attitudes of approach, not necessarily skills for doing. We will succeed only when we apply the simple formula of individual persuasion by personal precept and example.[16]

## THE CHURCH AND DELINQUENCY

According to Max Grunhut, the first establishment of record that was specifically created for the corrective treatment of delinquent youth was opened by Pope Clement XI in Rome in 1703. It was called the Hospice of San Michele and was designed along monastic lines. Over the outside door was the inscription, "For the correction and instruction of profligate youth, that they who when idle were injurious, when instructed might be useful to the State." And over the central hall, the inscription: "It is of little advantage to restrain the bad by punishment, unless you render them good by discipline."

The routine was most severe. The boys were chained by one foot and under a strict rule of silence, had to listen to pious readings; they spent the night in small separate brick cells. The incorrigible boys were separated day and night, and whipping was a frequent penalty for "past mistakes" as well as for non-performance of the daily task.[17]

Early Protestants likewise took a dim view of delinquent behavior in children. As reported and quoted by Ellingston, the associated doctrine of original sin held that a tendency to evil is born in each of us, inherited from Adam as a consequence of his sin in the Garden of Eden. And so John Robinson, an English Puritan divine stated in the early 1600's: "And surely there is in all children, though not alike, a stubbornness, and stoutness of mind arising from natural pride, which must, in the first place, be broken and beaten down . . ." And in colonial America the criminal code of the Province of East Jersey, adopted in 1688, could decree that a child convicted of assaulting or cursing his parents or of persistent disobedience or stubbornness should be hanged.[18]

According to Carr, the role of the Protestant churches in this effort is handicapped by the preaching of "old-fashioned," individualistic, personal salvation. Not infrequently some church leaders convey the impression that active interest in delinquency problems is "worldly" and "belittling." Ultra-conservative administrations have driven Boy Scouts out of church basements and slashed young people's work budgets to increase expenditures on the choir. Ministers have been called, supposedly to enlightened churches, for the express purpose, as one church official put it, of "ending this infernal monkey business," namely, the somewhat noisy presence of groups of youngsters in the church parlors on weekdays.[19]

A satisfactory definition of the role of the church in preventing delinquency is by no means easy of formulation. Among the sources of the difficulty, one author stresses the following: (1) the lack of agreement upon the legitimate aims and methods of organized religion itself, stemming from sectarian controversy; (2) the confusion concerning the proper scope of religious activities in relation to the work of other institutions, involving seemingly artificial distinctions between the "sacred" and "secular"; and (3) the traditional view that the historic mission of the Protestant churches is to teach religious principles almost exclusively, depending upon their beneficial effects upon individuals for the solution of social problems.[20]

The difficulties marked in the Protestant denominations, are not as manifest in the Roman Catholic Church. The social teachings of the latter are rooted in authoritative and scholarly encyclicals and there is agreement concerning "secular" programs—a situation greatly abetting effective work.

The Catholic Youth Organization has as a major objective the prevention of juvenile delinquency and works toward this goal with one of the most extensive and popular youth programs in the United States today. Both the Sisters of the Good Shepherd, dedicated to the correction of delinquent girls, and the late Monsignor Flanagan's Boys Town, Nebraska, have inspired similar programs among Catholics and non-Catholics.

Protestant Church activities are not nearly as extensive. The Northern Baptists, the Protestant Episcopal Church, various Lutheran bodies, and the Congregational Church, however, have instituted or, as is more often the case, sponsored programs directly designed to curb delinquency.

The church is the one institution that inculcates respect for personality. The primary role is to give spiritual guidance so as to prevent delinquency. However, there is little evidence to support such a contention. In the well-known study by Hartshorne and May[21] a few decades ago, in testing children for lying, deceiving and the like, there was found no significant relationship whether children attended church and possessed Biblical information or had not attended church. Church attendance and knowledge of the Bible do not necessarily insure proper character growth. The child seems to profit but little in morality from community institutions outside his family. Religious training apparently fails because morality develops at a slower pace than the tempo in which religious institutions can function.

There are more churches, ministers, and religious programs than ever before, yet somehow they have failed, as have other community institutions, to prevent juvenile delinquency. There seems to be a wide gap between listening to the Bible and practicing the religious principles enunciated.

Sometimes the church is the target for juvenile delinquency and criminality. In a book edited by Charles Hamilton, criminals recalled how they used to exploit the church:[22]

> Pete and I used to go to mass on Sunday morning, and put a bad five dollar bill in the collector's box, taking out four dollars and ninety cents in change, in good money. We irreverently called this proceeding, robbing the Dago in Rome.
>
> ... With my big rosy cheeks and bright eyes and complexion, I suppose I looked, in those days, very holy and innocent, and used to work this graft for all it was worth. I remember how, in church, I used tracts of the Christian Advocate as "stalls." I would hand them to a lady as she entered the church, and while doing so, pick her pocket.

Research subsequent to the findings of Hartshorne and May

tend to show inconsistent or contradictory findings. William W. Wattenberg suggests that the real questions to be raised could be like these: With how many youngsters in trouble do religious bodies now have contact? What part is religion playing in the lives of those with whom such contact exists? What can be done to make this contact more vital? In the Detroit sample reported by Wattenberg, if the "regular" and "occasional" groups of churchgoers are combined, the churches can claim some marked degree of contact with roughly two thirds of the boys in trouble.[23]

Wattenberg concludes that the influence of church attendance on juvenile misconduct lies, then in lowering the general likelihood that a boy will get into trouble rather than in specifically strengthening resistance to particular offenses. This would seem to bolster the previous findings that church attendance is part of a way of living which generally reduces tendencies toward juvenile misconduct.

As previously indicated, Sunday School and church training do not seem greatly to deter juvenile delinquency. From the available evidence to date there seems to be little relationship between Biblical information and the different phases of conduct by juveniles, delinquent or otherwise. This is true regardless of denominational category or regularity of attendance by young people. Such evidence probably warrants the conclusion that there has not yet been devised part-time, religiously-oriented, character-building programs for young people that will adequately substitute for the day-by-day relationships of parents and children. This conclusion means that churches probably can be used more effectively than has been the case to date in the prevention and control of juvenile delinquency and criminality. Some seminaries are pushing training of ministerial students as counselors and in work with delinquents.

## THE PRESS AND DELINQUENCY

Despite the continuing expansion of radio, movies, and television, the newspapers still remain the most important avenue of information to the public. The means of handling news concerning juvenile delinquency and criminality have been criticized by practitioners in the various fields having to do with delinquency.

Some of the criticisms of the press have been listed by Neumeyer. Crime news may be responsible for stimulating criminal behavior by describing the techniques of crime; by making crime seem common, attractive, glamorous, and profitable; by adding prestige to criminals and contributing to the hero worship of criminals and creating sympathy for them; by appealing to the lower impulses and by sensationalism; by making escape from justice seem easy; by ridiculing the machinery of justice; by conducting "trials by newspapers" and by advocating types of treatment that might stimulate crime and adventure. The alleged "crime waves" that appear periodically have grown out of undue publicity given individual cases and types of crimes.[24]

The amount of written material on the subject of juvenile delinquency is enormous. There are thousands of articles and dozens of volumes published each year on the subject. It has been stated that next to treatises on the Bible and Shakespeare, more has been written on juvenile delinquency than on any other matter.

Many journalists in writing of crime and delinquency permit their imagination to run riot. Newsmen give a "build-up" to criminals by thinking up sensational and descriptive names, such as the "Purple Gang" of Detroit, the "Sphinx Woman," the "Hammer Slayer," the "Tiger Murderess," and Willie Sutton was described as the "field marshall of big crime." Then, to the other extreme, newsmen will describe youthful offenders a "pimply-faced hoodlum," or a "sniveling delinquent," all of which have little or no bearing on the reality of the situation. Juvenile delinquents have no more of a monoply on pimples than have Boy Scouts or junior high school students. As a result, a stereotype is created in the minds of the reading public regarding both adult criminality and juvenile delinquency which is largely untrue.

Press distortions may titillate the imagination of the reading public. When a Detroit newspaper reported that one of the conditions of probation granted to two girls had to do with "no dates," hundreds of readers wrote protesting letters; one wrote to the President of the United States, proclaiming that such an order was unconstitutional, and that it interfered with the inalienable rights to life, liberty and the pursuit of happiness. Not often are the general public stirred from their apathy.[25]

Some newspaper editors print the names of juvenile offenders giving their readers full particulars on serious juvenile crime. They are against any censorship in news. Some newspaper publishers believe that "if a juvenile is old enough to rape a girl, he is old enough to get his name in the paper."

Regarding publicity for juvenile offenders and the alleged deterrent effect of such publicity, there is considerable disagreement in this area. Many police officials believe that publicity tends to glorify the offender in the eyes of his peers. Using their names in the newspapers may give them status. Some delinquents display scrapbooks with clippings about their misdeeds. Juveniles themselves are not in agreement on this matter. Some believe that too much publicity tends to hurt the parents or siblings of the offenders; others take a middle position; publicity for major crimes, no publicity for minor crimes.

Many journalists write with candor, honesty and insight, and as such often make a real contribution. Some social scientists would agree with Ray Sprigle's view of delinquency and crime in the future:[26]

> "Nobody's going to do very much about it. Oh, there's going to be plenty of talk, plenty of research, plenty this and that . . . most of it useless. Each year the tide of crime will wash higher. You are going to see more juvenile delinquency, more criminals, more police, more and bigger penal institutions, all costing the taxpayer more money. Complete coordination of all existing agencies of law enforcement, police systems, courts and probation systems, local, state, federal might accomplish something, but where is the optimist who thinks he'll live long enough to see that? Anyway, if you got it, you'd be pretty close to a police state."

Like Will Rogers, who remarked one time that "All I know is what I read in the newspapers," millions of Americans likewise draw from the same source of information. The widespread interest in reading newspapers is indicated by the fact that in 1958 there were 1755 English language daily newspapers in the United

States, with a total circulation of nearly 58 million, 544 Sunday newspapers with a circulation of over 47 million, and 8268 weekly newspapers with a circulation of nearly 19 million. The circulation of periodicals, and magazines runs into additional millions, to which must be added book and pamphets. If only a fraction of the various publications dealt with news of crime and delinquency, the total impact would be immeasurable.[27]

The press can perform many useful functions, including the right to criticize society's approach to crime and delinquency, but it should always be based on fact, objective surveys and responsible reporting. Only through an enlightened press can the present research in juvenile delinquency be "sold" to the tax-paying newspaper reading public. Otherwise, much of the research remains unexploited. The "Fourth Estate" has a profound obligation to both the reading public and the social sciences.

## RECREATION AND DELINQUENCY

Delinquent behavior tends to increase after school hours and after supper-time hours, primarily because the lack of adult supervision. Children sometimes fill in leisure hours with lawless activity and most juvenile crimes are committed during the hours which are unsupervised. There are high delinquency rates, at times, in areas containing social centers, swimming pools, youth centers, and settlement houses.

Nevertheless, it has been stressed by at least one authority that energetic young people may get into trouble when searching for entertainment. Professor Ruth S. Cavan, for example, notes that boys arrested for building a shack in the park were not malicious; neither were the children who burglarized sports equipment from a country club, nor those who stole a motor boat ride on the river, nor those who sneaked into the moving pictures without buying tickets. In their hunt for recreation, they became court cases.[28]

Sometimes more drastic consequences are in store for youngsters seeking entertainment. Juveniles may actually be killed as a result of indulging in certain forms of "play." For example, in the game of "Chicken" (played by a group in a moving automobile) the driver speeds the car faster and faster until one of the group finally is scared into telling him to slow down; this one is labeled as "chicken." Such puerile activities of young people have been aptly called "teenicide."

There appears little correlation between sports, supervised recreation and character building. One myth of long standing is believed by many individuals that participation in sports acts as an antibiotic in juveniles and that lack of interest in sports means potential delinquency. Many juvenile delinquents are above average physically and many have excelled in athletics, understood the value of teamwork, and cooperated very well. In Tacoma, three top students, one an Eagle scout, confessed to scores of burglaries. This situation can be duplicated in any city in the United States.

Some forms of music have been linked to delinquent behavior. I. Sablosky in July, 1944 stated that popular music is corrupting the youth of America. But Frankie Lane was of the opinion that no youngster who enjoys Bing Crosby, Dinah Shore or Patti Page could go for delinquency. Mr. Lane praised President Eisenhower for inviting well-known athletes to a breakfast, July 11, 1955, to discuss delinquency, among other things, and suggested that the President repeat the gesture by extending a breakfast to crooners too.[29]

Juveniles who get into trouble are not interested in supervised recreation. In one survey in New York City as reported by James R. Dumpson, not more than 10 per cent of the total adolescent age group in the area studied were participating in adult-sponsored leisure time activities. No amount of adaptation of services on the part of leisure-time agencies alone can prevent or control juvenile delinquency. To seek the answer in recreation is to deny the subjective meaning of anti-social behavior.[30]

In an earlier community project as reported by Fred A. Romano, emphasis on recreational and play projects were more successful in the Chicago Area Project. The first undertaking was an attempt to find and create play facilities for the children of the community. Approximately thirty young men from the community were selected to serve as leaders for the children in these recreational centers. Gradually a year-round program of activities for boys was developed in this district, which included volley-ball, touch-football, table games, handicrafts, kite contests, marble tournaments, roller-skate derbies, educational tours, Boy Scouting, Cubbing, camping, swimming and movies. More than 75 per cent of the community boys between the ages of ten and seventeen participated in this program.[31]

Of more than passing interest was the success in this Chicago Area Project of Scouting. Five years prior to the Project there were no Scouts in the district. Scouting was regarded by the boys as a "sissy" activity and parents were afraid it was a military program. Scouting was promoted and soon there were seven troops and five Cub packs and a total Scout membership of 255 boys. Apparently much depends upon the amount of funds available, type of leadership that can be utilized from the community itself and the close availability of the services. Frequently, Park Commissions will boast that a playground for every child is within a mile of their homes, but what child is going to walk a mile?

Since World War II, street club projects have appeared, usually sponsored by neighborhood or settlement houses. Trained group workers work with youthful gangs and attempt to furnish constructive ideas, activities and socially-accepted goals to gang members. Much success has been reported in Chicago and New York City by qualified observers of these street club projects.

Mention has been made of the apparent increase in sadistic acts by today's juvenile offender. Some of the victims are circus clowns that suffer from brutal treatment from juvenile customers of the circus. According to the Houston *Press,* July 4, 1956, clowning is getting to be risky business, for instead of laughing at him, many juveniles now throw anything from peanut hulls to iron staples at him. Aerialists come off their rigging with blood on arms and legs where staples struck them. Kids, even grown-ups, stomp on clowns' shoes and some times they shoot marbles from slingshots at these circus entertainers.

Youthful recreation suggested by the radio, television, motion pictures, and comic books may at times lead to delinquent behavior, particularly in the case of susceptible youngsters. With this possibility in mind, one national radio hook-up banned until after 9:00 p.m. all programs which might encourage the adolescent generation to participate in criminal acts. Such approaches probably serve to encourage many children to wait up for the broadcast. *Time* (March 3, 1952) reports that a group of San Francisco mothers similarly interested in the possible effects of the mass media, observed children's television shows for four hours, recording thirteen murders and assorted killings and sluggings, six kidnappings, five hold-ups, three explosions, three instances of blackmail and extortion, three thefts, two armed robberies, two cases of arson, one lynching, one torture scene, and one miscarriage. In a half-hour serial, the mothers clocked 104 gunshots; in another serial death was "shudderingly described" fourteen times in twenty minutes. What kind of behavior will result from exposure to this type of entertainment?

Various attempts have been made to answer this question. For example, in 1932, by means of questionnaires and written accounts of personal reactions, Herbert Blumer and P. M. Hauser undertook a study of the motion pictures and delinquency. They obtained information from 874 delinquents and 878 grade and high school boys and girls. Their conclusions showed that motion pictures seem to have a deleterious influence on 10 per cent of the males and 25 per cent of the females.[32]

Motion pictures, of course, depict the good and virtuous as well as the bad; and some of the best literature, not excluding Shakespeare, contains references to "evil" behavior. According to Judge Camille Kelley of Memphis, in approximately fifty thousand cases which came before her, less than six could be blamed on the motion pictures. Whatever the hunches, not very much is yet known about the impact of motion pictures, radio, and television.

While there is little consensus, many practitioners in the field of law enforcement and control, tend to blame delinquency, even poor police morale on television because of the exposure to crime, mayhem and violence. Others have stated that television crime programs are potentially more injurious than movies, radio, or comic books because television demands no physical efforts, no money, and no strong imaginary projection. Then too, television programs often depict life as cheap and depict judges, lawyers and police as dishonest, incompetent and stupid and not as handsome as the crooks they are supposed to capture.

Most of the television movies are old movies cut down to television time lengths. The quieter scenes have been cut out, which results in more unrelieved sadism and brutality. About twenty-five murders are committed in New York City during an average month, but television shows some thirty killings per day. During the first half of 1955, Los Angeles had forty-eight actual murders, but in a single week there were 120 murders on television. There are more killed each year on television than die annually by murder and non-negligent homicide in the six largest cities of the United States. However, television has a better record than the police, for every television law-breaker is "brought to justice." Many parents do not seem to object to such violence, even in the movies. A Mother may call the box-office and ask "What's playing." The manager may reply, "Well, there is a lot of violence, gunplay, murder in the picture," but the Mother, in one instance, interrupted with "Oh that's all right, as long as it isn't full of sexy stuff."[33]

The comic books and comic strips have also been cited as exercising an undesirable influence upon those children who avidly read them. Comics are read, according to some estimates, by four out of five children over six years of age. They appear in some fifty million copies of daily newspapers. About forty million comic books are sold every month. Their specific influence, however, is not clear—although dramatic cases are occasionally brought to the attention of the public. Thus is read the story about two twelve-year-old Oklahoma boys, who, stimulated by a comic book strip, stole an airplane, flew it 120 miles, and brought it down without mishap. They said they learned how to fly by reading the funnies.[34]

In the December 6, 1948 issue of *Time* is the story of two Canadian boys, eleven and thirteen years old, accused of robbery and murder. At the hearing they said that they got their ideas for their crime from the forty to fifty comic books they were accustomed to reading each week. The presiding judge commented: "I agree as to the influence of the literature these boys have been subjected to. A concerted effort should be made to see that this worse than rubbish is abolished in some way." Most adults probably sympathize with this plea. But there seems little doubt that the influence of comic books has been over-emphasized frequently by adult authorities and by juvenile offenders themselves. A comic book code, not in operation, set up by the publishers themselves may further alleviate this problem.

According to an article by John R. Cavanagh,[35] the first of the modern comic books was published in 1933. Each comic book is read by several people and 75 per cent of all comic books are purchased by children out of their own funds—an outlay of $300,000 a month or $3,600,000 per year. Between the ages of 6 and 11, 95 per cent of boys and 91 per cent of girls buy comics as a steady diet. During World War II, the combined sales of *Life, Reader's Digest,* and *The Saturday Evening Post* were exceeded by the comic books by a ratio of 10-1.

In an attempt to approach the problem of comic books realistically, Dr. Cavanagh points out that day dreams of children and adolescents are consistently filled with episodes of crime, violence and death or such erotic trends as love and marriage. These thoughts have been present in the minds of children since history began. The comic books do not place them there. The normal aggressive reactions find release in the phantasies stimulated by the comic books which thus become the means by which children are able to work off their hostility towards their parents and others without the development of guilt which they might otherwise feel. Many have commented on the quieting effect of the comics, the "marijuana of the nursery," usually in the belief that this is harmful. It seems more likely that the child is merely projecting himself into the story and releasing his aggression in the realm of phantasy than becoming noisy, troublesome or indulging in other overt aggressive behavior.

Another element which probably contributes to a child's interest in the comics is the Gestalt factor. The child likes pictures which help him to grasp the meaning of the words, to give him a better Gestalt—a better view of the whole meaning.

There are comics which are undesirable. These are in the minority. The group known collectively as "jungle adventure comics" typify this class. Here are found the scantily clad females, the chained females and the sexually suggestive situations which are the comics' most objectionable feature. However, young children, contrasted with mature folk, are not interested in sex as suggested by posture and scanty clothing. The comic book publishers, being business men, give their public what it wants. No one has conclusively demonstrated that the comic books are detrimental in any way. No normal child under the age of twelve is likely to be harmed by them.

In 1956, twelve states enacted new laws to curb objectionable comics. In Montana, it is a misdemeanor to sell or distribute offensive comics and a jail sentence for the second offense is mandatory. Nevada banned objectionable comics, but failed to set up standards to determine just what is objectionable.[36] Due to these and other failures in establishing "controls," censorship on comics is probably not more than 50 per cent successful.

To be sure, illegal conduct, adult and juvenile, is often undeservedly glamorized by the motion pictures, by radio and television, and by the comics. There can be no quarrel with those who decry this situation—or with those who condemn the tabloid publicity that so often gives crime and delinquency a kind of prestige. But the causes of delinquency and the reasons for its persistence are many and complex. Mass media and recreational institutions play their part. The effective control of delinquency and its abatement, however, call for inclusive measures that meet the community organization and the life of the individual at many points.

## REFERENCES

1. Carr, Lowell J.: Organized Efforts in Crime Prevention, *Federal Probation,* Vol. VI, July-September, 1942, p. 51.
2. Romano, Fred A.: Organizing a Community for Delinquency Prevention," 1940 *Yearbook,* National Probation and Parole Association, pp. 1–12.
3. Bloch, Herbert A. and Flynn, Frank T.: *Delinquency: The Juvenile Offender in America Today,* New York, Random House, Inc., 1956, pp. 198–202.
4. Wertham. M.D., Fredric: *The Seduction of the Innocents,* New York, Rinehart & Company, Inc., 1953, pp. 151–152.
5. Fancelow, John: *The Northern Star* (DeKalb) Northern Illinois University, April 22, 1960, p. 2.
6. Quoted in Problems in Education, *Social Problems,* T. Lynn Smith and Associates, New York, Thomas Y. Crowell Company, 1955, p. 352.
7. *Ibid.,* p. 354.

8. Bogus Bomb Scares in Schools, Point of View, *Journal of Social Therapy,* Vol. 2, Fourth Quarter, 1956, p. 295.
9. Johnson, Jr., Arthur C.: "Our Schools Makes Criminals," *The Journal of Criminal Law and Criminology,* Vol. XXXIII, July-August, 1942, pp. 310–315.
10. Axelrad, Sidney: Negro and White Male Institutionalized Delinquents, *The American Journal of Sociology,* Vol. LVII, May, 1952, pp. 569–574.
11. Kahn, Alfred J.: Who Are Our Truants, *Federal Probation,* Vol. XV, March, 1951, pp. 35–40.
12. *Ibid.,* p. 36.
13. *Ibid.,* p. 40.
14. Reinemann, John Otto: The Truant Before the Court, *Federal Probation,* Vol. XII, September, 1948, pp. 8–12.
15. Ellingston, John R.: *Protecting Our Children from Criminal Careers,* New York, Prentice-Hall, Inc, 1948, pp. 285, 290.
16. Johnson, Jr., Arthur C.: *op. cit.,* p. 312.
17. Grunhut, Max: *Penal Reform,* Oxford, The Clarendon Press, 1948, pp. 21–22.
18. Ellingston, John R.: *op. cit.,* p. 14.
19. Carr, Lowell J.: *Delinquency Control,* New York, Harper & Brothers, 1950, pp. 370–373.
20. Smith, Philip M.: Role of the Church in Delinquency Prevention, *Sociology and Social Research,* Vol. XXXV, January, 1951, pp. 183–190.
21. Hartshorne. Hugh and May, Mark A.: *Studies in the Nature of Character,* New York, The Macmillan Company (3 vols.), 1928-1930.
22. Hamilton, Charles (Editor): New York, *Men of the Underworld,* The Macmillan Company, 1952, p. 76.
23. Wattenberg, William W.: Church Attendance and Juvenile Misconduct, *Sociology and Social Research,* Vol. 34, January, 1950, pp. 195–202.
24. Neumeyer, Martin H.: *Juvenile Delinquency in Modern Society,* Princeton, New Jersey, D. Van Nostrand Company, Inc., 1961, p. 218.
25. Weihofen, Henry: The M'Naghten Rules in its Present-Day Setting, *Federal Probation,* Vol. XVIII, September, 1953, p. 10.
26. Sprigle, Ray: Crystal Balls Slightly Clouded, National Probation and Parole Association *News,* Vol. 34, September, 1955, p. 6.
27. Neumeyer, Martin H.: *op. cit.,* p. 220.
28. Cavan, Ruth S.: *Criminology,* New York, Thomas Y. Crowell Company, 1950, p. 114.
29. Sports and Character Building, National Probation and Parole Association *News,* Vol. 34, September, 1955, p. 5.
30. Dumpson, James R.: An Approach to Antisocial Street Gangs, *Federal Probation,* Vol. XIII, December, 1949, p. 23.
31. Romano, Fred A.: *op. cit,* pp. 9–11.

32. Blumer, Herbert and Hauser, Philip M.: *Movies, Delinquency, and Crime,* New York, The Macmillan Co., 1933, p. 37.
33. Hard to Believe Department, Random Shots from the Editor, *Law and Order,* Vol. 4, January 1956, p. 46.
34. Teeters, Negley K. and Reinemann, John Otto: *The Challenge of Delinquency,* New York, Prentice-Hall, Inc., 1950, p. 188.
35. Cavanagh, M.D., John R.: The Comics War, *The Journal of Criminal Law and Criminology,* Vol. XL, May-June, 1949, pp. 28–35.
36. Leonard, V. A., (Editor) : *Current Notes,* Action Taken to Control Distribution of Objectionable Comic Books, *The Journal of Criminal Law, Criminology and Police Science,* Vol. 46, January-February, 1956, p. 688.

# 5

## SPECIAL PERSONALITY AND BEHAVIOR PROBLEMS

JUVENILE DELINQUENCY is usually symptomatic of an underlying disorganization of the individual's personality or of his social environment or of both. It is not a disease or a clinical entity. Juvenile delinquency is a descriptive term referring to asocial or antisocial behavior.

Delinquency is not necessarily the overt manifestation of basic personality disorganization. Although the available evidence is not conclusive, it is possible that there is not an appreciably higher percentage of emotionally maladjusted boys in reform schools than among those on probation, in detention homes, or in the general population. On various personality tests, reformatory groups do not suffer much by comparison with noninstitutionalized youth. The stereotype of the juvenile delinquent as a mentally or emotionally "deficient" should be discarded.

In *Unraveling Juvenile Delinquency,* a study in a distinguished extreme) of a "dynamic" offender which is diametrically opposed series of investigations by the Gluecks present a pattern (possibly to the frequently held image of the delinquent—the weak, skinny, pasty-complexioned, who skulks about in a furtive manner smoking the inevitable cigarette. They describe this "typical" juvenile delinquent as follows:

> The delinquents, as a group, tend toward the outline of a solid, closely knit, muscular type, one in which there is a relative predominance of muscle, bone, and connective tissue.
>
> On the whole, the delinquents are more extroverted, vivacious, impulsive, and less self-controlled than the *nondelinquents*. They are more hostile, resentful, defiant, suspicious, and destructive. They are less fearful of failure or defeat than the *nondelinquent.*
>
> It is evidently difficult for them to develop the high degree

flexibility of adaptation, self-management, self-control, sublimation of primitive tendencies and self-centered desires demanded by the complex and confused culture of the times.[1]

Very likely this description approaches the misleading view of a counter-stereotype. Yet it serves as a warning that any fixed notion of the delinquent as a "personality type" does not square with the facts. This does not mean that psychological and psychiatric knowledge is unimportant in understanding and working with delinquency. Certainly the specialist should have technical competence in the field of personality disorders to plan any program of rehabilitation for the delinquent. This very competence provides child guidance clinics, whose personnel utilize techniques developed in medicine, psychiatry, psychology, and social work, one of the principal tools essential for effective work.

Ruth S. Cavan in her Presidential Address [2] to the Midwest Sociological Society, April 28, 1961 shed new light on the problem of delinquency by raising some interesting questions: "Are there gradations in delinquency?" If so, where along the line of gradation does a child become so out of line that his behavior merits calling him a delinquent? If delinquent behavior has gradations, does good behavior also have gradations?" Perhaps comparisons made between the "bad" boy and the "good" boy have been unfair and unrealistic. The "good" boy may be as much "out of line" and may suffer from even more personality problems than the "bad" boy. The delinquent might better be compared to the "All American Boy" who is represented in Figure 1, under Section D, (Normal conformity).

Figure 1. represents the social structure, the framework of which consists of the institutions and less formal but fairly permanent organizations, that operating together, carry on the functions of the society. Area D represents the central part of the social structure, where institutions are found that set the formal standards for behavior and exert the formal means of control. The base line represents the extent of deviations from the central social norms.

Human behavior falls into a continuum, yet in most instances

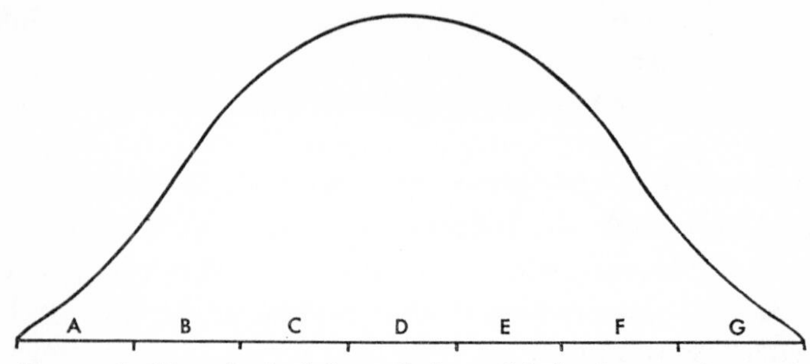


**Figure 1. Hypothetical formulation of behavior continuum.**[4]

A. Underconforming contraculture
B. Extreme under-conformity
C. Minor under conformity
D. Normal conformity
E. Minor over-conformity
F. Extreme over-conformity
G. Over-conforming conformity

it is described in terms of dichotomies. There is the sinner and the saint, the devil and the angel, the juvenile delinquent and the model child. Behavior has many intermediate shades of gray.

Area D is an area of tolerance provided that the social organization itself is not threatened. "Misbehavior" is overlooked on "Moral Holidays," such as Halloween, "V-J Day," and New Year's Eve. Most people find in area D a satisfactory way of life. Complete conformity to the social norms is rarely demanded.

Professor Cavan points out that in many research studies, the delinquent children (area A) are compared with near-perfect children (area G) as was done by the Gluecks in their *Unraveling Juvenile Delinquency* previously referred to. The Gluecks matched each of 500 correctional-school boys with "control boys" who for the most part had participated in no delinquency and whose behavior was exemplary.

Difficulty was encountered in finding 500 "perfect" boys, so included in the control group were a few boys guilty of hopping trucks, sneaking into movies, drinking, and running away from home. It would seem that the control group is fully as deviant from normal conformity (area D) as the delinquent group but in the opposite direction.

As Cavan indicates, the boys in area A are often called hoodlums, punks, bums, or little gangsters, while boys in area G have been referred to as wet blankets, sissies, teacher's pet or squares. Contrasted to both areas A and G, the area D youth is "all boy" the all-American boy; he can take care of himself; he is ambitious; he is a good sport. He may borrow small things and forget to return them, he may cheat on tests in school, may do property damage, lie for his own advantage, but always staying within the tolerance limits. He is developing, even in misbehavior, traits that will help him fit into the adult competitive D pattern of behavior, moving toward the social expectations for his future as an adult.

Areas A and G represent detachment from social norms and opposition to them, for these areas are *contracultures,* one of which is built up around disregard for the social norms. The term itself replaces the term subculture when applied to extreme deviating types of behavior, for subculture does not connote behavior that is in conflict with the main culture. The term contraculture was proposed by J. Milton Yinger.[3] It refers to values and modes of conduct that are in conflict with the prevailing social norms of area D. The values and behavior of the contraculture are not only different from, but are opposed to the social norms.

Area A youths are referred to as the "hard core" or "real" delinquents. The school may expel them permanently, the judge may commit them to a prison or a reformatory. In his group in area A, he is approved for stealing, and committing acts of hostility.

Area F youths have been criticized, ostracized, and rejected by area D Groups. There are those in area F who become the conscientious objectors to war, refuse to salute the flag, refuse to send children to school as required by law, and the like. Some overconforming contracultures are content to withdraw into isolation; some attack the general social norms through propaganda or legislation, even physically attack members of symbols of the general culture.

Any analysis of special personality and behavior problems is complicated by social class norms. The difference between middle- and lower-class definitions of behavior is especially pertinent, since most school officials, law enforcement personnel, district attorneys and judges represent the values of the middle class. Youths from areas A and B tend to come from lower class levels. The "well-adjusted" personality of an area A boy would be "out-of-step" and considered to be maladjusted by the standards of area D.

Personality and behavior problems are frequently *a function of cultural* factors which can contribute to delinquency. The value system of various groups cannot be internalized effectively by the youth or the conflicts such value systems present when they clash with value standards of the larger society. *Social* factors refer to the youth's functioning social relationships with others. Many come from common religious, ethnic, and economic backgrounds, but whose dissimilar patterns of family organization produce different types of problems often leading to personality and behavior problems that may ultimately be reflected in juvenile delinquency and criminality.[5]

## PHYSIOLOGICAL FACTORS AND PERSONALITY

Personality disorganization may be aggravated by various physiological circumstances. Consider the case, reported a few years ago, of the sixteen-year-old offender, bald as a cue ball, who faced the court charged with burglary. The judge being convinced that the conspicuous hairlessness played a part in the boy's delinquency, had him fitted for a toupee and released him to relatives in another county, rather than committing him to an institution. The restoration of a more normal appearance may account for the fact that no further trouble from him was reported. Similar physiological defects have been witnessed in court cases—such as a very large nose, eyes of two colors, acne, a club foot. An there seems little doubt that these "deformities"—as defined by the youngsters themselves and by some of their fellows—often play an important role in encouraging individuals to "fight back" through delinquent acts. Such physical characteristics may induce special psychological difficulties within individuals and self-conceptions that are socially unacceptable and individually and socially harmful.

There is no consensus among practitioners who are identified with the field of juvenile delinquency that physical conditions are associated with delinquency in any positive way. The literature on juvenile delinquency is replete with theories, opinions and data on physical conditions and the incidence of juvenile misbehavior, even adult criminality. Lombroso's concept of "physical deficiency," Victor Nelson's "compensation" theory, Smith and Schlapp's "glandular dysfunction" theory, Hooton's "biological inferiority" theory, even the relatively obscure "Lame, Halt, and Blind" theory have been attempts to establish a definite connection between physiological disabilities and delinquent and criminal behavior. Such a "cause and effect" relationship has not been established between physical conditions and criminal behavior and the exact relationship may be incapable of demonstration.

## NEUROTIC AND PSYCHOTIC FACTORS AND PERSONALITY

In an address by Dr. Sydney R. Smith,[6] on observations of juvenile offenders made in the psychological clinic, the following characteristics were noted: the delinquent child is apt to be unreflective; to be projective; to indulge in much oral pessimissm. Delinquents are suspicious of people who are good and kind, and in a cynical manner believe them to be soft-hearted, or soft-headed. There is much family disruption present; the mother's depression is contagious and often affects the child; the parents are often immature, resembling infantile personalities. The delinquent's parents are often pre-occupied in thoughts and plans that do not include their child, hence the child "loses" his parents over and over again.

The neurotic individual evidences dysfunction of behavior due to emotional stress as a result of frustrations, conflicts, deprivations, and feelings of great personal insecurity. The basic characteristic is *anxiety*.

The neurotic is not likely to commit spectacular crimes; he is more of a nuisance than a social menace. Neurotics "suffer" out experiences, they tend to have too much conscience, to be over-restrained and to use non-realistic means to achieve their goals.

Because of the seemingly irresistible nature of their acts, the offenses committed by neurotic and psychotic offenders are only incidental to the satisfaction of the inner urges that are imperious to their demands. Neurotic categories would include several types.

(1) *Anxiety*-reaction is shown by hypochondria, running away, bumming and committing petty crimes. (2) The *obsessive-compulsion* reaction may manifest itself in kleptomania (compulsive stealing), pyromania (compulsive fire-setting), exhibitionism, even suicide. (3) The *phobic* reaction is predicated on abnormal fears of dirt (mysophobia), blood (hematophobia), high places (acrophobia), darkness (nyctophobia) to name a few. (4) The *conversion* reaction would include hysterical or functional blindness and deafness for which there exists no organic basis. (5) The *dissociative* reaction would include amnesia or fugue, in which the individual may commit bigamy, evade taxes, change his name, or sell mortgaged property. (6) The *traumatic* reaction in which the individual may resort to "goldbricking" or malingering in hospitals, often at public expense. (7) The *philiac* reaction has reference to abnormal loves, as in pedophilia (children), zoophilia (animals), gerontophilia (elderly people) and the like. (8) The *homosexual* reaction, erotic attraction of the same sex, is usually thought of as being the result of a deep childhood neurosis or of infantile frustrations. According to Edmund Bergler,[7] the homosexual wallows in self-pity, collects "injustices," so as compensation he cuts "moral corners." This galaxy appears universal regardless of the I.Q., cultural background, or education.

The neurotic, unlike the psychotic, is more of a nuisance than a danger to himself and others. Outstanding traits include his marked inefficiency and his inadequacy in adjusting himself to his environment, as well as deep feelings of uneasiness and guilt. The neurotic's misbehavior is an act of compromise, so that any direct attack upon his misconduct is apt to be futile. Arrest, conviction, and imprisonment only tend to reinforce his own feelings of inferiority. But neurotic or psychotic personality conflicts, it should be remembered, do not lead *inevitably* into crime. Most criminals, in fact, are not maladjusted mentally or emotionally, and most psychologically maladjusted persons are not criminals. Most juvenile delinquents are "normal."

Probably most deviated sex offenders of the compulsive variety are neurotic, not psychotic. Very few of the following categories are found among juvenile delinquents. The *fetishism* or what

Reinhardt[8] calls "The Insatiable Substitution," refers to one whose eroticisms have been focused upon some object that stands as a symbol of the real sex object, such as shoes, lingerie, hair, or clothing. It could be a rose, or a gardenia, even a mere picture of the fetish object might do. William Heirens, the juvenile murderer of three women was obsessed by the fetishism of feminine lingerie, which incidentally supplied the motivation for over two hundred burglaries while a sophomore at the University of Chicago. The fetishist makes a good police suspect in a pointless burglary.

The *partialism* or so-called body fetishist is one who is sexually fixated on some part of the human body. Partialism is often complicated by the appearance of other sexual cravings. *Fetishisms* constitute a perversion peculiar to males. It is a "flight from woman." The fetishist renounces women and anatomy too. Due to body-fetishism, women who are deformed, crippled, or one-legged have more appeal than would men similarly handicapped, since fetishism is a male type of perversion.

*Narcissism* refers to self-love, named after the Greek youth, Narcissus who fell in love with his own reflection in a pool of water. For many individuals, it is the beginning of a life-long romance. *Voyeurism,* (Peeping Toms) must "see" in order to be sexually gratified. Voyeurism often begins as childish curiosity. Most voyeurists are harmless. However, laws are not specific on sex offenses, and as Karpman [9] has pointed out, people have been arrested for carrying in their pockets pictures of nude men and women that differ in no wise from pictures published in nudist magazines, many of which are allowed to go through the mails.

*Frottage,* is a form of sexual perversion which may manifest itself in "patting" female posteriors. These individuals are often encountered in elevators, street cars or in crowded stores. They may have a fetish for some form of clothing their victim happens to be wearing or some portion of the victim's body.[10] However, these "patters" are comparatively harmless, but legally troublesome. One man was arrested time after time for this offense, and cheerfully paid the fines which ranged from a dollar to one hundred dollars. Finally, he was asked why he continued to break this law after being fined so many times. His reply: "It was worth it."[10]

*Sadism* and *masochism* should be considered together, as they are virtually two sides of the same coin. As de River[11] suggests, it is well to remember that every sadist (one who inflicts pain on others) is a masochist and every masochist (who enjoys pain inflicted on him) is a sadist. The term "algolagnia" from algos (pain) and lagneia (lust) has been used, then subdivided into active algolagnia (sadism) and passive algolagnia (masochism) as more appropriate terms. The sadist may be the sex murderer who finds sensual gratification in mutilation of his victim. The masochist who loves "Queen Pain," enjoys both mental and physical punishment; some go to great lengths to witness their own demise. The professional prostitute has in her repertoire pins, needles, pinchers and high heeled shoes to accommodate her masochistic "tricks" (customers). The acme of sadism is murder.

*Transvestism* or what Reinhardt terms "Nature's Cruel Paradox," usually starts in childhood and refers to the desire to be identified with the opposite sex. The male's dress, manner, interests are designed to enhance his feeling of being a woman. He is not a homosexual in the realistic meaning of the term. As one subject expressed it: "I want a man to think of me as a woman . . . and to be attracted to me because he thinks I am a woman." [12] This drive may originate with "Mother's little helper," or when parents, who wanted a girl, got a boy instead. The guise of a woman is so expert, that occasionally, policewomen in "shaking down" "female" prisoners find a transvestite.

*Exhibitionism,* which de River calls "The Spectacular Complex," [13] causes the subject to expose himself to the opposite sex or the general public. Not only does the exhibitionist wish to be seen and appreciated, but often the desire to dominate is also present. In one sense, this perversion could be considered with voyeurism as one says, "I want to show you what I've got," the other states, "I want to see what you've got." The behavior of exhibitionism is compulsive. There is the need to reduce anxiety, rather than exhibition for pleasure, and it is usually accompanied by masturbation ("one day neurasthenia").

*Pyromania,* compulsive fire setting, identifies the "fire-bug" who is basically narcisstic and preoccupied with his neurotic drives. A small percentage of firesetters are pathological in that they set fire to buildings due to jealousy or rebuff. The true pyromaniac's motive seems to be for status; the sex pyromaniac motive concerns sexual gratification. The crime of arson has two psychological components—starting the blaze and extinguishing it. Fire marshals are aware of the close relationship between fascination with fires and sexual excitement in male arsonists who compulsively return to watch fires they set.[14] The record holder seems to be Dale Segree whose case was reported in Time magazine, July 19, 1954, who set fire to Ringling Brothers and Barnum and Bailey Circus at Hartford, Connecticut; 169 people were killed in six minutes. Segree had a long record of arson, starting as a youth, which included a school house, a store and a Salvation Army Center. A "flaming red rider on a fiery red horse" made him do it.

Among the paraphilias are *zoophilia* (sodomy, bestiality) which represents extreme examples of sexual inhibition and timidity. *Necrophilia* (sexual possession of a dead body) is repugnant to all cultural standards. Even cannibalism is more understandable. Necrophilia is intimately associated with extreme sadism.[15] *Pedophilia* (sexual possession of a child) refers to child molestation. The typical pedophiliac is often impotent, and is satisfied with the substitute act of fondling or masturbation by the victim. The pedophiliac has a "way with children," exploits the "parental attitude" and can be found in every community.

In addition to the neurotic disabilities, problems of a *psychsomatic* nature may be found among juvenile delinquents, such as *anorexia nervosa* (malnutrition, inanition), *bronchial asthma, constipation, finickyness, migraine* and *enuresis (bed-wetting).* Enuresis is fairly common among juvenile delinquents. According to Captain Frank Popello of the Maricopa County Sheriff's Office (Phoenix) Arizona, nearly half of the county jail youthful inmates are enuretics. Jail officials have to burn several hundred dollars worth of mattresses every year.

Neurotic disabilities have a history, usually a long record of previous difficulty. Many of the listed neurotic categories have their genesis in childhood. The obsessions and compulsions of the neurotic offender must be held partially responsible for a proportion of juvenile delinquency and criminality.

The juvenile offender is seldom psychotic. The truly psychotic offender is divorced from reality. The psychotic's dysfunction of behavior is due to emotional stress brought about by delusions and hallucinations. He has little insight into himself or into the conditions responsible for his crime. The paranoic, for example, may burn the house of one who is "working against him." or he may murder his enemy's entire family, even his own, as he labors under delusions of grandeur or persecution. The schizophrenic is most likely of all psychotics to commit a crime. Simple schizophrenics are characterized by indifference to society, and frequently are found among hobos, vagabonds, and those committing petty larceny. Paranoid schizophrenics plagued by unsystematized delusions, may murder because they have heard the "voice of God" commanding them to do so. Some of their offenses may be bizarre in nature, as breaking into a school house at 4:00 A.M. in zero weather to steal ice cream. The encephalitics have the highest specific relation to crime, resulting sometimes in grotesque suicide, self-mutilation, and violent destruction of property. Senile dements engage in crimes of rage and temper and sex offenses against children. Paretics (those reaching the terminal stage of syphilis) sometimes commit assault and murder. Manic-depressives may pass worthless checks in the manic phase or commit suicide during the depressive phase. Juvenile offenders, when psychotic, are most apt to be schizophrenic; significantly, schizophrenia was formerly known as dementia praecox.

The number of cases that fit the different neurotic and psychotic categories depends in part upon the particular clinic or psychologist involved. Diagnoses in the field of psychiatry, not being an exact matter, are highly variable, sometimes diametrically opposed. For example, one or more psychiatrists may testify for the prosecution in an insanity plea and find the defendant "sane"; in the identical case, other psychiatrists for the defense may find him "insane."

Michael Hakeem, an outstanding critic of the psychiatric approach to crime, states that psychiatrists may have enriched our vocabulary and produced prodigious literature, but much of it is propaganda. It is characterized by incautious, immodest effusions, misrepresentations, contradictions, illogicalities, biased data selection, and tautological trivialities. The concept of neurosis can have reference to either a theological dogma, a philosophical premise, or a bodily disturbance. Much depends in psychiatric diagnosis upon the relative social class position of both the therapist and the patient.[16]

The psychiatric school of criminology is predicated on the fact that law violators have deep-seated emotional problems and that a certain organization of the personality, developed entirely apart from criminal culture, will result in criminal behavior regardless of social situations. Yet in an article by Messinger and Apfelberg [17] recently published, these psychiatrists stated that out of 71,000 examinations of approximately 57,000 persons involved in felonies over a quarter of a century of continuous study, that most of these persons were not significantly psychotic, neurotic, or even intellectually deficient in the ordinary clinical sense. Approximately 1.5 per cent are psychotic, less than 1 per cent are significantly neurotic, and about 2.5 per cent are mental defectives. Thus, only about 5 per cent of all persons convicted of felonies need to be considered for special treatment for psychotic, neurotic, or mentally deficient states.

On the other hand, American jurisprudence has failed to keep step with dynamic psychiatry. This lag helps to account for the fact that it may be decreed that one offender is a "neurotic" and thus not insane, while another is a "psychotic" and therefore *ipso facto* not responsible for his acts. But what is the difference, it has been asked, between a schizophrenic who walks around naked because "voices" have told him to do so and the exhibitionist who, without hallucinations but through some obscure and irresistible inner urge, feels driven to expose himself in public? Insofar as basic motivations are concerned, is one more or less "insane" than the other? Frequently questions of this order face officials and others who deal with juvenile delinquency.

Ideally, of course, competent clinicians in the juvenile delinquency field should decide whether the offender should be treated as a "mental" case or not. The crime's very nature, especially if it is of a bizarre type, may reflect emotional disorders of the culprit and as such should be thoroughly investigated by professionally competent personnel. For the jailing or imprisonment of compulsive offenders, including, for example, many homosexuals, is not only a cruel measure from a humanitarian point of view but precludes the type of remedial work essential for adequate correction.

## MENTAL RETARDATION AND DELINQUENCY

Probably the greatest impetus to the American "feebleminded school" of delinquency came from the writings of H. H. Goddard who many years ago suggested that all criminals and delinquents are feebleminded, that the criminal type is really a species of feebleminded, and due to personal and social pressures may be driven into crime and delinquency for which persons of this type are "fitted by nature." [18] The inadequacy and misleading nature of such views is, of course, now an elementary lesson in social science. However, even today many people believe that there is a high correlation between feeblemindedness and delinquency. Furthermore, there is considerable confusion generally in properly distinguishing between mental diseases and mental deficiency. And in some cases, there is no clear-cut distinction between the two phenomena, since they both may be found in one individual. The criterion between the feebleminded and the mentally deficient is the ability to function in the group, which is something the feebleminded category cannot do. Mental deficiency refers only to mental test level. Feeblemindedness refers to an inadequacy in personal social adjustment —to get along in school, make an independent living—without special assistance or supervision.

According to Harry Manuel Shulman,[19] the study of the relationship of intelligence and delinquency began with the early 19th century neo-classical criminal justice doctrine that stated, since crime was a rational choice of conduct, mental defectives in common with infants and the insane, were not legally responsible for their actions.

The relation of intelligence and recidivism, i.e., repetition of offenses, has been given some attention. In the United States, roughly one quarter of all children arraigned as juvenile delinquents had previous arraignments. Both superior and dull children tend to higher incidences of behavior disorder than children of average intelligence, the bright group tend to "unlearn" much of their maladjusted behavior, while the dull continue, even increase, their misbehavior problems as they grow older.

The bases of determining feeblemindedness appears to change with the years. During the Goddard "era" many studies reported that 50 per cent of the delinquents were feebleminded. By 1930, the percentage of feebleminded delinquents had dropped to around 20 per cent, and in 1960, the percentage has further dropped to only 5 per cent incidence of feeblemindedness among delinquents.

Mentally deficient offenders are usually found in institutions about five times their proportion to the general population because of their susceptibility to suggestion. Frequently, the mentally deficient boy or girl is the "patsy" for others who may plan and organize the offense. Intellectually handicapped offenders have been sent to jail or prison for car theft although they could not drive a car. They are easily caught off guard. In the July 5, 1954 issue of *Time,* a mentally deficient offender identified his holdup victims, when they were unable to identify him!

In Shulman's discussion of *Intelligence and Delinquency,* an important comment is made relative to *social intelligence* and rehabilitative possibilities of juvenile offenders. Social intelligence refers to the capacity for social adjustment as differentiated from the ability to learn from experience. One may learn from experience, but not necessarily in the direction of benefit to society. During the 1920's, trade and vocational education were utilized as a delinquency rehabilitation programs. Today, educators seem to recognize that competence in trade and vocational careers calls for more than competence in such skills *per se.* Stable temperamental and personality characteristics are of primary importance. The frequent mental dullness, emotional instabilities, and reading and writing disabilities of a large proportion of delinquents make them poor risks for industrial training.

Mental defectiveness, though rarely an immediate cause of unlawful behavior, is nevertheless associated with it. Usually more suggestible than the average youth because they lack developed critical faculties, the mentally deficient appear among serious delinquents much more frequently than in the general population. About one in eight seems to be the ratio of the number of feebleminded children among all the cases brought into court as defendants. Within a year a total of about fifty thousand mentally deficient boys and girls will appear in court.

Shulman mentions some research in the area of juvenile delinquency that traced certain relationships between types of juvenile offense and intelligence level. One investigator found intelligence positively correlated with forgery, lack of parental control and malicious mischief; and negatively correlated with sex offenses, truancy and vagrancy. Stealing, on the other hand, was found to have no significant relation to intelligence. Another investigator found that for children aged five to 12.9 years, the offenses of stealing, fire-setting, forgery, incorrigibility, truancy and escape from an institution, increased with IQ increase. Personality problems tend to increase as the IQ increases and conduct problems tend to increase as the IQ decreases. Bright children tend toward personality problems and dull children toward conduct disorders.

Feeblemindedness does not cause delinquency, but mental deficiency and delinquency tend to be correlated in court statistics. One reason for this correlation, in all likelihood, is the fact that the brighter children in many instances not only are saved from the reformatory experience, but also quite frequently manage to avoid detention, court arraignment, or even arrest by the police.

## THE PSYCHOPATHIC DELINQUENT

The *psychopathic* delinquent seems to be in a psychiatric no-man's land, "psychopath" being a wastebasket term to explain human behavior that is adjudged not to be normal, neurotic, psychotic, or feebleminded, current terminology favors terms like the "sociopath," or "anti-social reaction," in place of the term "psychopath," nevertheless, this personality character disorder persists regardless of appellations. Unlike psychotics and neurotics, psychopaths appear to have no irresistible impulse to commit delinquencies, no delusions, no hallucinations, no memory defect, and no organic disease of the central nervous system. For this reason, they are usually held legally responsible for their unlawful acts.[20]

The outstanding characteristics of the psychopath are impulsiveness, irrationality, superficiality, and the inability to foresee the consequences of his own action.[21] He has "undisturbed" intelligence, is not distracted by emotional problems or guilt feelings, and has repeated unexplained failures in school, marriage or business. He is irresponsible and unable to accept blame. There is persistent antisocial behavior for no reason, and he would rather lie than tell the truth. The psychopath has no capacity for any deep, personal attachment to any thing, person, or even cause, and his sex proclivities are for purely recreational reasons, and highly superficial.[22] He will commit a crime for astonishingly small stakes, apparently just for the "Hell of it."

Much psychopathic behavior is bizarre behavior such as imitating the dog at fire hydrants when told that "he's in the dog house," urinating in bureau drawers, or in roommate's shoes, or out of library windows, setting horses tail afire, or throwing lighted matches in baby buggies. One boy sold his mother's new coat to the first passerby for $1.00. Despite these antics, the psychopath is frequently a person of great charm and appeal to women, and many make good marriages to capable women, who seem to sense they have a "baby" but often fail to realize that the "baby" will never grow up.[23]

The "typical" psychopath appears to commit quite unrelated crimes. The juvenile psychopath may drown chickens in the local pond while being truant from school. He may pour acid on a puppy's tail, or stab another child. Such individuals have been called "morally insane" or "social imbeciles," for they seem to be unable to learn from experience.

Recent studies indicate the probability that the personalities of adult criminal psychopaths have reached only the pre-adolescent stage of development. Under this "analysis," the so-called "normal" child progresses through five psycho-sexual levels of growth and development, beginning with the *autoerotic* stage (wants to be warm, dry, and well-fed), the *narcisstic* stage (3-5; becomes interested in his own body), the *Oedipus-Electra* stage (5-7; interest, sometimes over-attachment to parent of opposite sex), *homosexual* stage (7-11; interests restricted to own sex), and the ultimate *heterosexual* stage (from puberty on, interests transferred to the opposite sex, in conformity with social norms and expectations). Under this theory, the psychopath presumably stopped his emotional growth and development at the end of the autoerotic or narcisstic stage, but may have continued to develop physically and intellectually until adult standards were achieved.

If the psychopath possesses the emotional nature of a two year old baby, he will lack opportunity to emotionally identify with either of his parents, and as a result never develop any conscience. If that is the case, he will live under his own code, with no remorse or guilt feelings ever asserting themselves. With this emotional equipment, or rather the lack of it, the psychopath makes an excellent blackmailer, embezzler, forger, and above all, confidence man or woman, and probably accounts for more than his share of "hit-and-run" drivers. The dream life of the psychopath appears to have a unique quality, the dreams themselves being almost completely free of guilt so commonly found among neurotics. Verified knowledge, however, about the psychopath as an identifiable single "type" is still quite skimpy.

Nevertheless, in the field of delinquent and criminal behavior, characteristic traits of the psychopath are discernible. His crimes usually reflect no planning, not even discernible rewards. The psychopathic child may smash his own toys. Psychopathic delinquents often commit offenses for what appear to be silly, trivial reasons. These traits are illustrated in a textbook by accounts of two seemingly senseless, probably psychopathic crimes. One fourteen year old boy strangled the baby he agreed to tend as a baby sitter. A Chicago boy killed his young sweetheart while they were witnessing a gangster movie—and insisted he did not know why he did this. These crimes seemed to lack discoverable motives, and brought their perpetrators no financial gain.[24]

In a series of articles by Victor Cohn, of the Minneapolis *Tribune,* concerning children who kill, the lack of motivation, financial gain, or remorse suggest the psychopathic personality. Bernard S., nineteen, murdered three people in four days. First, a seventy-year old farmer who had "squealed" on him for running away from the St. Charles, Illinois reformatory. The next day, Bernard killed a policeman. "He tried to get me for when I'm sticking up a couple, no cop does that to 'ol Bernie. I aim for his forehead and shoot him. That's his tough luck." On the same afternoon, he shot a companion. "Sure, I shot him. I wanted him to help me hold up a hotel but he got yellow." When the death penalty was pronounced, he said to the judge: "To hell with you, I can take it." [25]

Cruelty to animals is frequently found in the behavior patterns of psychopathic children. *Life* in the October 20, 1952, issue relates an example of juvenile cruelty:

> Three boys, aged ten to fifteen, were prowling through a half-constructed house in South Bend, Indiana on a weekend. While there, their attention was struck by some bricks, a bag of plaster and a stray cat. They put the bricks together to form a crude bathtub, mixed the plaster with water to fill it and then dropped in the cat. After a while they went away, leaving the cat in its plaster cast. A construction employee found the cat on Monday morning, chiseled it out and brought it in pitiful but still living shape to a veterinarian. The vet cleaned off the rest of the plaster, gave medication to fight the gangrene in the rear feet and tail which had set solidily by that time and put a soothing ointment on the burned right eye. By Friday, the patient was walking around like a normal cat. The parents of the boys are paying for the cat's medical bills, and their thoughtlessly cruel sons may face juvenile court charges.

Placing the psychopathic boy or girl in a reformatory, jail, or a house of correction, contributes little to his (or her) rehabilitation. Hospitalization and psychiatric treatment are indicated in these cases. The psychopath knows the rules intellectually, but hasn't accepted them. He cannot apply moral principles to himself, but he can verbalize on it easily. He has no insight. Psychopathic offenders are seldom reformable, at least with present methods, and if they commit criminal acts persistently, it is often argued that they should be permanently segregated for their own benefit and for the protection of society.

## ALCOHOLISM AND DELINQUENCY

Alcoholism is a morbid condition resulting from the inordinate or persistent use of alcoholic drinks, rendering the victim mentally ill and afflicted with a body allergy. This condition should not be confused with occasional heavy drinking. The alcoholic constitutes a special problem in crime and is an excellent example of the repetitive offender. Dipsomania is not, in principle, a police problem, but in the absence of other agencies to cope with it, nearly 50 per cent of police time is expended on "drinking" cases. Drunkenness is the charge in about 60 per cent of all police arrests in Milwaukee, a large number of whom are probably alcoholics, and produces between 70 and 75 per cent of all admissions to the Milwaukee House of Corrections.

Sufferers from such conditions as alcoholic hallucinosis, alcoholic delusional psychoses, or polyneuritic psychoses, to use the technical terminology—itself suggestive—may find their way into criminal behavior in much the same manner as the drug addict who commits a crime. The alcoholic seems to be driven by inner compulsions beyond his control, the crime or the deed being only incidental to the psychic condition. Thus the need for professional psychiatric aid is strongly indicated in cases involving actual alcoholics. Considerable drinking among young and older people alike is not necessarily indicative of alcoholism.

It is difficult to determine the extent and intensity of juvenile drinking. Many high school boys and girls consume alcoholic beverages, irrespective of socio-economic status. Both the extent of drinking among minors and the number of delinquencies committed as a result of intoxication are in the realm of guesswork. According to various reports from metropolitan police departments less than five per cent of juvenile arrests involves the charge of drunkenness. There is considerable recidivism among some juvenile offenders due to alcoholic liquor. Persistent alcoholism, it should be stressed, is more likely to be symptomatic of some unresolved emotional conflict than merely the desire to experience the euphoria that often accompanies drinking.

In an article by Jessie F. Binford, then Executive Director of the Juvenile Protective Association, Chicago, it was found that the sale and excessive use of alcohol presented one of the greatest problems to the Association. Two thirds of the complaints received on community conditions were about the illegal sale of liquor to minors in taverns and liquor stores. In a large percentage of individual cases the excessive use of liquor by parents, especially mothers, and by minor boys and girls was significant.[26]

Presumably, this problem appears in most of the urban areas, but with great variation between places and times, depending upon various administrations of city government. Many taverns become centers for gambling, prostitution, lewd and obscene entertainment, often controlled by syndicated interests. As such, they contribute to excessive drinking, broken homes, neglect of children, prostitution, delinquencies and crimes of minors.

On both the juvenile and adult level, alcoholism continues to be a serious problem. Not only are many crimes committed by persons while under the influence of alcohol but alcoholic intoxication is itself legally a misdemeanor. And drinking, of course, results in much "disorderly conduct." Adult drinking often contributes to the lack of adequate parental supervision which in turn frequently stimulates a child's initial act of delinquency.

## DRUG ADDICTION AND DELINQUENCY

If drinking and alcoholism represent severe problems in the lives of many young people, an even larger departure from conventional mores is the practice of drug addiction. Addiction is itself "delinquency"—as witness the "blue-grass commitment" by which an individual may incarcerate himself in Kentucky by admitting that he is addicted to the use of narcotic drugs. In such instances, probation may be granted, provided the individual submits to the treatment made available at the Hospital for Narcotics maintained by the federal government at Lexington.

Because of the expense involved in obtaining narcotics, drug addiction is related to other forms of delinquency; in many instances, the addict must steal in order to obtain the necessary funds to support the drug habit. Many young people may steal from their own homes, appropriating books, jewelry, clothing, radios, and the like, in order to convert them into cash they can use to purchase drugs. Juvenile addicts sometimes buy and sell drugs on a commission basis in school hallways and lavatories, or they may become "mules" acting as messengers or delivery boys, intermediaries between the user and peddler of drugs.

There is a strong tendency to exaggerate the "tie-in" between crime and delinquency and drug addiction. The "crazed" drug addict on a crime rampage is a fairly familiar stereotype reported in the press. Yet out of 5,200 drug addiction cases which appeared in the Chicago court—the only one of its kind in the world—there were only 158 "boosters" (shop-lifters), 58 "cannons" (pick-pockets), 191 burglars, 206 larcenists, 195 murderers, 46 purse snatchers, 47 confidence men and 7 sex assaulters. The balance, 4292 persons or roughly 90 per cent, were charged *solely* with drug addiction.[27] These figures are consistent with other findings that indicate that relatively few addicts are prone to crimes of violence or, for that matter, engage in habitual criminal behavior of any sort.

It is difficult to ascertain the extent of juvenile addiction. In the past it has been a convenient "whipping boy" for social reformers, "do-gooders," crusaders, and sometimes authorities themselves; and it is always "good copy" for the tabloids. Possibly the threat of juvenile drug addiction has been overemphasized. In the 1960 *Uniform Crime Reports,* out of 3,959,559 arrests, only 27,735 were for violation of narcotic drug laws. Yet some newspapers and "authorities" state that 25 per cent of all crime is due to drug-crazed addicts. Drug addiction per capita has been decreasing since 1900. Most known drug addicts reside in the following states, New York, California, Illinois, and Texas, in that order.

Maurer and Vogel suggest a convenient frame of reference in listing narcotic drugs:[28]

I. *Opiate sedatives considered addicting*
   1. Opium ("elephant," "rooster," "55").
   2. Morphine ("Mary Anne").
   3. Codeine.
   4. Heroin ("boy," "h," "horse," "foolish powder").

II. *Non-opiate sedatives considered addicting*
   1. Barbiturates (Nembutal, Sodium amytal, Seconal).
   2. Chloral hydrate (knock-out drops).

3. Paraldehyde
4. Bromides
5. Marihuana ("weed," "reifers," "Mary Jane").

III. *Stimulant drugs*
1. Cocaine ("girl," "c," "snow," "coke," "nose candy").
2. Benzedrine
3. Peyote

Drugs used by juveniles include marihuana, heroin, cocaine, morphine and opium, among others. One of the easiest and cheapest drugs to procure is marihuana which is not habit-forming in the physiological sense, but which is habit-forming psychologically. One girl explained why she enjoyed marihuana: "Because it kicks. It's just like being a lush only you don't have a hang-over and you're not sloppy and getting sick, maybe going out and drive a car and kill somebody like a lush, and its cheaper than Scotch." Marihuana's effect upon individuals is unpredictable. Furthermore, marihuana serves as a stepping stone for the jaded drug user to try something different; hence he may graduate to heroin or cocaine.

Users of marihuana report the time element seems extended, with the minute having 180 seconds. Things seem funnier, arms seem 80 feet long, the user of marihuana can do anything like stepping over street cars or out of sixth story windows, or from a moving automobile at 75 miles per hour. The marihuana user feels no pain or has no fears; the boxer on marihuana will continue fighting even though his hand is broken. Marihuana is not a true aphrodisiac; marihuana users happen to be at the height of their sex power, which is unleashed and which accounts for the unusual sex activity in many instances.

Of all narcotic drugs, heroin is most often preferred, although it is expensive and accounts for approximately 60 per cent of drug offenders appearing before the Chicago drug court. Cocaine is the luxury item of the drug trade. Cocaine tends to induce revery rather than the depraved acts sometimes reported by the press. The cliche of the underworld in this area is "Never team up with a Cokey." Cocaine users become too apprehensive and see policemen at every window, behind bathtubs, even hiding in match boxes. Cocaine users have conspicuous habits—an itchy nose and a general air of furtiveness. Morphine tends to impart in the user a feeling of increased mental and physical vigor. (Morphine sometimes actually benefits particular individuals, such as the chronic alcoholic or the psychoneurotic.) Morphine is a specific for pain. Each of these drugs, perhaps costly cocaine to the least extent, is used by some American youths; and the behavior thus induced has become a part of "normal" juvenile life in some circles.

The symptoms of drug addiction are summarized by Kenney and Pursuit[29] as watery eyes, restlessness, fast walking, upset stomach, unusual or abnormal ideas, undesirable friends, no interest in working, frequent yawnings, stooped shoulders, abs on skin, and arms, wearing long sleeves even in summer time to hide tell-tale marks made by the needle, pillow wet with perspiration, remaining in bath room for long periods of time, burnt finger tips, body stench, increased need for money, personality changes, wearing colored glasses to conceal reddened eyes, and dilated pupils.

According to Cloward,[30] the point of transition from adolescence to adulthood is also a point at which drug-use rises. Many former "bops" do not make this way up to adult adjustment. There is not much satisfaction in shifting from the status of juvenile gang leader to the degrading adult status of being unemployed. During the late 1940's and 1950's, conflict gangs were rampant in New York. Public outrage forced their breakdown by the police and courts, and the conflict gang has tended to fade away. In its place, a more troublesome problem arises now in sharply increased rates of drug use. Drug use has now become the primary delinquency problem in New York. By restricting access to one form of deviance without providing the social resources for functional but conforming alternatives, one form of deviance was simply converted into a worse form, drug addiction.

Most remedial programs of the past and many of the present tend to be punitive in character. The conviction that "there ought to be a law" is still widely held. But with the passage of each restraining law, the price (and profit) tends to rise, which financially benefits the peddler of the drugs. One reason for the punitive attitude toward drug users is because, in the United States, drug addiction is relatively prevalent in the "underworld" and is thus associated with crime and its correction, in contrast to drug addiction in Europe which is viewed primarily as a problem for the medical and allied professions.

There are hopeful signs that in the future remedial programs will tend to become more realistic, especially as research findings are made available to those in charge of such programs. Alfred R. Lindesmith, one of the many social scientists working in this area, has made worthwhile contributions to a better understanding of the drug addict and has done much to invalidate the commonly accepted stereotype so familiar in sensational literature. The drug user is rather a miserable and harassed person.

The Division of Narcotic Control of Illinois reports success with the Nalline test as a worthwhile adjunct in the rehabilitation of narcotic users. Nalline is derived from opium, but is an antidote, having a reverse action to it. If the pupil of the eye dilates after Nalline is injected in the suspect, it means that drugs have been ingested within seventy-two hours. Addicts seem to approve of the Nalline test because they can *prove* they are "clean," instead of trying to convince someone orally. At the present time (1961) there are over 300 former addicts in the program of Illinois, and 80 per cent have stayed "clean" for two years.

Both alcoholism and drug addiction are related, at least in some instances, to the sexual activities of adolescents, which likewise have been highly publicized in the tabloids of today.

## SEXUAL PRACTICES AND DELINQUENCY

The breakdown of traditional sexual mores and the drift and diversity of changing opinion about sexual morality affect individuals in different ways. Although contemporary sexual attitudes appear to have become highly liberal, as compared with the views of our forebears, it is not at all certain that modern youth is as profligate as "public opinion" sometimes appears to suggest. Differences in sexual orientation and practice, however, may reflect differences in socioeconomic and class standards. For example, Dr. Winston W. Ehrmann's[31] survey at the University of Florida, a five-year study of college youth, indicates that 61 per cent of the men and 91 per cent of the women "draw the line" within conventional moral limits in their current dating behavior. This finding is fairly consistent with Kinsey's surveys of the sexual practices of American men and women, in which he reports class and educational differentials which indicate that sexual intercourse itself is engaged in at an earlier age and more frequently among the less educated who, however, tend to avoid the "petting" preliminaries that are so marked among college youth.

Ball and Logan[32] in their research with lower-class girls in a Kentucky state reformatory, tend to confirm the above findings, also tend to confirm Lejin's concept of "conformist delinquency," in the area of sexual misconduct. The girls involved in this study were aware of the middle-class norms, knew promiscuity was socially undesirable, were not hostile to such social norms, but were motivated by the desire to maintain status within their own adolescent subculture. There was no evidence of unusual circumstances or pathological behavior. The majority of the girls lost their virginity while on automobile dates and the principle reason given was "liked the boy very much." Nearly a fourth of the girls admitted it was the first date. Subsequently, sex was a part of dating as "the boy expected it," or "nothing else to do," for fun or pleasure. Other rationalizations included "had been drinking," "would be considered chicken otherwise," or "everyone was doing it." At least 70 per cent of the girls questioned admitted they knew it was wrong, and all of the girls were slightly below average intelligence. They had dated actively from age thirteen and had no interest in supervised recreation.

Many juveniles, despite rather extensive sexual experiences, may be incredibly naive in many aspects of biological import. Sessions in group therapy with both boys and girls in institutions seem to confirm this observation. For example, David Dressler reports how astonishingly childish were some of the notions juvenile parolees had regarding sex. At one time a youthful parolee stated he didn't drink coffee because "it gets you syphilis." When asked to explain, he added: "Yeah. You drink coffee and you get noivous. Coffee leads to smoking; smoking leads to drinking; drinking leads to goils; and goils give you syphilis. No coffee for me."[33]

Partly as a reflection of the contemporary cultural current accent on sex, the public is easily titillated by accounts of sexual escapades—a fact on which the newspaper have capitalized. Consequently, many notorious sex cases have tended to overemphasize sex as an offense. One club of four girls admitted their activities were devoted to the "seduction of bus drivers." Nearly three hundred synonyms for "love making" indicate the prominence of this activity ranging from "spooning" in the 1890's to present-day terminology of "bubblegum tag," "goat roping," "spoogling in the dingly weeds," "schnooking," and the like.

There are interesting sex differentials that should be taken into account when handling juvenile offenders. A fifteen-year-old girl is more mature than a fifteen-year-old boy. The boy may not know if he is a man or still a child, but the fifteen-year-old girl knows she is a woman. Boys are easier to handle than girls, girls cannot be bluffed. Girls feel the loss of status with peers more than do boys. If a girl is caught in delinquency, other girls' mothers won't let their daughter associate with the "bad" girl, hence the female offender has a "bad girl" role. Many sex offenses of juveniles are relatively unimportant and are often due to a fixed morbidity or adolescent experimentation. However, society is upset by the promiscuous girl, but the promiscuous boy is only "sowing wild oats."

In some disorganized areas and families, the opportunities for sexual exploitation of young boys by adult homosexuals are quite extensive. Influenced by promised financial rewards, boys have been known to aid and even to seek out older males who prefer them as sex objects. There is also the problem of females who use youngsters for normal as well as deviational sexual gratification, a practice which is often known to the police of metropolitan areas. However, sex deviation and juvenile delinquency are far from synonymous. It must be remembered that sex deviation is widely practiced among nondelinquents. On the basis of present evidence, it may be asserted that sex or sex deviation *per se* neither causes nor is the cause of juvenile delinquency.

## REFERENCES

1. Glueck, Sheldon and Eleanor: *Unraveling Juvenile Delinquency,* New York, The Commonwealth Fund, 1950, pp. 274, 275, 278.
2. Cavan, Ruth S.: Presidential Address, The Concepts of Tolerance and Contraculture as Applied to Delinquency, *Midwest Sociological Society,* Omaha, Nebraska, April 28, 1961.
3. Yinger, J. Milton: Contraculture and Subculture, *American Sociological Review,* Vol. 25, October, 1960, pp. 625–635.
4. Cavan, Ruth Shonle: The Concepts of Tolerance and Contraculture as Applied to Delinquency, *The Sociological Quarterly,* Vol. II, October, 1961, pp. 243–258.
5. Bloch, Herbert A., and Flynn, Frank T.: *Delinquency: The Juvenile Offender in America Today,* New York, Random House, Inc., 1956, p. 98.
6. Smith, Dr. Sydney R.: Annual Meeting of the Arizona Conference on Delinquency Prevention Control, Arizona State University, January 10, 1959.
7. Bergler, M.D., Edmund: *Homosexuality: Disease or Way of Life,* New York, Hill and Wang, Inc., 1956, p. 49.
8. Reinhardt, James Melvin: *Sex Perversions and Sex Crimes,* Springfield Thomas, 1957, pp. 237ff.
9. Karpman, M.D., Benjamin: *The Sexual Offender and His Offenses,* New York, Julian Press, Inc., 1954, p. 478.
10. Drummond, Isabel: *The Sex Paradox,* New York, G.P. Putnam's Sons, 1953, p. 135.
11. de River, M.D., J. Paul: *The Sexual Criminal,* Springfield, Thomas, 1950, pp. 3–12.
12. Reinhardt, James Melvin: *op. cit.,* p. 78.
13. de River, J. Paul: *Crime and the Sexual Psychopath,* Springfield, Thomas, 1958, p. 143.
14. Bromberg, M.D., Walter: *Crime and the Mind,* Philadelphia, J. B. Lippincott Company, 1948, p. 165.
15. Karpman, M.D., Benjamin: *op. cit.,* p. 358.
16. Hakeem, Michael: A Critique of the Psychiatric Approach to Crime and Correction, *Law and Contemporary Problems,* Autumn, 1958, Duke University School of Law, pp. 650–682.
17. Messinger, M.D., Emanuel and Apfelberg, M.D., Benjamin: A Quarter Century of Court Psychiatry, *Crime and Delinquency,* Vol. 7, October, 1961, p. 343.
18. Goddard, H. H.: *Feeblemindedness: Its Causes and Consequences,* New York, The Macmillan Co., 1914, p. 37.
19. Shulman, Harry Manual: Intelligence and Delinquency, *The Journal of Criminal Law and Criminology,* Vol. XLI, April, 1951, pp. 763–781.

20. Hurlbert, H. S.: Constitutional Psychopathic Inferiority in Relation to Delinquency, *Journal of Criminal Law and Criminology,* Vol. 30, 1939, pp. 3–31.
21. Cleckley, M.D., Hervey: *The Mask of Sanity, St.* Louis, The C. V. Mosby Company, 1950, pp. 355–356.
22. Kalina, Roger K.: Management of the Psychopath, *Proceedings of the 1960 Congress of Correction,* Denver, Colorado, Aug. 28-Sept. 2, 1960, p. 268.
23. Cleckley, M.D., Hervey: *op. cit.,* pp. 220–221.
24. Teeters, Negley K., and Reinemann, John Otto: *The Challenge of Delinquency,* New York, Prentice-Hall, 1950, p. 517.
25. Cohn, Victor: Minneapolis *Tribune,* series of articles, Why Children Kill, December, 1947–1948.
26. Binford, Jessie F., Postwar Problems of Youth, *Federal Probation,* Vol. XI, October-December, 1947, p. 9.
27. Cited by Lois L. Higgins, *Bureau of Crime Prevention,* Chicago, Illinois, in her address to the American Prison Association Annual Meeting, Biloxi, Mississippi, October, 24, 1951.
28. Maurer, David W., and Vogel, M.D., Victor H.: *Narcotics and Narcotic Addiction,* Springfield, Illinois, Charles C. Thomas, Publisher, 1954, pp. 47–116.
29. Kenney, John P., and Pursuit, Dan G.: *Police Work with Juveniles,* (2nd Ed), Springfield Thomas, 1959, pp. 144–149.
30. Cloward, Richard A.: Address to the Governor's Conference on Youth, Sherman House, Chicago, Illinois, April 13, 1961.
31. Ehrmann, Winston W.: Influence of Comparative Social Class of Companion upon Premarital Heterosexual Behavior, *Marriage and Family Living,* Vol. 17, (1955) pp. 48–53.
32. Ball, John C., and Logan, Nell: Early Sexual Behavior of Lower-class Delinquent Girls, *The Journal of Criminal Law, Criminology and Police Science,* Vol. 51, July-August, 1960, pp. 209–214.
33. Dressler, David: *Parole Chief,* New York, The Viking Press, 1951, p. 144.

# 6

## JUVENILE GANGS

GREGARIOUSNESS IS A persistent feature of human relationships. It is a common trait manifested in "consciousness of kind" and the hunger of the social person for comradeship and in his fear of aloneness. Juvenile gangs are phenomena of gregariousness, to be sure. They illustrate much more about society and culture than this universal trait. Their study also reveals some important factors in the development of juvenile delinquency and criminality.

### JUVENILE GANGS AND THE SOCIAL STRUCTURE

Juvenile gangs, both their frequency and the type of behavior in which their members engage, reflect the social structure of the community. Studies made in recent years have documented, for example, the extent to which the class system of the local city or town determines the associations of people in general, including the grouping of youth in cliques, bunches, and gangs. Both the well-known investigations of "Yankee City," a New England town of some seventeen thousand population, and of "Elmtown," reveal that adolescents generally intermingle, fraternize, and form informal but cohesive groups largely along class lines.[1] When it is kept in mind that the norms of behavior deemed socially appropriate in the United States are largely those established by and reinforced by the "middle classes," the class restriction of youth groups can be seen to play an important role in the determination of conduct, delinquent or otherwise.

The most clear-cut illustration of the influence of class and neighborhood influences is to be found in the larger cities. For many years it has been observed that socially and physically deteriorated urban areas are marked by both high delinquency rates and numerous juvenile gangs, many of which engage in antisocial and criminal conduct. A quarter of a century ago an impressive contribution to the understanding of juvenile gangs was made by

Frederick M. Thrasher. Professor Thrasher studied 1313 gangs containing twenty-five thousand members, concentrated around Chicago's Loop—the central business district. He concluded that gangs are characteristically found in geographically and socially interstitial areas, often in a section where expanding industrial plants encroach upon the city's older residential quarters. At the time of the study, this "delinquency area" was concentrated around the business district. Numerous subsequent studies have borne out Thrasher's findings: that in such divisions of the city lack of family control and of adequate community recreational facilities encourage youth to form their own play groups and gangs, which, without proper guidance, may establish their own norms of behavior, including delinquent behavior.

Some individual delinquency is a phenomenon of the middle-class norms according to Talcott Parsons [2] in an article appearing a few years ago. Middle-class children are isolated from adult males as the females handle the discipline and set the standards of good conduct in both home and school. Hence the middle-class boy unconsciously identifies "goodness" with femininity, and being a "bad boy" may become a positive goal for some middle-class boys in an effort to assert their underlying masculinity and to play a male role.

In a sort of follow-up to this "explanation" of delinquent behavior along class lines, Albert K. Cohen [3] has advanced an interesting and provocative thesis of juvenile delinquency that there is a persistent subculture in certain sections of our urban areas. By subculture is meant a culture within the larger culture of society. Juvenile gang behavior may be explained in terms of urban society class structure. Juvenile delinquency, a product of this subculture, is prevalent in the lower socio-economic classes. Many unlawful juvenile activities are non-utilitarian, negativistic and malicious. The lower class boy is handicapped in many ways by lack of opportunity to compete with middle-class boys. Hence the delinquent subculture offers some solution to the problems of working class boys. The subculture gives him status, since he is frequently unable to meet the middle-class standards.

Bloch and Niederhoffer [4] suggest that delinquency is not best explained in terms of a struggle between social classes but rather due to major changes in the economic patterns in moving from a rural to a highly industrialized urban life. They relate gang behavior of urban youth to the absence of a definitive role structure in urban society. "Hedonistic" behavior is not the peculiar province of lower class delinquency, but may be found in juvenile misbehavior at all social levels.

Of course, not all city gangs bring about delinquency. Cliques of various sorts, male and female and mixed, arise in all sections of the city and in smaller communities as well. But there seems little doubt that in those areas where deprivation is greatest and where the "Gold Coast" symbols of affluence are physically nearby but socially distant, there exist the most compelling encouragements for youth to engage in law-breaking activity.

Even in these sections of the community no two gangs are alike. But there are basic similarities in their leadership hierarchies, their group loyalties, their search for adventure and excitement, and their oftentime first-hand knowledge of the underworld, whose representatives they may admire. That the latter factor is widespread is suggested by Thrasher's findings: of the 1313 gangs, 530 were characterized as "delinquent" or "criminal" and only fifty-two gangs were described as having no demoralizing effects on their members.

## GANG ACTIVITIES

Delinquent behavior, as viewed by the members of the gang themselves, is not always "demoralizing"—often quite the contrary. Oftentimes respect in the group and hence self-respect depends upon some degree of prowess, or at least willingness to engage, in acts defined as delinquent by outsiders. And often these acts have their origin in play itself. This situation is illustrated by the groups of boys who "went stealing" for recreation, as reported to Clifford Shaw during a famous study he conducted several years ago.

> When we were shoplifting we always made a game of it. For example, we might gamble on who could steal the most caps in a day or who could steal in the presence of a detective and then get away. We were always daring each other that way and thinking up new schemes. This was the best part of the game. I would go

into a store to steal a cap by trying one on, and when the clerk was not watching, walk out of the store, leaving the old cap. With the new cap on my head I would go into another store, do the same thing as in the other store, getting a new hat and leaving the one I had taken in the first place. I might do this all day and have one hat at night. It was the fun I wanted, not the hat. I kept this up for months and then began to sell the things to a man on the west side. It was at this time that I began to steal for gain.[5]

This quotation also suggests the role played by group pressure in determining behavior patterns in gang life. Delinquencies, as well as nondelinquent acts, are commonly committed by youth operating in small groups; the "loner" is relatively a rare case. For in the age demarcation of the gang, internal group pressures and loyalties tend to compel the more youthful and less prestigeful members to engage in behavior patterns established by the bolder and older leaders. To join one gang in New Orleans, an applicant had to jump on and off a moving freight train, smash street lights, and hit a Negro on the head with a brick. These gang leaders, if they live in certain areas of the city, often find *their* models rooted in local tradition, tradition giving sanction to delinquency and crime.

And here is seen the gang functioning as an important educational agency. If members of these quite natural boyhood (and girlhood) associations learn how to play marbles or stickball they also learn other and less innocent group-ways. For the gang may teach—and quite effectively in this school of deeds—how to "roll drunks," steal from railroads or buildings, "boost" from stores, fight gang "wars" and so on. All of these, in a word, may be part of the group's way of life.

According to Kenney and Pursuit, a juvenile gang is defined as "three or more youth banded together, through mutual interests or companionship." There is the "old gang" that has existed a long time, usually boys, often girls fifteen years or older, that engage in serious, unlawful acts. The "new gang" is just getting started, usually boys, but occasionally girls, fifteen years or under, engaging in the more petty types of delinquency.[6]

According to one investigator, Friday night is the crucial night in gang life, the night they drink, give parties, "needle" rivals. Saturday afternoon is another critical time when rival gangs attend the same movie. And summer evenings, when the weather is fine, seems to be the peak time for "rumbles" and gang conflict.[7]

Usually originating in play groups, the juvenile gang gains group solidarity in its conflicts with school, police and the larger community. Crime techniques are often disseminated and may themselves symbolize the gang's uniqueness and its value for its members. Group identification and morale are further enhanced by the adoption of a special language: the members may be "on the bop" when looking for a street fight, "give them the Douglas" when kicking a prone person in a fight, or "wash a cat away" when beating up someone, and "jockey-boxing" when prowling glove compartments of automobiles. They may be heading for a "session" when going to a dance, or may be imbibing "Sneaky Pete" when drinking a mixture of gin and wine.

The activities of delinquent gangs have constituted a serious civic problem in large cities. As reported in the February 26, 1961 Chicago *American,* there are approximately thirty-five teen-age gangs out of more than 200 gangs, in Chicago that cause police trouble. During 1958, police arrested forty-one youths for murder, 120 for rape, 951 for robbery, 340 for assault, 1,396 for burglary, 3,291 for larceny and 1,231 for car theft. These arrested youths were not necessarily gang members.

World War II witnessed the growth of many "combat" gangs. Our culture pattern seemed to support the thesis in World War II that total violence was the solution to world problems. So juvenile delinquents turned to violence to solve their own problems. As stated in the August 19, 1957 issue of *Newsweek,* every city has its "juvenile jungles" or teen-age strongholds, the new urban blight. One gang reads of a rival gang killing and their reaction is: "We're just as tough as those guys." Community buildings bare scars too. A branch of the New York public library had to close because vandals kept heaving bricks through the windows. The librarian termed it "a beleaguered fort" in an "area of desolation."

The recent years have witnessed the growth of many gangs, some of which were responsible for such crimes as "mugging," rape, homicide, and various types of racketeering. In the 1920's, Thrasher had reported forerunners: the "Murderers" whose members stole from delivery wagons, broke into boxcars, and stole automobiles for joy rides; the "Dirty Dozen," an especially aggressive gang that deliberately provoked ethnic groups as well as rival gangs and "earned" its money by bootlegging and stealing. In more recent years, these patterns have been repeated—with the gangs acquiring more lethal weapons, including knives, guns, knucklers and chains. And these weapons, unfortunately, have been put to use quite frequently by teen-agers as reports in such cities as New York, Chicago, and San Francisco reveal.

This grim picture, however, should not lead to the conclusion that all or most members of juvenile gangs prey upon society without compunction. According to one study made in World War II years, of those youth brought into juvenile court only about ten per cent should be classified as vicious, hardened, habitually delinquent. This minority includes the youngsters who adopt delinquent behavior as a career and the gang as a medium of "protection, comfort, and training for effective operation." [8] And these are the young people who so frequently become "hardened criminals" in later life.

## GANG "MORALITY" AND ORGANIZATION

Much has been written of gang "morality." And certainly it is true that the juvenile gang, like other close-knit small and intimate social groups, has its own social norms, its own "code." A large part of this code, as publicized by such motion pictures as "Knock on Any Door," is supposed to be expressed by the slogan: "Live fast, die young, love all the girls, hate all the cops, and have a good-looking corpse." While this is no doubt a somewhat misleading expression of the gang's code, it is clearly the case that, in order to survive in a hostile world, the gang must follow a fairly severe set of rules. And of central importance in the gang's code is the insistence upon loyality to the group. Thus the adult criminal principle of "Never squeal or burn your partner," is matched in the juvenile gang by the rule "Don't rat." The obligation to follow the rule is supported by a privilege: it is better to take a beating at the hands of the police (headbeaters) than to disclose gang information, and in turn the members of the gang will do as much for *you*. Probably most boys join gangs for a definite purpose for otherwise the boy might be unprotected. He often finds acceptance into a world that otherwise rejects him.

The code of the gang is closely related to another of its essential components: its system of internal organization, usually informal but none-the-less effective. As previously mentioned, almost all juvenile gangs (like their adult counterparts) develop a hierarchy of control, descending from the recognized leader down through such positions as "war-general," "light-up" man (in charge of the arsenal), the funny one or jester, the "dumb" one, the "goat,"—names used by the members of a corner gang in Italian neighborhood, reported in *Street Corner Society* by William Foote Whyte (Chicago: Univ. of Chicago Press, 1943 and 1955). Both the "officials" of juvenile gangdom and the group loyalties holding the gang members together, it should be noted in passing, are sometimes exploited by local political machines, as Whyte brings out in his study, for their own ends. For here are already well-organized potential henchmen at the service—for a price— of local "bosses."

Not only is the gang marked by internal organization, but its "working" relations with outside groups, including other gangs, are sometimes quite extensive. As related in *Time,* April 7, 1958, the Bishops, a gang of Brooklyn, New York, had five divisions, 150-200 members between ages thirteen to seventeen and claimed a territory (turf) which extended two miles along Fulton Street in Brooklyn. The older gang members were known as the "Big People," and the junior members the "Little People." Many juvenile gang members, for example, "graduate" to more mature law-breaking groups. In New York City, it has been reported that older gangs often have junior auxiliaries or "Tiny Tims." Very young boys, serving their apprenticeships in these junior groups can look forward—much as Cub Scouts look forward to more senior status—to becoming regular members of gangs with such picturesque names as the "Forty Thieves," "Swamp Angels," "Slaughter Housers," "Hudson Dusters," and "Musketeers."

Quite frequently the gang's name illustrates its ethnic composition. When it is remembered that lower-class residential areas are often also the living-centers of concentrated ethnic groups, "racial" and national and religious, it is not surprising to learn that juvenile gangs themselves take on an ethnic stamp. Thus in New York, among other gangs, are found the "Gestapos," "Bombinos," "Latin Counts," "Puerto Rican Eagles," and "Irish Dukes"; in Detroit, the "Little Jewish Navy" and "Purple Gang"; in Los Angeles the "California Daylighters," who, at times, terrorized "enemy" ethnic groups.

In a survey of juvenile gangs in Tucson, Arizona by Lieut. Charles P. Smith of the Pima County Sheriff's office, (1958), many gang appellations reflected interests other than ethnic or racial, such as "Shades" (members wear dark glasses, even at nighttime), "Sidewinders" (mostly Davis Monthan Air Force Trainees), "Sad Sacks," "Hot Rodders," "Black Widows," "Baby Dolls," "Black Ants," "Non-Virgins," "Non-Virgins, # 2," "Aces," "Moonglows" (stealers of hub caps), "Pep Cats," "Bombers," and "Catalinas."

Not all juvenile gangs with impressive names are highly organized or in continual combat. Distorted publicity by the press is often misleading. As Yablonsky points out, the boy's gang in reality is often a sort of impermanent "near-group," having characteristics somewhere between a mob and a well-organized social group. One gang, the "Balkans" was so disorganized it actually had no name. When the group became involved in a fight, policemen kept asking the members who they were, and finally one gang member, who was studying history in school, spoke to the gang, "how about the Balkans," so they told the officers, "We're the Balkans," and that was it.[9]

The United States possesses no monopoly on juvenile gangsterism. Russia has its "stilyags," Japan its "apuray," with over 400 gangs in Tokyo alone, of whom it is reported, that they do not waste time slugging it out among themselves but keep busy making money by intimidating shop keepers, collecting "protection money," and shop-lifting. In Chile, they are called "colericos" (angry ones), who wear jeans, plaid shirts and ride around in convoys of motor scooters. In Australia, the male delinquent gang member is called a "bodgie-boy" and his female companion a "widgie." England has its "Teddy-Boys" on whom *Time* reported in the September 24, 1956 issue as crashing theater doors, throwing bottles, heaving over automobiles, ripping out seats of movie houses, turning on fire hoses on movie audiences. "Teddy-Boys" for the most part were born of poor parents in Britain's slums, they had very little education and their home life was practically nonexistent. Their hair cut ranges from the D.A. (Duck's arse) to the TV roll and the Tony Curtis. As part of their jargon, a "frog" is a road, a "whistle" a suit of clothes, and a "bird" is a girl.

One should not conclude, however, that juvenile gangs are always stamped by ethnic alikeness or that all spring from the most deprived sections of the population. Some gangs contain representatives of two or more ethnic groups, for example, several in New York City, in a sense, are little melting pots," and the members of many others come from families considerably more affluent than "lower class." Similarly delinquency is not restricted to the latter groups by any means. According to Louis P. Spitz, former head of the Juvenile Division, Reno Police Department, delinquency is fairly widespread through that community. (Reno is probably not an especially representative city), involving at times children of Reno's "best" families. Delinquency and juvenile gangsterism, then, are not merely problems of concern to welfare officials who work among families on "the other side of the tracks." As community concerns, however, it must be remembered that middle-class children not only have much greater opportunity to channel their energies in law-abiding group activities but also rarely, as compared with their more deprived peers, become deeply enmeshed in either the temptations of the criminal world or the police agencies organized to cope with that world.

Over the past decade, considerable effort has been expended to conduct experimental therapy with juvenile gangs, in an attempt to change their attitudes, if possible, toward the larger society. According to Cloward and Ohlin [10] workers in this area should be aware that there are three more or less distinct types of delinquent subculture among male adolescents in the slums of large urban areas. One is essentially a "criminal subculture"—a type of gang which is devoted to theft, extortion, and other illegal means of securing income. A second is the "conflict subculture"—a type of gang in which the manipulation of violence predominates as a way of winning status. The third is the "retreatist subculture" a type of gang in which the consumption of drugs and other illicit experiences is stressed. Although these subcultures are rarely found in pure form, they do generally exhibit sufficient differentiation to warrant being separately classified. Resources for combatting deviance are always limited. There seems to be much more public concern about conflict subcultures than about the "retreatist" groups. Gang delinquency seems to be equated in the public mind with conflict behavior, and warfare in the streets has become the dominant symbol of lower-class male delinquency. The criminal and conflict gangs have occupied most of the attention of workers using therapeutic techniques in an effort to better understand juvenile gangs.

Ernst G. Beier,[11] writes of the experience a two man project encountered, designed to develop techniques for dealing with nonconformist juvenile gangs not easily reached by social agency programs in upper Manhattan. Rapport had been established by a friendly entrance into the lives and activities of about fifteen boys, ranging in age from fourteen to seventeen, in their street corner hangouts, and on their own level of entertainment, such as crashing movies. The boys were encouraged to take certain tests and in the Rorschach, the majority of the members showed extraordinarily few signs of phantasy or inner life, nor did they show signs of affectivity. It was interesting to note the dearth of imagination in these boys. One remarked that what he wanted most was a million dollars so he could build a house with a pool table in every room. After fourteen sessions, a notable change occurred in the appearance of these neglected boys. They began to dress neatly, to shave and have haircuts. One afternoon, when the therapist accompanied the boys to their old corner restaurant hangout, one boy remarked, "Oh, Christ, back to this damn place again." They were beginning to see themselves in a new perspective. They had always pictured themselves as "rough and ready guys," and their lives were going the way things were meant to be. But now they no longer seemed bound by this inevitability; they were beginning to wonder just why they had to live that way. All experiments in gang therapy are not as successful. As Yablonsky indicated, the usual therapy is for the community worker to try to "redirect" the mob's activities into constructive channels, such as forming a baseball team, but what happens . . . . many of the boys meet each other for the first time and start to talk about organizing gangwar activity. Where there was a "near-group" before, the community worker may innocently help organize a gang.

James R. Dumpson [12] discusses the success enjoyed by a privately financed welfare council in New York, which managed to infiltrate into four of the most troublesome gangs in central Harlem. It was learned that newspaper and magazine articles gave a distorted picture of the frequency of the groups' participation in antisocial behavior. Participation in sports, movies, parties, dances take up a much larger part of their time. Just "hanging around" and visiting their girl friends are important activities of all the gangs. For the worker, the area of antisocial behavior is the most difficult to handle, and he must use great skill in defining his difference from the boy and still maintain a useful relationship with him. The end result of this project was that sex offenses were minimized and gang warfare stopped. Only four workers participated in this experiment; hence a permanent group of workers might go far in solving permanently the city's gang problem.

In an effort to better understand young people who seem able to adjust well to their peer groups (gangs) but get into trouble with the larger social organizations, Wattenberg and Balasterieri [13] studied the records of some 5878 adolescent boys contacted by the Detroit police. It should not be assumed that gang membership is a sign that something is wrong in the lives of the boys or girls concerned. These investigators concluded from their study that socio-economic indices had greater value in predicting recidivism in the case of gang members, while family indices were of greater value in the case of non-gang members. Those boys who belonged to gangs differed from non-gang boys in showing evidence of coming from easy-going homes and living in socio-economically low neighborhoods. The non-gang boys displayed indications of coming from tense or depriving families. These findings might provide a clue to treatment strategies. Where delinquency could be traced to tensions arising out of early family history, individual psychotherapy would be indicated. On the other hand, where delinquency resulted from a too free interaction with the peer culture or a poor neighborhood subculture, the unit of treatment or prevention would appear to be the social group or the neighborhood.

## GIRLS AND GANGS

Delinquency and gangism are not, of course, confined to the male sex. However, somewhat in keeping with the persistent tradition of male superiority, girls in juvenile gangland seem to play special and somewhat subordinated roles. Nor do boy juvenile gangsters, especially when they have attained adolescent years, reject female fellow-members. To the contrary, girls are recruited into gangs. Many become members voluntarily and apparently with enthusiasm, though some enter only under threats of physical violence. Sometimes the membership of these female auxiliaries is indicated by secret symbol, such as a spider tattooed on the left hand, attesting affiliation with "The Spiders" of Los Angeles, or a red dot used by "The Cherries" of the same city. Or the girls may have designs "carved" on themselves, especially if they are defined by the boys as subsidiary members. It has been reported that parents who object to their daughters joining gangs run the risk oftentimes of juvenile revenge, such as the slashing of the tires of the family automobile, the tearing-out of ignition wiring, or the filling of the fuel tank with sugar or sand. But it is probably true that most girls who find their way into youth's gangdom do so without the aid of such dire measures. Girls no more escape the compelling circumstances of their lives than the boys themselves.

What are the functions of the girl gangster? In some degree, of course, she is the juvenile counterpart of the much-publicized "moll" of adult "mobsters." Gangsterettes are often expected to submit to the sexual advances of the boy members; young girls, not infrequently by force, are initiated into "adult" sex practices. They sometimes assist boys in gang fights, illustrated a few years ago by girls using their then-popular high pompadour arrangement of hair to conceal such weapons as knives and finger-nail files. Girls have been used by gangs in New York City to waylay leaders of rival groups—the traditional "decoy" technique. These seem to be the principal activities of even those girls who organize their own female gangs—the "Robinettes," "Chandeliers," the "Shangri-la-Debs" and so forth. Thus Bernard summarizes:[14]

> Only rarely does the girl gang function without affiliation. In the great majority of cases it exists as the auxiliary of some boy gang, to which it gives fierce loyalty. One important duty is to act as weapons carriers to the boys, who thus escape seizure and charges. The girls also supply alibis, claiming that a suspect boy was with them at a "session" or in bed at the time of the crime's commission. Principally, however, the young ladies act as camp followers, supplying the lads with such sex as they require—and fulfilling duties as lures and spies.

Juvenile girl gangsters have come into the public limelight especially since the years of World War II. Around Naval bases and Army camps, for example, they have at times been used by their civilian companions as bait to lure service men into out-of-the-way places, where the latter were "rolled" and robbed. Apart from the publicity given to such cases, it appears that the number of female gangsters has been on the increase in recent years. Gang offenses among girls between the ages of fourteen and seventeen appear to be higher than during the peak delinquency war years. In spite of their subservient position in boys' gangs and the fact that their own gangs are usually viewed as auxiliary to the male groups, these young women are reported to be more difficult to handle than the boys themselves. New York police have been reported to comment, for example, "These junior gun-molls are tougher than the guys."

## THE APPEAL OF THE GANG

Why do young people join gangs? Several of the background factors already have been indicated. But an important part of the picture of juvenile gangism would be missed if the fact were overlooked that gang activities, from the viewpoint of young people themselves, are fun. Everyone values recreation as an important function of gang affairs, both law-abiding and law-breaking, is to provide recreation for its members.

Ruth S. Cavan reports *(in Criminology)* the case of one small gang of boys, all under eleven years of age, who persistently stole equipment and contents from unlocked cars—whether they had "use" for the loot or not. Their real gain was derived from the excitement and anticipation of their final act: leaving in the cars small printed cards reading "Lock Your Car. The Nighthawks." Imagination was at work here. Sometimes imagination and the youthful search for adventure leads to serious violations of the law, as illustrated by this story from *Life*:[15]

> In Bakersfield, California, six youngsters ages eight to thirteen and a dog named Butch left their slum district called "Billy Goat Acres," and set out on foot for excitement. When they got hungry, they broke into a fruit store, then smashed some windows in a used-car lot, found an unlocked car, and started West across the Tehachapi Mountains, but after twenty miles, sideswiped a truck, blew out two tires, had to abandon the car. They found another in a rancher's garage, but 104 miles later near Los Angeles, they skidded into a soft shoulder, had to leave the car, but in a matter of moments, picked up another car. But this time the owner called the police.
>
> At 95 miles an hour they roared onto Los Angeles' Sepulveda Boulevard followed by two radio patrol cars; the cops opened fire and after eleven shots, the car stopped. Police approached warily, guns drawn against what they fully expected was a carload of adult desperados. Out popped the unhurt and tousle-headed members of the Billy Goat Acres mob.

The search for fun, then, often leads to delinquent acts. These acts may become established in patterns of behavior receiving at least some sanction from the adult world, even from certain of its more prestigeful members. When, for example, during World War II, one newcomer to a gang objected to stealing tires on the ground that, according to press and radio, such behavior was akin to treason due to the rubber shortage, the leader, one Knifey Joe, replied "G'wan home, punk. Treason! Look at them big shots and politicians riding around on new tires and getting all the gas they want. Don't be a sucker!" [16] When the prevalence of more immediate law-breaking adult models who inhabit the local breeding-grounds of delinquent juvenile gangs, including often enough members of the youngsters' own families, are considered, it is not surprising that illegal patterns of behavior are taken up by youth groups–sometimes in the cause of "play."

Glane [17] discusses the element of "play" relative to East Los Angeles gangs. Play groups crystallize into neighborhood gangs. Conflict in congested areas over territory, play spaces may weld members of a gang into a social unit, in which a "we" feeling is acquired. These play groups are not systematically organized, although natural leaders emerge and are looked up to with great respect, even in the classroom. Traditions are originated through such practices as identical tattoo marks on the face, hands, and arms, and fraternity-like initiations. School administrators in the area hope to provide supervised activities for the children so that they will be less strongly attracted to gang life. A large gymnasium building is slated to be open evenings so that boys and girls need not "roam around looking for excitement elsewhere."

Youngsters are also attracted to neighborhood gang groups because their own homes lack attraction. Many disorganized families have created such a problem in East Los Angeles. Cultural conflict between alien-born parents and children of Mexican descent and American birth is common here. To quote a school attendance and child welfare supervisor: "The parents, by and large, are still law-abiding and docile, whereas the children feel they can get nowhere with their docility. In a study of Mexican-American gangs in Los Angeles, Emory S. Bogardus attributed gang formation to a sense of differences due to language difficulties, academic problems in school, contrasts in child-control methods, race discrimination, and low economic status." [18]

Wattenberg and Balisterieri list the opinions of sociological researchers as to the reasons why the gang exerts such strong appeal and just what or who should be blamed. There is little consensus. W. F. Whyte, in *Street Corner Society*, points out that home plays a very small part in the daily routine of a full-fledged gang member. C. Himber [19] is inclined to blame broken homes and weak religious ties, as well as social conditions. Going somewhat more deeply into personal factors found in gang leaders, Miriam Van Waters [20] sees rejection in school, church and social clubs as putting youngsters in the position where the gang is their only road to prestige and status. The other gang members are likely to give promise of filling psychological needs not met by the adolescent's own parents.

F. Redl[21] states that pre-adolescents have a deep need to form cliques and gangs among themselves. Most writers assume that it is normal for pre-adolescents and adolescents to join groups. C. B. Spaulding[22] sees the gang as necessary to satisfy wishes for response and security. A. S. Beckman[23] believes that suggestibility is higher in gang groups due to broken or disturbed homes and retardation in school increases their willingness to accept suggestions of truancy.

D. B. Harris[24] states that delinquent gangs arise in areas in ecological transition and largely take on the standards prevalent in such areas. Healy and Bronner[25] found that the delinquent who came from families in which there were non-delinquent siblings, was in 91 per cent of the cases extremely disturbed emotionally, largely because of poor relationships within the family. The delinquent's lack of social restraint was due to lack of affectional identification with a good parent.

R. Topping,[26] in what she calls the "pseudo-social boy" states gang membership may be an attempt to compensate for a sense of effeminacy or of physical or mental inadequacy. She observes that, on the basis of wide clinical experience, there is often a dependent attitude, on the part of the gang member, toward the mother and an indifference or resentment toward the father. She further notes the possibility that such gang members often come from large families.

Frederick M. Thrasher[27] concluded that gang membership was due to inadequate family life, poverty, deteriorating neighborhoods, ineffective religion, poor education, and inadequate recreation; such is Thrasher's "Matrix" of gang development.

Many boys and, increasingly, girls idolize and imitate great outlaws of the past, from Robin Hood to the James brothers.

In juvenile gangs there is often hero worship of outlaws of the present, the adult gang leaders. The fact that so many of these youngsters are poverty-bred and slum-fed helps to account for the "big-shot" ideal. Moreover, under these conditions, there are numerous handicaps facing youth, disadvantages of descent, limited education, sometimes even illegitimacy or physical disability. In keeping with the ubiquitous success norms of the greater society, the aspirations of these young people call for rapid advance up the social ranks, if possible. In the minds of some of them—those especially impressed by the "big-shot" models—social barriers can be hurdled and fame and fortune achieved quickly by adopting the ways of the criminal or near-criminal world.

The appeal of illegal and extra-legal short-cuts to "success" complicates and aggravates the problem of the delinquent juvenile gang. People coping with this problem—parents and social workers and community leaders—often couch their appeals to follow conventional and legitimate paths in terms of abstractions that do not compete successfully with the concrete and immediate and "real" lures facing young people who are growing up in "delinquency areas." These areas, moreover, encourage attitudes of bitterness and cynicism, so frequently found among gang members.

Typically, in juvenile delinquency as epitomized by gang membership, is a disdain for work and legitimate economic goals. There are dreams of quick success, with emphasis on "pull" or looking for the "soft job;" hence monotonous routine jobs of office, store, or factory are avoided at all costs. Juvenile gang members attack property as a form of play, may hide the loot of bread-wrappers in the back yard. The gang gives an opportunity for both verbal and physical assaults, an outlet for aggressions. Through such behavior, the gang member has an "audience," with whom he can establish a "rep," can prove he has "heart," and the ability to "take it," as well as hand it out. The gang furnishes opportunity for excitement and thrills and "kicks" of which delinquents seem to be in perennial search. Supervised recreation is not the answer for delinquents, most of whom would not be "found dead" in such a program. The needs of the delinquent for aggressive activity, excitement, thrills, avoiding work and monotonous routine of the more conventional life seems to be met by participation in gang life and partially accounts for the tremendous appeal of the juvenile gang.

If youthful aspiration is to be constructively channeled, if the glamor of the big-time criminal is to be lessened and legitimate means of achievement are to be followed, if cyncicism is to be replaced by confidence in socially constructive values, and if the juvenile gang is to be just that and not a breeder of delinquency—if these goals, essential in an adequate reform program, are to be achieved in any substantial degree—social science and the community must join hands in a more concerted and realistic effort than has yet been made.

## REFERENCES


1. See Warner, W. Lloyd and Lunt, Paul S.: *The Social Life of a Modern Community,* New Haven, Yale University Press, 1941; and A. B. Hollingshead, *Elmtown's Youth,* New York, John Wiley & Sons, 1949.
2. Parsons, Talcott: Certain Primary Sources and Patterns of Aggression in the Social Structure of the Western World, *Psychiatry,* Vol. 10, May, 1947, p. 172.
3. Cohen, Albert K.: *Delinquent Boys: The Culture of the Gang,* Glencoe, Illinois, The Free Press, 1955.
4. Bloch, Herbert A., and Niederhoffer, Arthur: *The Gang—A Study in Adolescent Behavior,* New York, The Philosophical Library, 1958.
5. Shaw, Clifford: *Delinquency Areas,* Chicago, University of Chicago Press, 1929, p. 35.
6. Kenney, John P. and Pursuit, Dan G.: *Police Work with Juveniles* (2nd Ed.), Springfield, Thomas, Publisher, 1959, p. 136.
7. Salisbury, H. E.: The Shook-up Generation, *New York Times,* March, 24–30, 1958.
8. Doshay, Lewis J.: The Challenge and Solution of Juvenile Delinquency, *Journal of Clinical Psychopathology and Psychotherapy,* Vol. VI, April, 1944, p. 187.
9. Yablonsky, Lewis. The Delinquent Gang as a Near-Group, *Social Problems,* No. 2 (1959), pp. 108–117.
10. Cloward, Richard A. and Ohlin, Lloyd: *Delinquency and Opportunity,* Glencoe, Illinois, The Free Press, 1960.
11. Beier, Ernst G.: Experimental Therapy with a Gang, *Focus,* Vol. 30, July, 1951, pp. 97–102.
12. Dumpson, James R.: An Approach to Antisocial Street Gangs, *Federal Probation,* Vol. XIII, December, 1949, pp. 22–29.

13. Wattenberg, William W. and Balistrieri, James J.: Gang Membership and Juvenile Misconduct, *American Sociological Review,* Vol. 15, December 1950, pp. 744–752.
14. Bernard, William: *Jailbait,* New York, Greenberg, 1949, p. 93.
15. By permission, from *Life,* February 11, 1952, (c) *Time,* Inc.
16. Reported in Pamphlet No. 300, *Children's Bureau,* U. S. Department of Labor, 1943.
17. Glane, Same: Juvenile Gangs in East Side Los Angeles, *Focus,* Vol., 29, September, 1950, pp. 136–141.
18. Wattenberg, William W. and Balistrieri, James J.: *op. cit,* p. 745.
19. *Ibid,* p. 744.
20. *Ibid,* p. 744.
21. *Ibid,* p. 744.
22. *Ibid,* p. 745.
23. *Ibid,* p. 745.
24. *Ibid,* p. 745.
25. *Ibid,* p. 745.
26. *Ibid,* p. 745.
27. *Ibid,* p. 745.

# 7

## APPREHENSION AND DETENTION

It is estimated that there are more than a million laws, including both felonies and misdemeanors, on the statute books in the United States; there are more laws than people—about seven for every man, woman, and child. As laws increase in number, violations tend to increase. There often appears to be a growing spirit of contempt for the law enforcement system, on both adult and juvenile levels. During World War II, parents sometimes boasted, in the presence of their children, of patronizing the black market. It is difficult to control behavior merely through laws.

In many delinquency areas of urban communities, lawlessness has become almost a tradition that is handed down from one generation to another. Owing to the pervasive nature of the "spirit of delinquency," detection and apprehension are exceedingly difficult, for more often than not the police receive little cooperation from the citizens in urban delinquency areas.

The law itself recognizes only the chronological age of the offenders, ignoring the mental, emotional, and physiological ages as if they had no existence. Legally, responsibility for one's acts is presumed to increase with the years. Witness the differential treatment accorded the juvenile delinquent, the young adult offender, and the adult offender. From one viewpoint, the law ignores children completely, for they are not even mentioned in the Constitution of the United States.

Paradoxically, civil law holds that anyone under twenty-one years old is legally incompetent to enter into contracts. He may not hold or dispose of property; and yet let him commit a crime and the only question asked by the law is "Does he know right from wrong?" If the answer is affirmative, he must pay his "debt to society." He may be sent to jail or prison, or even executed for his crime, although according to the civil law of the state he may not be responsible enough to marry or to drink alcoholic beverages.

Such inconsistencies constitute one of the many reasons why there is so much disregard for the law in general, particularly in reference to the activities of juvenile delinquents. They know they live in an adult world in which there are different standards of morality for young people and adults. The mother pleads a "sick headache" to avoid playing bridge, but the child is punished for telling a little "fib." This "double standard" is one reason why adulthood seems so attractive to children.

## THE POLICE AND YOUTH

When police deal with the juvenile by handcuffing and jailing him they aggravate a resentment he may have against society. Also the manner in which the police handle child offenders may determine in a large measure the juvenile's attitude toward legal authority. Occasionally the police officer takes the attitude that the violation is a kind of personal affront, and may testify against the boy to "get even." Enlightened police administrators recommend treating juveniles with consideration in order to gain their confidence and respect. The juvenile officer should learn to be firm, fair, and friendly and talk the language of the juvenile delinquent if he can. Probably the greatest requisite is patience. Encourage the juvenile to talk, he'll give more information that way than asking him questions.

When interrogating the boy, learn the names of those the youngster respects, as a teacher, a minister, since the third party approach is helpful. Ask him whom he likes the better, Mother or Father, and if it's Mother, keep Dad out of the conversation, as it would be a waste of time. Interrogation of a serious crime should be made at the station house, not at home in front of his parents. Privacy is more important for juvenile interrogation than in adult interrogation. The juvenile officer should be in civilian clothes, not in police uniform. Never lie to a juvenile. Juveniles tend to be more belligerent than adults when in police custody. It is well to watch out for knives. The "Dallas" or "Fort Worth Special," a curved knife, with a match stick under the blade high enough, so when the knife is removed from the pocket, the blade is already open. The juvenile offender frequently acts on impulse, may run, or even fight the officer.[1] Some juvenile offenders need the sympathetic approach, with others, it would only be a waste of time. Certainly no policemen should resort to vulgarity, profanity, or obscenity—yet such behavior on the part of the "guardians of the law" is by no means rare.

The policeman often dispenses monitory justice (warnings). Typically he settles and decides more violations than he takes into court. He "judges" thousands of cases every year—such as petty thefts, breaking windows, and starting fires in alleys. Because he is often the child's first personal contact with the law, he should conduct himself with dignity, impartiality and competence. Kenney and Pursuit recommend that the juvenile officer be neat of dress at all times, since the whole police department may be evaluated by this one representative.; the officer must not be a "tobacco chewer" or one who "dips snuff."[2]

Stallings and Dressler confirm the accepted dress pattern of the juvenile officer, who is supposed to always wear a tie and coat. This has brought forth some ridicule from brother officers who have referred to juvenile officers as "dude undertakers," and "altar boys." Other appellations include "social detectives," "kiddie cops," who have to "stamp his library card," or "suspend his lollypop privileges." Over the past several years, juvenile officers have been maligned with criticism and ridicule.

While kindness may be a good rule to follow in extracting information from juvenile offenders, such as offering a "coke" or even cigarettes, in many instances kindness and consideration backfire. In one case, a young girl of seventeen, with a record of twenty-three arrests from prostitution to armed robbery, and escape from a reformatory, was permitted to walk down the street with officers minus handcuffs, in deference to some public opinion. The moment opportunity presented itself, this prisoner kicked off her shoes, sprinted away, with citizens deliberately blocking the pursuing officers. At a busy traffic intersection, the officer on duty there chose not to stop her either, and the girl got away. When the traffic officer was later asked why he didn't cooperate in stopping this run-a-way prisoner, the reply was, "Nuts! I work traffic."[3]

Police frequently encounter instances of parental cruelty and sadism. One parent hit his child so hard he broke his neck; in another case, parents had left a baby's diaper on so long, the safety pin had rusted, and became embedded in a sore on the baby's stomach.[4]

Delinquents' parents may pose a problem for the juvenile officer. According to Charles P. Smith, Juvenile Officer, parents present four reactions when their children become a police matter: (1) We don't care, send him to the reform school; (2) What can we do to help our child? (3) Parents may become abusive to their own child, and (4) Parents may become belligerent, even assaultive to the police officer.[5]

In keeping with the principle of dignity and competence, the University of Southern California's Delinquency Control Institute designs courses of study to help the police officer understand the causes, treatment, control, and prevention of juvenile delinquency and crime. He is taught how to approach young people and how to interview them, so that they may see in him a source of help, rather than a threat. Research has indicated that of all the "authority" figures in police and correctional work, juveniles dislike the police most of all.[6]

At least five per cent of police strength should be assigned to juvenile, but this minimum standard is attained only once in two hundred times. In spite of the seriousness of juvenile delinquency and the need for specialized knowledge of this constantly increasing area of misbehavior, there are no special police officers assigned to juvenile cases in fifty per cent of all cities of the United States where the population exceeds ten thousand, according to the February 2, 1960 edition of the Memphis *Press-Scimitar.*

The Chicago *American,* November 1, 1960 reported that "Hit-and-run Juveniles Flee on Bicycles," and in recent months have victimized forty-five women and six men in robbery and beatings, with most offenders under fifteen years of age. One youth slammed into a pregnant mother with his bike, knocked her down, managed to steal 30 cents from her. Another bicycle brigand robbed, then attempted to rape his victim on Michigan Avenue and 16th Street and passers-by walked on despite her screams. Under today's impersonal and anonymous characteristics of urban society, the victim of crime is apt to stand alone.

As Donal E. J. MacNamara has indicated many times, specialized knowledge in handling teen and sub-teen offenders is of prime importance to the juvenile police officer. Many specialized courses are given at Northwestern Traffic Institute and Yale University's Bureau of Highway Traffic. Perhaps the most outstanding illustrations of this type of training are to be found in the Federal Bureau of Investigation's educational activities at the National Police Academy and in the preservice police training programs pioneered by August Volmer and now regularly scheduled at nearly a dozen colleges and universities, including the University of California and Michigan State, San Jose State and Fresno State Colleges, to mention but a few.[7]

Railroads and railroad police are plagued by juvenile delinquency and criminality, with trespassing as the principle difficulty. Railroads seem to hold a real fascination for youngsters. Georgia children ranging in age from ten to fourteen formed the "Dare Devel Club" with prerequisite for membership being able to tantalize a vicious bull or risk death by train, by laying their heads on ends of cross ties near running rails. A ten-year-old boy of Bloomington, Indiana jammed a ten inch bolt in a switch, caused a wreck of a locomotive and nineteen freight cars and the deadly steam from the firebox, penetrated by a torn-up rail, scalded to death the engineer, fireman and brakeman. The boy stated that he was "just playing." In August of 1953, a thirteen-year-old boy shot a .22 calibre rifle at trains, one bullet hit the brakeman, killing him instantly. In any given year, over 600,000 trespassers are found on railroad property and most of them are juveniles. Since 1935, the Erie Railroad and Atchison, Topeka and Sante Fe have officers lecture to school children by showing color films and have contacted in excess of five million children, especially in the schools along the railroad right-of-way.[8]

Many sincere but misguided efforts have been accorded the juvenile offender. Formerly, he was fingerprinted and photographed; now under a protective program which is followed in many communities, even his name is omitted when the crime he commits is reported by the press. However, inasmuch as the professional criminals often come from the ranks of juvenile delinquents, a reversal, in part at least, of the present "protective" trends seems to be in order. Proponents of finger-printing juvenile delinquents believe that it is the best method of identification, that it helps to protect the innocent, that it completes the records and enables the FBI to include nation-wide juvenile delinquency statistics in their *Uniform Crime Reports.* Fingerprinting, it might be argued, constitutes no more a stigma than going to juvenile court.

Some police departments have made an effort to counteract juvenile delinquency by establishing junior police systems in which youthful members become subject to call at any time. Juvenile police duties include such activities as assisting in traffic details near schools, churches, even down-town corners; attending regular meetings; learning the type of conduct appropriate for a police officer. This type of program has been tested in various communities, including Decatur and Mattoon, Illinois, and considerable success has been reported. Youthful members conduct themselves as "officers and gentlemen" or face dismissal from the junior police group.

In any consideration of official methods of delinquency prevention, mention should be made of the program of preventive activities of the New York police department. The recreational program of the Juvenile Aid Bureau in New York works through the Police Athletic League (PAL) which has been in existence since the early 1930's. PAL's chief aim is to substitute wholesome recreation for antisocial activities, thus helping to prevent incipient misbehavior. PAL has over one hundred thousand members of which 15 per cent are girls. However, there are many authorities in police administration who believe that recreation is not a police role or a police function. The real police role is "ordering and forbidding" and the police are about the only social agency that has this role. While many police personnel appear to prefer to specialize in "crime prevention," it may actually be symptomatic of a "flight from police work." or a search for personal publicity or glory. The police service should not necessarily include case work or crime prevention.

While the public should not expect police personnel to raise and be responsible for children other than their own, nevertheless, in their day-to-day activities they become fully aware of the pitfalls about which many parents fail to skirt which results in delinquency. In a recent brochure entitled "How to Raise Juvenile Delinquents," the Houston Police Department pointed up several mistakes or errors in child-rearing. For example, it is suggested, under the above caption, to avoid the use of the word "wrong" since it may develop a "guilt complex" in the child and the child may believe that society is "against him." When he picks bad or dirty words, laugh at him and make him think he is being cute. Praise the child in his presence to all the neighbors to show how much smarter he is than the neighbor's children. Pick up everything after him; his books, his shoes, and his clothes. Quarrel frequently in his presence. Give him all the spending money he wants and satisfy every craving the child has for food, drinks, and everything. Take his part against policemen, teachers and neighbors because they are all "prejudiced" against your child, and then when he gets into real trouble, always defend yourself and say: "I never could do anything with him anyhow."

The curfew as a means of police control seems to be a controversial issue, a much-discussed topic although only two articles appear in the literature from 1896 to 1943 on the subject. The "popular" view is given by Robert Ruark writing in the Miami *Herald,* August 29, 1955—in which he stated:

> I see nothing particularly horrifying about the nation-wide curfew for teen-agers, since I hear that juvenile delinquency is caused by lack of sleep. It would seem to me that it works best in the big cities, where the young gangsters clot the corners in savage knots, swagger around running people off sidewalks, and haunt the streets and parks for drunks to roll, and people to beat up for fun.

The weight of evidence strongly suggests that the curfew just doesn't work out, and is frequently subject to abuse, even poor judgment. For example, in September of 1958, two Detroit girls, both sixteen, enroute home at 1:30 a.m. were accosted by a strange man and in response to their screams, a neighbor called police, who promptly gave the girls tickets for violating the curfew law, instead of looking for the accoster.

In an article by Ben Solomon, many sound reasons are listed against the curfew as a tool of control for juveniles. The California Court of Appeals declared the curfew unconstitutional in June, 1961. Curfews are "Dead Letters" in over 3,000 cities, towns, counties and states. Many police regard the curfew as a "Nurse-maid's job," as it is difficult to determine girls' ages, and police cannot possibly know about all unofficial events, even agency meetings at which juveniles may have a right to be present. Curfew laws are not needed by the police to interrogate youngsters after dark, and most parents prefer to retain the right of determining how late their children should stay out.[9]

The police may interrogate juveniles under local, or state laws which are relatively unknown. For example in Arizona, no one under twenty-one may smoke tobacco, and most juveniles smoke tobacco. In Salt Lake City, a 1907 law prohibits anyone under twenty-one smoking tobacco and if the offender gets a ticket as a first offense, he has a choice of paying a small fine or attending a two hour lecture that features movies on "The Evils of Tobacco."[10] Chicago has a little-known ordinance, "General Principles," under which almost any charge may be lodged against an offender, such as calling an officer "names."

Most juveniles are law-abiding, and resent the publicity given their age category by the very few who do violate the law. In one survey reported by *This Week* magazine, November 27, 1955, from more than 5,000 teen-agers who recommended punishment for juvenile offenders, the favorite punishment and recommendation was "crack down on them, hard." Some juveniles suggested five year jail sentences, and one proposed that the juvenile offender and his parents be locked up in the same cell. Not one listed comic books, gangster movies, or TV programs as any spur or incentive to juvenile delinquency.

Some law-abiding juveniles have occasional experiences that tend to produce cynical attitudes toward law enforcement and adult "justice." As reported in the Tucson *Daily Citizen,* April 23, 1958, a sixteen-year-old boy in Chicago came home from school, surprised a burglar in his home, and chased him to a bus stop, screaming, "Help, Robber" but passers-by did nothing. When the bus arrived, the boy again asked for help, saying to the bus driver and passengers, "Someone help me, this man has got my little brother's bank in his hand." The bus driver summed up everyone's feelings by saying: "Listen, I'm not a cop," then took the burglar's change, and gave him a seat. The boy stood there helplessly watching the bus drive away!

Adding women to the law-enforcement agencies has greatly improved police efficiency—even in such matters as estimating the ages of girls, when required. In California the police are not permitted to transport females between the ages of five and eighteen except in the presence of a woman. Interrogation of girls and women is conducted with a woman present. According to Mrs. Jo Deason, policewoman of the Tucson Police Department, the main job is to handle runaway girls, usually twelve to fourteen years of age, and nearly all become the victims of assault or rape.

According to Lois Lundell Higgins,[11] the first police *matrons* were appointed to take care of female prisoners in New York City in 1845, but it was not until 1910 that Alice Stebbins Wells of Los Angeles was appointed the world's first regularly rated policewoman in Los Angeles, California. Her appointment attracted wide newspaper comment because she was an educated woman, a social worker, a theologian and had deliberately sought the opportunity to work in a police department. To the question, "How could you make an arrest?" she replied, "I want to keep people from needing to be arrested, especially young people," thus introducing a new concept into police work.

Policewomen of today successfully perform certain specialized functions—interrogation of women offenders and victims and juveniles—that cannot always be as readily handled by men. They are particularly effective workers in the field of crime prevention.

This involves work with the families of adult male offenders, with female offenders, with girls in danger of becoming prostitutes, and, in some cases with young boys.

Some prejudice remains against policewomen, and they account for about one per cent of total police personnel. Instead of "checking" on night-time activities of boys and girls on the streets, for example, policewomen may be restricted to clerical duty. But in the coming years, policewomen will occupy a larger niche in police service and in public appreciation.

Police departments have also established juvenile bureaus specializing in handling juvenile delinquency cases, variously called Crime Prevention Bureaus, Youth Guidance Bureaus, Special Service Bureaus. This type of agency was initiated in 1913 when Portland, Oregon, established the first juvenile bureau in the United States. Despite forward-looking programs such as these, adaptation of similar agencies and techniques and, in general, progressive police work in the youth field have been disappointingly slow in the majority of the communities in the United States. As Donald Imler[12] of the Delinquency Control Institute has pointed out, police administrators are deeply concerned with the problems they face in their efforts to professionalize the service. Even the rookie patrolman looks forward to the day when police will be considered in the same professional class with lawyers, doctors, engineers, and educators. However, before this can come about standards must be raised, a code of ethics universally established, the body of knowledge concerning police activity must be made available, research must be engaged in to establish these, and practice must be refined through the training of both neophytes and experienced officers.

## JAIL AND DELINQUENCY

A picturesque and revealing definition of a jail is that given by a one-time jail inspector for the federal government:

> *Jail:* An unbelievably filthy institution in which are confined men and women serving sentences for misdemeanors and crimes, and men and women not under sentence, who are simply awaiting trial. With few exceptions, having no segregation of the

> unconvicted from the convicted, the well from the diseased, the youngest and most impressionable from the most degraded and hardened. . . . A melting pot in which the worst elements of the raw material in the criminal world are brought forth blended and turned out in absolute perfection.[13]

Many jails have improved since 1923 when Joseph Fishman wrote of the then-current conditions of jails throughout the nation; but a substantial number continue to fit his description.

Daily some 750,000 men, women and children are compelled to drag out their hours in the idleness of a narrow cell or a common pen of the local jail. Jail thus fails to serve law and order and becomes a laboratory of delinquency and degeneracy. The judge who assigns an offending person to a jail "to teach him a lesson" is either cynical or ignorant or possibly both.

In spite of forbidding stipulations in state laws, at least fifty thousand children are detained in jail every year. One western state maintains a statute prohibiting the detention in jail of children under twelve years old; yet it was revealed in 1947 that in a period of nearly four years three local jails, all in one county, built up a record totaling 1,430 days of child-incarceration. According to Austin H. MacCormick[14] thousands of children, some of them as young as eight or nine years of age, are confined every year in county jails in the United States for periods of a few hours to several months under abominable conditions. In one jail, "a boy of ten found by an inspector, beseeched pitifully: 'Mister, please get me out of here. I'll be a good boy.' The child seemed to be a chronic school truant. The jailer referred to him as a "habitual criminal." Practically every state has some adaptation of the Standard Juvenile Court Act, and jail detention of children is forbidden by statute in 28 states and the District of Columbia. However, these laws "are more honored in the breach than in the observance."

Children are assigned to jail in most communities, however, because there are no other places to detain them. And here they are all too often subjected to disgraceful conditions. In one community, for example, girls who had been charged with truancy were discovered sharing quarters with experienced prostitutes; and in another community twelve-year-old girls and boys were held with adults in a dirty jail from June to August, waiting for the juvenile court to reconvene after the summer vacation.[15]

A seven-year-old boy was held in jail for twelve days in a California community as reported in *Time,* January 17, 1955 on the charge "in danger of leading a lewd and immoral life." He had placed his hands under the dress of a five year old girl. When a newspaper man publicized this case on a local television station, there was an immediate response with over 700 telephone calls, 1,000 letters and several petitions even sent to the Governor of California. Finally the boy got a hearing and was sent home to his parents.

There are numerous instances of children incarcerated in jails. In Anchorage, Alaska a twenty-month-old baby boy was found "insane," and lodged in the federal jail at Ketchikan in 1954. The infant had been given a hearing and found insane by a jury. The baby was transferred to the Ketchikan hospital shortly after the hearing, but was still listed on the jail records as an insane convict.[16] The Florida *Times-Union* (Jacksonville) on December 12, 1952 reported that two youngsters, ages three and five, had spent forty-eight days in jail in Johnson City, Tennessee because the juvenile court judge had "forgot" about them.

The Detroit *Free Press* on February 29, 1948 reported that through some legal quirk, girls could be committed to the Detroit House of Correction if picked up for some minor offense without benefit of trial, attorney, or jury. One girl had been confined for eighteen months and the matron said: "I don't know why she's here, but you can't get her out, it's the law." Attorney Frank MacLean found eighty-five girls unjustly and unlawfully imprisoned, and in one day released seventeen girls on writ of habeas corpus. Only two states, Connecticut and New Hampshire claim never to use jails for children; the former state operates three regional homes that serve the entire state.[17]

Cases such as these underscore the fact that the jail, presumably an aid in the maintenance of law and order, frequently has the opposite function of serving as an educational setting for delinquency and crime. And sometimes the lessons are taught with telling effect, abetted by such procedures as the inmate-created "kangeroo court." This tribunal, termed by one authority a "perverted form of self-government," is headed by a "judge" who is usually one of the worst prisoners. Penalties are brutal and the "court" imposes fines of a few dollars on newcomers called "fish" for "breaking into jail." One young inmate who died while in a western county jail, due to epilepsy according to the jail physician, lost his life in fact because a degenerate nineteen-year-old kangeroo court "judge" had severely beaten him for threatening to report the sexual assault and tortures practiced upon him.[18] Until conditions permitting such occurrences as these are changed, the jail system will continue to labor under the opprobrium the "Shame of America."

The jail was originally instituted as a place of detention until trial. It still fulfills this function, of course, as a temporary abode behind bars for men and women. But the jail also often imprisons, and sometimes for long periods of time, impressionable children and youths. Juveniles steel themselves to hide emotion, buying onions, lemons to bite into, try hard to make no facial grimaces, as they attempt to emulate some of the characteristics of the "hardened criminal." And the lessons learned in jail guarantee, in some cases, at least, the launching of careers in delinquency and crime.

To eliminate the abuses of children in jail, MacCormick states that this problem cannot be attacked effectively on the local or county level alone. It virtually would be impossible to inform, convert, and stimulate to action the people and officials of over 3,000 counties, and approaching the problem on the federal level would be deemed interference with both county and state rights. The state level of approach thus emerged by elimination. The shame of our aptly named common jails has been tolerated far too long by public officials to whom the jail is only another pawn in the political game, and by professional penologists who state frankly that the "jail problem has got us licked," but, in truth, have never given it a real fight.[19]

## DETENTION OF THE DELINQUENT

Juvenile court philosophy maintains that young people should be detained in special quarters prior to their appearance in court.

*Detention* refers to temporary care of children removed from their homes pending investigation and the court's decision. *Shelter care* refers to emergency and temporary out-of-home care of children where physical restraint is not necessary, contrasted with detention which involves security features to insure the child's safekeeping.

Detention means different things to different children, depending upon the child's previous experiences and life patterns. For most boys and girls held by the law, detention connotes food and shelter. For others, it suggests indiscriminate contact with other detainees. Palmieri lists the various types of children coming to detention—the defiant child, the chronically disturbed child, the recessive child, the over-restricted girl and boy, the handicapped child, the victim of sibling rivalry or a broken home or gangster associations.[20] Some have committed a minor offense, others a major offense. Some are only truants or runaways or they may be neglected, dependent or even lost children. In some detention facilities the girls' wing faces the boys' wing permitting both groups of inmates opportunity for mutual exhibitionism. Occasionally, newcomers will be isolated the first twenty-four hours with no reading material or games, so that "meditation will be encouraged." Not infrequently, detention is a degrading experience, especially where untrained, under-paid, and unqualified staffs treat detainees as inferior persons. Moreover, detention usually means idleness—time wasted in so far as any rehabilitative efforts are considered. Detention has been described as the weakest link in the rehabilitative process.

A survey conducted in 1945 by the National Probation and Parole Association revealed a failure of some official agencies to obey their own state laws in providing detention homes rather than jails for juvenile offenders. The survey showed that for the most part detention homes were understaffed, overcrowded with children, and inadequately supervised by untrained officials. There were fewer than 150 detention homes in the United States. In the fifty-eight counties in the state of Caloifornia only thirty-two have separate children's facilities, which is approximately twenty per cent of the entire nation's detention home facilities. Some detention homes throughout the nation are maintained as "show places" rather than as establishments for constructive community services. Too many officials are not deeply concerned with the welfare of their charges, since they apparently feel the youthful offenders are headed for the reform schools anyway.

A recent survey limited to twenty-one county detention facilities located in fourteen states and scattered throughout five geographic regions of the United States has been published by the Children's Bureau in Pamphlet #10 together with some pertinent conclusions:

> One inevitable conclusion of the above analysis is that in the larger urban jurisdictions there is a strong likelihood that a significant proportion of the money expended by detention institutions would not be required if detention police, procedures, and programs conformed to sound standards. It is clear that many children held in detention should not have been detained at all, and that others are being detained for periods far too long to serve well the needs of the child, the court, and society. This situation has developed because of failures in the screening and referral processes of juvenile units of the police; failures to provide the proper quantity of rehabilitative institutions of various types in which delinquent children can be placed, and a failure in the court processes to utilize detention carefully and to study and make disposition to accommodate any of these failures is expensive and, more importantly, may jeopardize the entire rehabilitative process. Available funds at all levels of government should be directed toward the remedy of these failures in order to permit much-needed reorientation and improvement of detention services in keeping with the concept and philosophy of the system of juvenile justice generally recognized in this country.[21]

Despite the gap between 1945 and 1960, the realms of theory and practice are too far apart. Detention facilities seem able to defy substantial improvement.

On the positive side, detention homes offer excellent possibilities if proper attention is given to such items as the physical plant, location, administration, personnel, services to the child, information to the court, length of detention, and planning for detention facilities. Many juvenile court judges boast of their detention facilities. According to the Tucson *Daily Citizen,* March 30, 1958, Judge Gilliam of Denver said: "We have the best juvenile home in the country. We had a boy in here who had been in eleven juvenile homes and he told us "this is the best." We call him the "Duncan Hines" of juvenile homes. In some of our tough districts, the kids play cops and robbers just like I did when I was little, but they use real cops. It's so tough down there a cat with a tail is a tourist."

In all detention homes there should be emphasis on cheerfulness, livability, and ease of maintenance. Ample room should be provided for indoor and outdoor play and game activities. Detention homes should be located within or near so-called "delinquency areas," and certainly not close by the local jails. Personnel should be well qualified, well paid for their jobs. Yet, a Note in the *National Probation and Parole Association Journal,* July, 1957, stated that in California where salary scales are among the highest, the assistants who work for the rehabilitation of juveniles are paid $2 a month less than the men who carry out the garbage to the trucks. The *services* to the child in a detention home that realizes its important function in the corrective process should include good physical and custodial care, medical examinations, psychological and psychiatric tests, child guidance and casework, and recreation and religious teaching. As Palmieri has stated, children in detention are not canned goods or automobiles which can be shelved or stored; handling children under detention home conditions is a delicate time and energy-consuming job requiring the skilled assets of the best staff.

Theoretically, the purpose of detention is to provide the child material and psychological security while authorities are studying his case and gathering information concerning his background. As stated before, there is a wide gap between the theory and practice of detention. Institutional confinement of any sort probably has some deleterious effect upon children whether they are "normal" emotionally disturbed, or delinquent. Detention, as it is exercised today, in a large measure, seems a relic of retributive penological thinking that disregards the possible consequences of detention for the child himself.

As Sherwood Norman, Detention Consultant has indicated, old

concepts of detention grew out of the notion that delinquent acts call for retaliation (lex talionis). A youngster who appears to be a tough customer must be shown that "we can get tough too." In the past and even today, many detention homes have little concern for the development of the child's personality. "The children are with us too short a time," we are told. Whatever the size of the detention home, personnel must be capable of meeting three basic program objectives: good physical care and custody; a full, varied, and creative activities program; guidance through intensive casework. A detention home worker must be a well-adjusted person himself. Unfortunately, small communities with populations of under 50,000 seldom are able to afford proper detention care for their children. Mr. Norman, one of the few recognized authorities in the detention home field summarizes the problem ahead:

> We might as well face reality. The jail detention of children will never be abandoned in this country unless the state constructs and operates specially designed, strategically located detention homes. These homes would supplement the local boarding home by taking only those children who require secure custody. State subsidies where tried have seldom been successful. In Virginia, for example where the state offers to pay almost the entire cost of operating a detention home, counties show a shocking indifference to juvenile detention.
>
> Regional detention centers operated by the state according to high standards and supplemented by local boarding homes are the only hope of ridding ourselves of the blight of detaining boys and girls under juvenile court jurisdiction in jail. Ideally these detention homes would be located in the same general areas as regional child guidance clinics. Ideally, too, they would be affiliated with a statewide juvenile court system as they are in Connecticut. However, we need not wait for a state juvenile court to meet a very urgent problem. If we care for our children we will act now.[22]

Palmieri stressed the belief that the child must be studied from many angles; and unless a proper approach is utilized, officers may obtain only a fraction of the complete story about the child. According to John McFarland, Superintendent of Mother Higgins Home, the detention facility for Pima County, Arizona, the personnel of detention homes must try and "process" just one case at a time, and not worry too much about theoretical and abstract considerations of juvenile delinquency "causes." The detention home worker must also realize that he is going to lose more cases than he is able to salvage, and the big tool is *talk*. His recipe for handling delinquent boys in detention: "Explain the rules, and if the boy is tough, you get tougher, show him you mean business, then once that's settled, he knows you're the boss, then you are in a position to be friendly, cooperative, even "permissive." However, if the detention home personnel used much of the "permissive stuff" found in textbooks, they wouldn't last long in any institution."

Bloch and Flynn report the lack of detention facilities in Illinois. As late as 1955, there were ninety-six counties out of 102 counties in the state, that were without specialized detention facilities. Quoting Fred Gross, an earlier investigator, who reported that from 1938 to 1942, 319 juveniles were held in the Cook County jail and only 10 per cent of these were held for less than five days, Bloch and Flynn indicate the seriousness of this situation. Gross uncovered one case, a fourteen-year-old boy found guilty of petty larceny on two indictments— the value of the property being $2.00 in one case and $8.00 in the other. Although hospitalized with pneumonia, this youthful offender was sentenced by the criminal court to two consecutive one-year terms in the county jail and assessed fines and costs of $300.00. He spent twenty-one days in jail awaiting court action, he served 666 days on his sentence, and another 200 days "working out" the fines and costs. He entered jail at age fourteen, emerged at age seventeen.

Bloch and Flynn presume, and probably presume correctly, that the sentencing judge thought this boy's formative difficult adolescent years should be spent in acquiring good citizenship traits in a jail then notorious as a "school for thieves," dominated by inmates, and without a single progressive program feature.[23]

In an article by Jean Dietrich which appeared in the Chicago *Sun-Times,* February 26, 1962, the Arthur J. Audy Home for Children is the legal detention facility for Cook County children. During 1961, 6,500 delinquents and 3,040 dependent children were processed, with a daily population in excess of 300 children.

According to Superintendent James M. Jordan, the Home is adequate to house the delinquents for which it should be used exclussively, but the city should have decentralized homes in various parts of the city or suburbs for the children who are only dependents.

Today, as in 1945, when the National Probation and Parole Association made its survey on the nation's detention facilities, in many detention homes the staff is still underpaid, untrained, and unqualified; knowingly or unknowingly, its members may even act as delinquency seducers. For many children detention is a bitter experience as they await their juvenile court hearing which sometimes drags on for weeks or even months. Unfortunately, the general public has only a meager understanding or appreciation of what the detention home is attempting to accomplish for youth in trouble. For this, as well as other reasons, community education is indicated as both desirable and necessary before the opprobrium of detention is removed.

## REFERENCES

1. Couston, Bruce: Juvenile Officer, Tucson Police Department, comments taken from an address to Criminology classes, University of Arizona, (Tucson), March, 1958.
2. Kenney, John P., and Pursuit, Daniel G.: *Police Work With Juveniles* (2nd Edition) Springfield, Thomas, 1959, p. 47.
3. Stallings, Harold L., and Dressler, David: *Juvenile Officer,* Springfield Thomas, 1954, pp. 35, 82–84.
4. *Ibid,* pp. 122, 171.
5. Smith, Lieut. Charles P.: Sheriff's Office, Pima County (Arizona) comments taken from an address to Criminology classes, University of Arizona (Tucson), February, 1959.
6. Chapman, Ames W.: Attitudes Toward Legal Authorities by Juveniles, *Sociology and Social Research,* Vol. 40, January, 1956, p. 173.
7. MacNamara, Donal E. J.: Police Training in Prevention of Crime and Delinquency, *Journal of Criminal Law and Criminology,* Vol. XLII, July-August, 1951, p. 263.
8. Dewhurst, H. S.: *The Railroad Police,* Springfield, Thomas, 1955, pp. 111–116, 165.
9. Solomon, Ben: Curfews: Valuable or Worthless?" *Police,* Volume 5, May-June, 1961, pp. 51–54.
10. Correctional Notes, *Utah, National Council on Crime and Delinquency News,* Vol. 40, November, 1961, p. 10.

11. Higgins, Lois Lundell: Introduction, *Policewoman's Manual,* Springfield, Thomas, 1961, pp. xiii–xiv.
12. Imler, Donald: Training Peace Officers to Understand and to Work with Youth, *Federal Probation,* Vol. XIII, March, 1949, pp. 42–44.
13. Fishman, Joseph Fulling: *Crucibles of Crime,* New York, Cosmopolis Press, 1923, pp. 13–14.
14. MacCormick, Austin H.: Children in Our Jails, *The Annals,* Vol. 261, January, 1949, pp. 150–157.
15. Ellingston, John R.: *Protecting Our Children From Criminal Careers,* New York, Prentice-Hall, 1948, p. 185.
16. "Jails": A Note in the *Journal of Social Therapy,* Vol. I, October, 1955, p. 198.
17. MacCormick, Austin H.: Keeping Children Out of Jails: It Can be Done, *Federal Probation,* Vol. XIII, September, 1949, p. 45.
18. Ellingston, John R.: *op. cit.,* p. 186.
19. MacCormick, Austin H.: *op. cit.,* p. 40.
20. Palmieri, Henry J.: The Child in Detention, *Focus, Vol.* 28, January, 1949, pp. 22–23.
21. Comparison of Expenditures and Estimated Standard Costs for Selected Juvenile Delinquency Services, *Children's Bureau,* 1960, Pamphlet # 10, p. 11.
22. Norman, Sherwood: New Goals for Juvenile Detention, *Federal Probation,* Vol. XIII, December, 1949, pp. 29–33.
23. Bloch, Herbert A., and Flynn, Frank T.: *Delinquency: The Juvenile Offender in America Today,* New York, Random House, Inc., 1956, p. 172.

# 8

## THE JUVENILE COURT

JULY 1, 1899, marks the official birth date of the juvenile court. On this date the law became effective in Illinois which established the first juvenile court in the city of Chicago. This was the first recognition of a separate area of legal control for juvenile behavior. By 1945, every state had passed some type of juvenile court statute.

From the beginning the movement was influenced by the juvenile court philosophy, an ideology sponsored chiefly by humanitarians, social scientists and a sprinkling of judges. This philosophy placed emphasis upon treatment consequence rather than upon behavior circumstances, the prevailing viewpoint of the criminal court. At the beginning, conflict arose in the legal profession as to whether or not the proposed policy of the juvenile court philosophy would violate the child offender's constitutional rights. Because of this conflict (and also because of the limited facilities of most juvenile courts) this philosophy has never fully materialized. Many criminologists now believe that the juvenile court is the principal experimental proving ground for changes in the entire crime-control system.

### DEVELOPMENT OF THE JUVENILE COURT IDEA

Many events in Illinois and in other states led to the passage in 1899 of the first juvenile court in the world. Charles L. Chute,[1] a long-time National Probation and Parole Association executive, traces the juvenile court since its inception. The first important event was the establishment of special institutions for child offenders, beginning with the New York City House of Refuge in 1825 and later, similar publicly-supported reform schools in Massachusetts, Pennsylvania and other states. In a number of states acts appeared providing for separate hearing of children's cases in the regular courts. In 1869 Massachusetts passed a significant act requiring the courts to give written notice to the visiting agent of the State Board of Charities before committing children. This is probably the first time that a social worker was given legal status as a court officer. In 1870, Massachusetts enacted a law requiring separate hearings for children in Suffolk County. In 1877, a similar law was approved in New York, and included certain provisions to prevent children from associating with adult offenders. In 1892, New York provided for special trials for those under sixteen. In 1898, Rhode Island enacted legislation similar to that of New York.

In Chicago, it was the social and civic organizations—notably the Chicago Woman's Club and the Catholic Visitation and Aid Society—that first urged a juvenile law. The Woman's Club actually had a bill drafted in 1895 for a separate court for children and a probation department, but their legal advisors told them it was unconstitutional, and they abandoned it. They and many other organizations kept up the agitation. Hull House under its leader Jane Addams, interested itself in the plight of the thousands of children then in the jails. The Illinois State Conference of Charities devoted its entire program in the fall of 1898 to "The Children of the State." Dr. Hastings H. Hart, Superintendent of the Illinois Children's Home and Aid Society, was a speaker and urged getting together on a juvenile court bill. The co-operation of the Chicago Bar Association was sought and they appointed a committee to prepare a bill that would secure the support of all interested agencies. The first draft of the juvenile court bill underwent much revision at the hands of the lawyers but finally was approved as the Bar Association bill and was introduced in the Illinois legislature by Representative Newcomer. After a hard fight, during which some compromises were made (especially in omitting a provision for paid probation officers), it passed on the last day of the legislature. Because no provision for paid probation officers was retained in the act, a citizens' committee, known as the Juvenile Court Committee, was formed. With the aid of the Chicago Woman's Club, the first paid probation officer was provided. Dean Roscoe Pound of Harvard Law School hailed this Juvenile Court Act of Illinois as "the greatest advance in judicial history since the Magna Charta."

Following the success of the Chicago court, the movement spread rapidly. In Denver, Colorado, Judge Ben D. Lindsey independently organized a juvenile court in 1899 under a so-called "school law" with limited jurisdiction over delinquent children of school age. A juvenile court act similar to that of Illinois was passed in Colorado in 1903 and Judge Lindsey became the best-known proponent of juvenile courts throughout this country and Europe. One of his greatest contributions was the securing of the first act in 1903 giving jurisdiction to the juvenile court to deal directly with parents and other adults contributing to the delinquency or dependency under either chancery or criminal procedure. The court thus became the first juvenile and domestics relations court.

Juvenile court laws or many of their provisions have been followed in most European countries, beginning in England with the passage of the Children's Act of 1908. A League of Nations study in 1931 showed at that time that juvenile courts or some substitute for them were established in thirty foreign countries.

Another important development concerned uniformity of standards between the many local courts and for state-wide coverage so that all children in need of care may have protection. A state-controlled juvenile court system was first established in Utah in 1908. In 1941, Connecticut became the second state to establish a state juvenile court. The third state to establish a state-wide juvenile court was Rhode Island in 1944. One state court with two full-time judges replaced twelve district court judges—all handling children along with criminal and civil court work. State juvenile courts are being discussed today in other jurisdictions, especially in Virginia and Florida. Utah has demonstrated that a state court plan is adaptable to large rural states as well as the smaller, more populous ones.

Although by 1938 nearly every state had juvenile court laws, no solution for separate, noncriminal treatment of delinquent children brought before the Federal courts was reached until the passage of the Federal Juvenile Delinquency Act of that year. This act authorized informal hearings for children under eighteen and, unless they are placed on probation, their commitment to the custody of the Attorney General for placing in federal or local institutions for juvenile delinquents or in boarding homes has been effective in many cases.

Juvenile courts increased rapidly, Wyoming being the last state to establish such a court in 1945. Juvenile courts are today still in the process of evolution, and new procedures and techniques are being developed.

## THE FUNCTION OF THE JUVENILE COURT

When the first juvenile court in Chicago began to function, it exemplified what Roscoe Pound described as "personalized justice." Destined to affect before the law not only the juvenile field but also the whole scope of human relationships under the law, it may be viewed as a twentieth-century approach to an age-old problem of human rights and responsibilities.

The underlying purposes of the juvenile court are two-fold: (1) to remove the child offenders from the ordinary criminal courts to equity courts, which consider the doer rather than the deed; and (2) to have this juvenile court render protection and treatment to *other* children needing both. Admirable as these purposes are in principle, they often fail to be carried out in actual practice.

In the juvenile court idea have been combined virtues of both the old common law and equity. Common law had established that children were not criminally liable if they were seven years old or under at the time of their offense. The juvenile court extended this earlier age limitation to eighteen years in most jurisdictions. Founded on the principle of *parens patriae,* namely, that the state must exercise guardianship over a child when the parents are unable or unwilling to discharge their full responsibility to him, the juvenile court, as a court of equity, avoids any stigma for a child which a criminal court contact might place upon him.

As indicated by Vedder and Maloof,[2] the juvenile court, since its inception, has functioned on this basic premise, that the youthful offender is to be treated, not as a criminal, but as a child in trouble, whose parents or guardians fail to discharge their responsibilities to him. Nonlegalistic, this court is characterized by informal procedure, with great powers of discretion invested in its judge. Still, although much antiquated thinking regarding juvenile misbehavior has been abandoned, the handling of delinquent children continues to be largely punitive in character, and after more than a half-century of juvenile-court philosophy and practice, most people still believe that the juvenile court is a place where they punish "bad" children.

Juvenile courts are the least understood and most misunderstood of all the nation's tribunals. Their distinctive philosophy, procedures, and approaches are features which few people appreciate; this is one reason why they have not been able to live up to the expectations of the public. Endeavors to curtail the functions of the juvenile court have been attempted through legislation and court decisions. The 1907 amendments to the Illinois juvenile court, for example, utilizes such terminology as "frequents," "patronizes," "habitually," "idleness," and "vulgar language," consensus on which is well-nigh impossible. Such terms mean all things to all people.

Restrictive legislation is usually proposed by persons who consider the progressive methods of juvenile court procedure as a scheme of "coddling" youthful offenders. Teeters and Reinemann cite a characteristic example of such assaults—the 1935 drive in Chicago (the court's birthplace!) to amend the law establishing the juvenile court so that all children above ten years of age and charged with felonies would be tried in adult criminal courts. The Supreme Court of Illinois, in considering the case of a fifteen-year-old girl charged with murder, declared that "it was not intended by the legislature that the juvenile court should be made a haven of refuge." Federal Judge William H. Holly characterized this statement as having decided that Cook County's juvenile court had no legal status, that it existed merely by license of the county's criminal court.

The Chicago *Tribune,* in an editorial of May, 1939, demanded that the criminal court assert its constitutional jurisdiction over young offenders. The editorial stated that the function of the criminal court is to punish offenses against the law—the juvenile court is not inflicting punishment, and the present maximum age for juvenile delinquents was too high. Today, the pendulum seems to be swinging the other way. According to Oliver J. Keller, Jr., of the Illinois Youth Commission, age thirteen will be substituted for age ten, as the minimum age that a child could be tried in the adult criminal court, effective as of January 1, 1962.

As Chute has suggested, perhaps the greatest defect in juvenile court laws has been their failure to provide complete jurisdiction over children. Twenty-one of our states (almost half) permit some offenses, either all felonies or only capital offenses, to be excluded from juvenile court jurisdiction or be shared concurrently with other courts. This is inconsistent with the original purpose of the juvenile court, which seeks to treat all children who are in need of care and protection, regardless of the offenses committed. In a few states the intent of the law to give exclusive jurisdiction over children has been thwarted by Supreme Court decisions. Illinois is one of them.

The National Probation and Parole Association published its first *Standard Juvenile Court Act* in 1925 to carry out juvenile court standards adopted jointly by the Association and the U.S. Children's Bureau in 1923. The act sought to give the juvenile courts exclusive jurisdiction up to 18 years of age in all types of children's cases needing court action. However, in many jurisdictions, if the act committed by the juvenile is repugnant enough, he suddenly becomes "responsible" and is tried in an adult criminal court, his adolescent age offering little or no protection.

In December, 1955, the Arizona *Republic* (Phoenix) criticized the Arizona juvenile court system, suggesting that juvenile codes and courts in innumerable instances may violate the child's rights, that in criminal prosecutions, the *accused* (including the child) is entitled to a speedy and public trial, an impartial jury, compulsory process for obtaining witnesses in his favor, the assistance of counsel at all times, and since these "rights" in the juvenile court are denied him, it contravenes the Sixth Amendment. A vengeful neighbor, merely by filing a petition, can take any child away from his parents by alleging the child is neglected, dependent, or delinquent and doesn't have to allege any facts.

The Juvenile Code of Arizona provides that a hearing be held but neglects to say when, so theoretically the child can be held until age twenty-one. It violates the First Amendment, that no law shall abridge the freedom of speech or of the press. If framers of the Arizona Juvenile Code can draw a veil of secrecy about juvenile misconduct, then the legislature can enact a law forbidding any mention of a public official accused of malfeasance .... and under the Juvenile Code of Arizona, a child found guilty of jay-walking could be taken from his parents, and placed in a foster home or a reformatory ... such is the potential power of the juvenile court judge. The juvenile court and its functions continue to meet the jaundiced eye of press, and because of it, a large segment of the public as well.

As far as the Federal Constitution is concerned, the minor offender is entitled to the services and counsel of an attorney. One ten-year-old offender was sent to a state reformatory for car theft, and after release, was charged with parole violation. He applied for a writ of habeas corpus, contending the original sentence imposed by the juvenile court was unconstitutional because the juvenile court at no time had informed him of his right to counsel, under the Sixth Amendment. The ultimate function of the juvenile court is to make an adjudication of whether the offender is a delinquent, or determine the guilt or innocence of the offender. The juvenile code statutes are designed to protect the child, not diminish the rights he already had, hence the superior court held for the juvenile appellant. The appellant court concluded that any deprivation of right of counsel violated the Sixth Amendment and constituted a denial of due process. The juvenile court statute is not itself unconstitutional, for it does not take away the right, but, any failure to advise juveniles of his rights or any attempt to have him waive his rights is a violation of the Sixth Amendment.[3]

As a result of the campaign of the Arizona press to "liberalize" the business of Arizona juvenile courts, the records and the proceedings of the juvenile court are now open to the press and the public. One danger to the cause of more "publicity," is the juvenile court and juvenile probation staff may prefer to omit some information of a highly confidential matter to protect the child. Hence, in some Arizona counties, to comply with the new law to make the records and proceedings open to press and public, and to protect the child, use is made of a "folder within a folder" system. "Court orders" and "court records" are bound permanently into the case folder, but, the case history, correspondence and other casework confidential materials are bound separately and when public inspection is requested, the inner folder is withheld. This appears to be legal, since the repealed section of publicity referred to the "records" and "proceedings" of the juvenile court.

The traditional, or the "American way" of obtaining justice as delineated by the Federal Constitution was through the fundamentals upon which the method of promoting justice was based, such as the right to a speedy trial, right to counsel, et cetera but the juvenile court was designed to ensure a superior justice by protecting the child, and to a great extent, has abandoned the very fundamental legal safeguards found in the Constitution. This is known as the "peculiar paradox" of the juvenile court and was recognized soon after its establishment, which took the form of inquiry as to the competence of the judge trained in the law and the problem of his determining the proper therapy in treatment cases, a province almost completely foreign to his specialized training. The conclusions of many appear to be that juvenile court judges are frequently not competent to pass on the "other than legal considerations." [4]

Although juvenile courts and their functions are known throughout the world, there is very little information available to the public in the various types of libraries. The juvenile court system is difficult to assess, since there is no one "system" but dozens of "systems," with great variation in time and place, even within the United States. Very few juvenile courts have a full-time judge, and most juvenile courts have inadequate knowledge of the youthful offenders appearing before them. Juveniles are unfamiliar with courtroom processes and terminology. In England recently, the oath was changed from "I swear by Almighty God" to "I promise by Almighty God," because juveniles misinterpreted the word "swear." Juvenile courts lack the power to impose the death penalty on any child under its authority.[5]

According to Tappan, processing the child through the juvenile court and its treatment facilities involves exposure to potentially injurious associations. Taking children out of the adult criminal courts has not solved the problem of contamination, for a child may learn more from his daring peers than he does from hardened criminals. Since the juvenile court represents a hazard to every case adjudicated, the court should be the last resort, and, whenever possible, the child should be dealt with first in non-judicial agencies.[6]

The functions of the juvenile court do not follow any charted path; "confusion in the court" better describes the situation at the present time. While appellate courts have decided that the youngster in the juvenile court is entitled to his "rights" as found in the Constitution, the Supreme Court of Pennsylvania recently held to the contrary, that "since juvenile courts are not criminal courts, the constitutional rights granted to persons accused of crime are not applicable to the children brought before them." This decision, cited by Professor Paul Tappan, was appealed to the United States Supreme Court on the grounds that the protections of the Fourteenth Amendment against deprivation of liberty without due process had been violated. The Court refused to hear the case.[7]

As Tappan points out in another article in *The Annals,* the statutory provisions relating to juvenile courts and their jurisdication are misleading. "Real" juvenile courts are relative rarities; they can be found for the most part in some of the large cities.[8] The best of these juvenile courts are sometimes part of a court of domestic relations. In forty states, juvenile authority is centered wholly or in part in courts that serve some other function: municipal, county, district, circuit, superior, justices of the peace, or probate courts. Most commonly the judge who sits as a juvenile court has criminal jurisdiction and devotes only a relatively small part of his time to children's cases. There seems to be considerable justification for the often quoted statement that "when the child needs the juvenile court the most, he gets it the least."

Relatively untouched, however, is the principle upon which juvenile courts were established: that children under eighteen years of age have not reached the state of intellectual and emotional development which make them fully responsible for their acts.

But there are qualifying provisions, which have been previously indicated, but worthy of repetition, that if the juvenile's act is sufficiently repugnant, the court can decide that the child is responsible after all and should not be tried by the juvenile court. The latter may then refer the case to the adult criminal court. Such a "decision" was handed down in the courts of Miami, Florida. The offender, a sixteen-year-boy received a five year prison term from the judge of the adult criminal court. The Jacksonville *Times-Union* on February 5, 1952, reported that this was the first case under the new Juvenile Court Act (which permits the judge to send to adult criminal court juveniles whom the judge considers "obstinate") in which a juvenile offender was tried by criminal court. Such cases, it should be noted, have not greatly lessened the over-all trend to utilize the juvenile court process.

## THE JUVENILE COURT JUDGE

Juvenile court literature stresses the view that the assumptions, terminology, and procedures of the criminal court are obstacles to the rehabilitive aims of the juvenile court. The phraseology of the criminal code should be avoided in dealing with a child. A child is not "arrested," he is "taken into custody," he is not "imprisoned," he is "detained," he is not "convicted," he is "adjudged," he is not "sentenced," he is "committed." He is not charged with a "crime" or found "guilty" of a crime, but he is adjudged a delinquent. Allegedly, a major reason for this situation is that the typical juvenile court judge has had criminal law training and experience which strongly influence the way he plays the role of juvenile court judge. When a juvenile is brought into court, the judge from then on is a part, a very important part, of the "environment" of that juvenile. If the judge's attitude toward the delinquent is wrong, then the judge himself may even become an obstacle in straightening out the juvenile. A hostile child can rarely be helped. A hostile judge can rarely be helpful.[9]

Because many judges assigned to the juvenile court find it difficult to shed the formality and atmosphere of the criminal trial when they hold juvenile court sessions, they often arraign the child at the bar as if he were a hardened criminal and often use the probation officers as if they were prosecuting attorneys. They sometimes think exclusively in terms of guilt or innocence.

As pointed out by Juvenile Judge Walter H. Beckham, of Miami who has enjoyed the rare privilege of presiding over a busy juvenile court for over twenty years without a single appeal from his rulings, the juvenile court is more a court of human relations than a court of law. The judge's chambers should be clean, bright, and cheerful, with inspiring pictures on the walls depicting happy family and child life. The furniture should be clean, comfortable with an easy chair, especially for mothers with young babies. The judge's chair should be on the floor level with other chairs in the room. The child and the parents should be seated together directly in front of the judge. No smoking should be allowed and everything should be quiet, neat, and orderly. A gentle, pleasant voice and friendly demeanor on the part of the judge and probation officer are highly important. It helps if the judge will nod and smile pleasantly at the parties in the case as they come into the room to be heard. The court should avoid having officers in uniform and carrying pistols or "billies.

The juvenile court proceeding is not a trial of anyone on criminal charge, but an "investigation" into the conduct of a young citizen to determine what action or program should be adopted for the welfare of the child. The court should never tear down the respect, love, and faith a child may have in his own parents, regardless of their behavior or misconduct. Discussion of sex offenses should be in refined language and not in the language of the street. The child is never called a "kid" or "brat," but by his given name and the parents should be addressed as "mother" or "father." The greatest qualification a juvenile court judge can have is a genuine love of people. He must have a real interest in their problems and an understanding and sympathetic heart.[10]

In a similar vein, Charles H. Boswell, Probation Officer, lists a few "Don'ts for juvenile court judges," such as don't play politics in court, don't permit derogatory testimony concerning the character of the child's parents in front of the child, don't respond to a hostile child with hostility, don't rely on a "bawling out" to accomplish much with an immature, misdirected or unhappy youngster who is brought into court, don't demand that either youngsters or adults meet unreasonable probation conditions, don't threaten the youngster by using the reformatory as a club over his head, for that is about as futile as a judge advising a juvenile with an I.Q. of below eighty that he could make grades of "A" or "B" in school if he would only try! The last "Don't" suggested is don't expect your probation officers to be able to accomplish a full and adequate social investigation overnight.[11]

Too many judges must rotate in assignments to juvenile court or must devote the major portion of their interest elsewhere; therefore their interest in the welfare of children can not be sustained. For example, one study indicates that in one juvenile and domestic relations court the judge claimed that 70 per cent of his time is spent on divorce cases, while the remaining 30 per cent is not devoted entirely to juvenile offenders. In another court, the judge stated that he was required to give as much as 85 per cent of his time to matters *not* concerned with juvenile delinquents. In yet another jurisdiction, the responsibilities assigned to the court were expanded into so-called "family" matters to the extent that even prostitution cases were included.[12]

In one western state the writer knows of a situation where judges formerly rotated the juvenile court assignment every six months. Some of the judges in this court had boys report to their offices in groups of four and lectured to them on the advantages of conforming to the rules of society! The same judges worked without trained probation officers; they relied upon volunteers to do the social case work—which means little more than a routine signing of the "book" by the offender. The situation illustrated by these cases is hardly consistent with the modern accent on professional specialization.

Juvenile court judges are either elected or appointed by state or federal executives. In either system of selection, political influences often determine the outcome, and there appears to be an enormous variety in the qualifications considered for the assignment. Before the passage of the Juvenile Court Act in Florida in 1950, for example, the governor could appoint anyone as judge of the juvenile court as long as the person possessed "high moral character." For the judgeship of this juvenile court, an appointee was not required to be either a lawyer or a social worker, nor to have special educational training or any experience in court. He merely had to be eight years older (or twenty-five years old) than the children he supervised, and must have survived three summers of Florida sunshine![13] This, of course, is an extreme case and has been rectified by recent legislation.

In 1941, the state of Missouri adopted a plan for its selection of juvenile court judges which plan has found favorable acceptance and is endorsed by the American Bar Association. Under this "Missouri Plan," the judge is appointed by the governor from three names submitted to him by a commission. The appointee, virtually "on probation" for twelve months, then runs for election for a full term, his success dependent upon popular vote.

Because he is "low man on the totem pole," in the judicial hierarchy the office of the juvenile court judge does not, as a rule, attract top-level personnel. And the short tenure of office in many jurisdictions often discourages qualified men and women from seeking this job. At the same time, the judge's position is of central strategic importance in the juvenile court, combining the role of dispenser of justice, with those of chief administrator, policy maker, and public relations official. In these capacities, he occasionally represents a curious picture of the juvenile court. For example, in the case of the two boys who pushed over about forty tombstones in Reno (reported in *Gazette,* July 14, 1948), the judge, for their punishment, ordered that twice weekly for several weeks each boy had to "patrol" the cemetery every evening, in addition to righting the tombstones.

Another judge in Brooklyn, delivered the following lecture to a seventeen-year-old-boy charged with soliciting alms from textile workers:

> What you need is for me to have you in a two-by-four room. What I would do to you! I'd blacken your eyes and give you some real American spirit and do for you what your parents should have done. We spend billions in this country for schools and what have we educated here—a mongrel and a moron! I have six kiddies myself and my oldest girl is ten. She knows who God is

> and the laws of the country. Down at my house we have a cat-of-nine tails. I show it, and that is all. Get out of this courtroom. You are not fit to be here.[14]

A statement on juvenile delinquency and its implications was reported by the Tucson *Daily Citizen* March 29, 1958, in which Juvenile Court judge Philip B. Gilliam of Denver was quoted:

> We have been sloppy in our thinking. We've been told there is no such thing as a bad boy. Well, these people are wrong. Most of the juvenile delinquents are meaner than hell. These kids are sick and they are mean. They see their drunken fathers beat up their mothers and the kids want to go out and shoot a cop or rob a drunk as a result.
>
> We must combat the rising American philosophy of "give me mine" and "don't be a sucker." We must make the good boy popular again. A "square" is really a nice kid who goes to church and studies, yet the terms "don't be a square" or "don't chicken" predominate, daring others to break the law. The cheapest way to handle juvenile delinquents is through probation which costs about $40 a year, contrasted to the $2500 to send him to an institution. "Every time a kid goes bad, a good man dies."

Many such cases could be assembled, illustrating the extent to which highly personal views may color official decisions of the judge. The judge of the juvenile court may be solicitous or he may be vindictive; he may be as impersonal as law itself or he may be highly personal. One teenager was arrested in the basement of a dowager's home and she had lectured the boy for two hours on the evil of his ways, and when the offender appeared before the local juvenile court judge, the judge stated: "you poor lad, two hours of Mrs. B's conversation is punishment enough for anyone. Case dismissed."

One woman judge of a juvenile court gave a girl offender two years in the reformatory when medical examination revealed that she was not a virgin. One thirteen-year-old boy was brought into the juvenile court on a petition signed by an eighth grade school teacher, who unsworn, told the judge, out of the presence of the boy and his parents, that a female classmate of the boy told her he had broken her living room window the previous Halloween, and she had "heard" he had done other mischief too. Although all hearsay, the judge placed this boy in the reformatory until "he was rehabilitated" but in no case to extend past his twenty-first birthday, a period of almost eight years.[15] This great latitude surely calls for men of professional training and of *judgment*—if there are to be effective judges of the young offender.

Of course, many juvenile court judges are highly capable, performing admirably even when greatly handicapped by limited funds and facilities. These superior officials characteristically concentrate on the offender's possible rehabilitation, not his punishment—"what are we going to do *for* him, not *to* him. When one juvenile court judge offered to shake hands with the boy defendant, the boy lifted his arm impulsively as if to ward off a blow, saying "I thought no one would shake hands with me." Many defendants have no idea what a juvenile court judge should look like. One boy remarked, "I thought I'd see some old sourpuss."

The competent judges of the juvenile court generally maintain an informal atmosphere in court; typically their speech, sympathetic and mild, reveals their quest to *understand* children. These superior judges would probably agree with David Bogen [16] that what is needed is not the complete rejection of "justice" which has been demanded by those who feel that the offense should not in the least control the disposition of the case, but rather an enlightened "justice" which will protect the rights of the community, and yet leave scope for modern individualized treatment of the youthful offender. Above all else, understanding the youth before him should be the judge's governing goal. William Healy, a physician, is a pioneer in the orthopsychiatric approach to problems of juvenile delinquency and he believes that the juvenile court is here to stay, representing as it does, justice for youth.[17]

So much has been said and published criticizing the juvenile courts that Harrison Allen Dobbs,[18] has written specifically in their defense. He emphasizes that fact that the court was no fly-by-night happening and was not the result of selfish and sentimental drives. However, the situation faced by the children's tribunal is a challenging one. Careful thought and action are required if the juvenile court movement is to go forward and not backward. In the future this young social institution certainly might make more lasting contributions to children's welfare.

This discussion of the juvenile court judge should not overshadow the fact that the judge himself is by no means the only potential weak spot in the juvenile court system. Perhaps of equal importance are the problems resulting from the failure of state and county agencies to provide the facilities necessary for carrying out the functions of the court efficiently. These are problems directly confronted by the judges themselves. They should become the concern of all citizens who are interested in the improvement of an institution so important in the lives of our youths—the juvenile court.

## INCREASE IN COURTS AND OFFENSES

Juvenile court business is becoming big business. The total volume tends to increase yearly. In 1937 the Children's Bureau reported that 462 courts serving 36 per cent of the population of the United States processed about one per cent of the nation's seventeen million children between ten and sixteen years of age. During 1937 these courts, in thirty states and the District of Columbia, reported 78,688 delinquency cases, about one-seventh of them girls and the remainder boys.

Because of the incompleteness of numerical data, only a general approximation of delinquency and juvenile court activity during World War II and the postwar period can be given. But most studies have shown that child offenses began to multiply during World War II, the rates of increase varying by states and by counties. Since 1943, courts have reported a continuous decline in girls' cases, but boys' cases registered an increase in 1945, following a decline during the preceding year. After a peak at the end of World War II (1945) juvenile court delinquency cases dropped in number each year from 1946 through 1948, a phenomenon which seems to be related to the improvements of the conditions associated with war. In 1949, for the first time since the end of the war, juvenile court delinquency cases reversed their downward trend and increased by four per cent over the previous year. That year it is estimated that almost three hundred thousand children, or about twelve in every thousand between the ages of seven and seventeen, came to the attention of juvenile courts because of delinquency and criminality.

Most juvenile courts have jurisdiction over actions involving dependent and neglected children. There was an over-all decrease of eight per cent in the dependency and neglect cases between 1946 and 1949, probably as a result of the high level of employment and general prosperity during the postwar years and the elimination or improvement of many war-associated conditions. Of the total number of children's cases handled by the 413 courts reporting in 1949, about twenty-four per cent were dependency and neglect cases. The median age was six and a half years, while for delinquency cases the median was fifteen and a half years. The United States Children's Bureau at that time estimated that if the volume of delinquency continued, even on the 1948 level, at least 275,000 children each year may be expected during the next several years to come before the nation's juvenile court.[19] This "projection" of 275,000 children was entirely too conservative.

In 1950, based on reports from 458 courts, the estimate rose to 435,000; and in 1956, based on reports from slightly over eighty per cent of the juvenile courts that reported, the estimate was 450,000, or 2.2 per cent of all children aged ten through seventeen. By 1959, approximately 483,000 cases were handled by the juvenile courts in that year.[20]

As summarized by Professor Neumeyer, the rapid decline of juvenile delinquency following World War II paralleled a similar decline after World War I. After the wars, people tend to settle down, families are re-united, regular work schedules are re-established in place of the three-shift basis, adults are more at home to supervise the children and youth-serving agencies increase their activities. However, the inordinate rapid growth of juvenile delinquency after 1948 is difficult to explain. The juvenile population has increased since that year, but the volume of delinquency has increased even faster. Increased prosperity is only a partial explanation.[21]

## APPEARANCE OF THE CLINIC AND THE COUNSELOR

Most delinquent children can be reclaimed; but their reclamation or correction demands continuity of treatment of each child as an individual. However, under the present standards, treatment is apparently not thorough enough for there appears to be no significant difference in the arrest rate for those receiving treatment compared with those not receiving treatment.[22] Nevertheless, extension of the functions of the juvenile court will materially enhance this endeavor. Some juvenile courts function with the assistance of guidance clinics or counselors.

A typical child guidance clinic which works with a juvenile court combines the skills of the psychiatrist, psychologist, and social worker, makes a diagnoses of each offender, and serves as a consulting agency to the juvenile court. The counselor serves as an assistant to the juvenile court judge, as he does the preliminary work of interviewing the juvenile offender, as well as contacting all persons concerned in the case. His recommendations as to final disposition of the case are usually accepted by the busy juvenile court judge. Many juvenile courts, however, function without the assistance of a guidance clinic or a counselor, primarily due to lack of funds.

According to Lowell J. Carr, the vast majority of American juvenile courts have no clinics, no counselors and the 2,000-odd small town juvenile courts don't know what a psychiatrist looks like. Nine out of ten juvenile courts are so far below grade as to be practically subterranean, which cannot be blamed on crooked politicians, hick voters or the moron public. It is a matter of economics; most communities in the United States are too poor to afford a juvenile court, much less a modern, clinic complete with a trained staff. Carr estimates that the typical small town juvenile court wouldn't average more than nine-tenths of a case per week. No small town can afford to maintain a special detention home, a child-specialist judge, a trained probation officer, a special diagnostic clinic—all to handle one delinquent every six or seven days. Rural counties cannot raise the money to pay for such standards. Six days out of the seven, the high-powered specialists would be playing checkers to pass the time. The delinquency business is simply not there.[23] Because of lack of funds and personnel facilities, many judges must attempt to combine many functions in one office—a severe handicap to proper remedial work.

Moreover, officials of clinics and juvenile court judges are not always in harmony. Some officials are of the opinion that the clinic should concern itself with the cases that come from the public school, the home, or social agencies, and lean to the opinion that accepting court cases injures the reputation of the clinic, due to the delinquency aspects involved. For example, the clinic may recommend treatment for dependency, neglect and personality problem cases; but in delinquency cases, the juvenile judge decides on the appropriate treatment necessary. Ideally, of course, the judge, the probation officer, the psychiatric social worker, and the psychologist should learn to work together for the sake of the child.

Another problem is posed because many parents appear unwilling or unable to understand the function of the clinic. Sometimes both the parents and the child consider the referral to the clinic as part of the punishment rather than a method of treatment. This attitude, often a consequence of inadequate education of the parents, may also hamper successful treatment.

One of the more recent adjuncts to the juvenile court, referred to above, is the much-needed counselor. The counselor tries to solve the problem first. Actually, in many communities, the quality of the juvenile courts is in large part a direct reflection of the capabilities of the counselors attached to them. The counselor should have an extensive acquaintance in the community, particularly among those who control the purse strings. Like the judge, he should have an understanding of, and sympathy for, both adults and children.

As Katherine F. Lenroot[24] has pointed out, when the first juvenile courts were established professional training for social work had not yet been started; child guidance clinics had not been thought of; child-saving and child-caring work, chiefly under private auspices, emphasized the removal of children from undesirable surroundings, chiefly for care in institutions or free foster homes, rather than the strengthening and rebuilding of family life. We must accept the fact that in treating the older and more aggressive youth there is a difference in the emphasis, approach, and skills required.

In the last analysis, the success of the work of the juvenile court is intimately related to the availability of adequate treatment resources outside the court. Such resources must include facilities for guidance and service to children in their own homes. Also required are effective resources for the treatment of children outside of their own homes, in foster homes, small study homes, or institutions. The whole area of treatment of juvenile delinquency is greatly in need of further study. The services of the juvenile court are an integral part of the broad and long-range program necessary to promote the well-being of all children as well as the protection of certain children who have special needs.

## EXTENSION OF THE JUVENILE COURT IDEA

Since 1899, when the world's first juvenile court law was enacted in Cook County, Illinois, this social institution has been gradually expanding. The development of probation theory, originated by John Augustus in 1841, lent itself to the spreading philosophy of the juvenile court. Also contemporary humanitarian influences made themselves felt in the reduction of capital penalties and cruel and unusual punishments. The juvenile court idea has been extended in specific areas. These areas include the establishment of adolescents' courts, youth correction authorities, and family courts. In addition, the pervasive influence of the juvenile court is reflected in the procedures of some of the criminal courts.

Judge Jacob M. Braude[25] traces part of the history of the Boys' Court of Chicago, in existence since March, 1914, the court having been designated as one of the specialized branches of the Municipal Court of Chicago, and deals with cases involving boys from the ages of seventeen to twenty-one.

Chicago has no special court for girls over juvenile court age because the Juvenile Court is given jurisdiction of girls up to the age of eighteen. When a girl reaches her eighteenth birthday, the law says she becomes a woman and if she gets into trouble she is dealt with in the Women's Court, except for felonies in which event she is brought to trial in the Felony Court.

The Boys' Court answers the need for a tribunal equipped to deal especially with the problems which late adolescence presents. The philosophy of the Boys' Court briefly stated is this: That, if the law curiously enough says that "every dog is entitled to at least one bite" then, certainly, every boy ought to be entitled to at least one chance and every effort is made to give to a first offender that one chance. Hence, under an extra-legal form of probation which is called "supervision," the defendant is placed with any one of four different agencies which cooperate with the court such as the Holy Name Society, representing the Catholic group; the Chicago Church Federation, representing the Protestant group; the Jewish Social Service Bureau and the Colored Big Brothers Organization. If the supervising agency reports the defendant has made an adjustment and is ready for ultimate discharge, the defendant is then officially discharged on the court records and to all intents and purposes there is no criminal record against him. The Boys' Court is established on the principle that the individual boy is far more important than the crime which he has committed.

Various agencies have been instituted to cope with adolescent delinquency. For example, the Wayward Minors' Act of New York (1923) provides that a person sixteen to twenty-one years old who is a habitual drinker or drug user, who associates regularly with undesirable persons or frequents houses of prostitution, may be deemed a wayward minor. This Act was intended as an aid to parents with incorrigible children who had passed the upper age limit of the state's juvenile court jurisdiction. Another adolescents' court in New York City, created in 1936, is a part of the felony court of the Borough of Queens. The Wayward Minors' Court, with city-wide jurisdiction over girls sixteen to twenty-one years of age, was at first a part of the Women's Court; since 1945, officially known as the Girls' Term, it has functioned independently.

Another type of agency working with adolescents is the youth authority. The Youth Authority program integrates under one governmental agency the several aspects of the treatment process; diagnosis and classification, institutional treatment, parole and delinquency prevention through community organization.

California has been in the vanguard in the establishment of youth authorities in the United States. Although the original

California law of June, 1941 which established a youth correction authority drew heavily upon the model act of the American Law Institute, there was at least one important difference, as the provision allowed the Authority to accept boys and girls from the juvenile courts (while the model act limited the Authority's function to youths above the juvenile court age).

Perkins criticizes the Youth Authority, in that it has too much authority (The Authority may dismiss an offender in a year, in six months, in six days, or *at once*), and gives a hypothetical case:

> Two boys A and B steal a car, are chased by the police, drive recklessly through the streets, try to jam the police car against the sidewalk and end in a smash-up in which an innocent bystander is killed. They are brought to Court, tried and convicted and admitted to the Youth Correction Authority.
>
> The Authority studies the boys. A is overwhelmed by what he has done, is penitent and anxious to avoid any mistake of this kind in the future. . . . B, on the other hand, is superficial and unstable, he expresses penitence, but it seems highly probable he may yield to temptation again. Both boys have similar background, and there is nothing to indicate that either is dominated by the other. Under Section 29 the Authority discharges A and keeps B under control, and sends him to the Reformatory.
>
> Here we have a law which not only permits discrimination between A and B without objective evidence, but also makes such discrimination mandatory, if the Authority forms a favorable opinion of A and an unfavorable one of B. . . . if there is anything in the world which produces flaming resentment and antagonism, it is *unfair discrimination*.[26]

The Youth Authority program came about because the traditional correctional processes failed to rehabilitate a large number of the youthful offenders who passed through it. California's pioneer effort was successful and soon other states followed with act incorporating the principles of the Youth Authority, such as Minnesota, Wisconsin, Massachusetts, Illinois, Kentucky and Texas. The first boy placed by California under the care of the Authority was received at the clinic in 1942; on its eighth anniversary (January, 1950), the California Youth Authority had cared for some thirteen thousand youths in its schools and camps. The numbers of youths processed since 1950 have increased substantially. Since that time California reports that the increase in delinquency is less than the population increase of the state. Despite some valid criticism, the Youth Authority seems destined to remain. As John Otto Reinemann[27] indicates, because of its underlying philosophy of a systematic approach to the youthful offender, the idea of the Youth Correction Authority has been called "the most revolutionary step taken in American penology since the establishment of the Elmira Reformatory," and much more promising than that innovation.

Some authorities believe that an extension of the present state juvenile court holds great promise. Most county juvenile courts located in small communities cannot afford a full time judge specially qualified for juvenile court work. The 1949 edition of the Standard Juvenile Court Act of the N.P.P.A. was the first to contain a provision for a statewide court established on a district basis, to assure special juvenile court judges for an entire state, as in Connecticut, Rhode Island and Utah. In each of these states there is a state juvenile court and a small number of full time, specially selected judges. No other judges sit in the juvenile courts in those states. Except for these statewide courts, according to Sol Rubin, only two per cent of the counties in the country have full time judges, and one-third of these are not specially selected to serve in the juvenile court.

Rubin distinguishes between the juvenile court and the equity court; for example, an equity court is bound by many formalities, including all the rules of evidence, while a juvenile court is informal in procedure and bound by very few rules of evidence. The equity court is concerned primarily with money and property affairs, while the juvenile court is mainly concerned with the personality and behavior of individuals; there the "remedy" is not a judgment between contesting parties, but an effort to find a mode of treatment. Therefore, a juvenile court is *not* an equity court, although it is based on equitable principles. It is a special, new type of court. An equity judge has no special experience that qualifies him as a juvenile court judge. The same is true for a court of law. Rubin concludes that the establishment of a state children's court does not solve all juvenile problems, but it does provide the best framework for the attainment of high standards in all phases of juvenile court action. More state juvenile courts may be anticipated within the next few years.[28]

Public Law 865, the Federal Youth Corrections Act—"to provide a system for the treatment and rehabilitation of youthful offenders" and "to improve the administration of criminal justice" —was enacted by the Eighty-first Congress and approved by the President on September 30, 1950. This legislation was the culumination of ten years' work by the Judicial Conference of the United States and its Committee on Punishment for Crime to provide the means and methods of training and treatment for young offenders.

The Federal Youth Corrections Act has been called the most forward step in law enforcement history. The Act defines a youth as a person under twenty-two years of age, and gives the courts greater discretion and new alternatives for dealing with him. It makes the Bureau of Prisons responsible for establishing classification centers, providing diversified institutional and treatment facilities, public or private, retraining and reeducation, and recommending to the Youth Division of the Parole Board the release of youths ready to return to their communities. Moreover, it is now possible to experiment with furloughing youthful prisoners who, without prejudice, can reenter the institution by choice or by necessity. Apparently a good many federal judges are looking forward to implementing this authority.

## IMPLICATIONS FOR OTHER COURTS

As indicated by Reinemann, the juvenile court idea not only has expanded vertically to include youth of older years and permeating criminal justice procedure in adult cases, but also has expanded vertically by influencing the treatment of many kinds of "family" cases including those pertaining to domestic relations, legal custody, adoption, illegitimacy, and related problems. Certain characteristics of juvenile court philosophy are singularly applicable to the procedure in family cases. The establishment of family courts has been aptly described as "socialized courts with socialized laws," to handle our unhappy and delinquent spouses much as we handle delinquent children. Often their behavior is not unlike that of a delinquent child, and for much the same reasons.

Judge George W. Smyth[29] notes that the problems of the parents and children are inseparable. No problem of a neglected or delinquent child can be treated successfully without also considering the attitudes and actions of the parents. An element of oversight, carelessness, disinterest, or ineptitude in the discharge of parental duties appears in almost every case. The juvenile court is nonlegalistic, has considerable flexibility, and is distinguished by informal procedure. Its judge enjoys powers of broad discretion. It is both a judicial and administrative agency. The juvenile court makes intensive use of the social sciences in its search of causation of juvenile misconduct, neglect, and dependency, and in its aim of rehabilitating the child, if possible, within the family itself.

The juvenile court also has had some impact on criminal administration. This influence may be particularly observed in the utilization of presentence investigation and the widened use of probation. Superior court judges are realizing, more and more, the desirability of knowing something about the defendant besides the grand jury indictment. It is hoped that in the years ahead additional characteristics of the juvenile court, such as the lack of formalism, the by-passing of "crime" and "convict" labels, the utilization of social science, and the wider and more comprehensive conception of moral responsibility, will be adopted by the adult criminal courts.

As Tappan so well points out, however, a note of caution is in order. There has been a tendency to exaggerate the contrasts between juvenile court procedures, pictured in glowing terms, and those of the criminal court system, viewed in a very critical and quite inaccurate light. In many places, especially in rural counties, juvenile courts do not approach adequate standards. Children's cases are handled much like other cases except for the proceedings' relative privacy and the fact that special attention is given to the allegations of the complainant-parent or police officer and to their common demands for the child's commitment. In urban areas as well there is great variation in the courts' conduct, much more so than in the criminal courts. This diversity is a reflection of the failure, thus far, to develop any firm consensus as to desirable goals and methods in dealing with children and adolescents.[30]

Although the following recognized objectives for the juvenile court of the future were suggested about a decade ago by Charles L. Chute, they are still valid and still unrealized in the vast majority of juvenile courts of the United States.

(1) Exclusive jurisdiction for juvenile courts in all cases of children who need the authoritative treatment of the state.
(2) Improvement of court staff. Probation officers and other social and technical staff members should all be appointed under civil service or other effective merit systems.
(3) The services of juvenile courts should be available to all children, especially to those in rural areas.
(4) More uniform extension of the powers of the court, and more use of its present powers, to deal with parents and other adults who contribute by acts or neglect to the delinquency of children.
(5) Juvenile courts should seek greater co-operation and co-ordination with other social agencies—public and private—with the schools, the police, and citizens' groups.
(6) The juvenile court, through its judge and entire staff, must participate in community movements for the development of co-ordinated agencies for child and family welfare and for the prevention of delinquency. It must seek to strengthen its services through interpretation of its vital work to the public.[31]

## REFERENCES


1. Chute, Charles L.: The Juvenile Court in Retrospect, *Federal Probation,* V l. XIII, September, 1949, pp. 3-8.
2. Vedder, Clyde B. and Maloof, Louis J.: Problems of Crime and Juvenile Delinquency (Chapter Six), *Social Problems,* (Edited by T. Lynn Smith) New York, Thomas Y. Crowell Company, 1955, p. 169.
3. Minor Appearing Before Juvenile Court is Entitled to Assistance under the Federal Constitution, (Abstracts), The Journal of Criminal Law, *Criminology and Police Science,* Vol. 46, March-April, 1956, p. 852.
4. Numberg, Henry: Problems in the Structure of the Juvenile Court, *Journal of Criminal Law, Criminology and Police Science,* Vol. 48, January-February, 1958, p. 503.

5. Savitz, Leonard D.: Capital Crimes as Defined in American Statutory Law, *The Journal of Criminal Law, Criminology and Police Science,* Vol. 46, September-October, 1955, p. 355.
6. Tappan, Paul W.: *Juvenile Delinquency,* New York, McGraw-Hill Book Company, Inc., 1949, pp. 220-221.
7. Tappan, Paul W.: *Crime, Justice and Correction,* New York, McGraw-Hill Book Company, Inc., 1960, pp. 390–391.
8. Tappan, Paul W.: Children and Youth in the Criminal Court, *The Annals,* Vol. 261, January, 1949, pp. 127–137.
9. Loevinger, Gustavus: The Court and the Child, *Focus,* Vol. 28, May, 1949, pp. 65–69.
10. Beckham, Walter H.: Helpful Practices in Juvenile Court Hearings, *Federal Probation,* Vol. 13, June, 1949, pp. 10–14.
11. Boswell, Charles H.: If I Were a Judge, *Federal Probation,* Vol. XV, March, 1951, pp. 26–30.
12. Schramm, Gustave L.: The Juvenile Court Idea, *Federal Probation,* Vol. XIII, September, 1949, p. 19.
13. Waybright, Roger J.: Chairman, Drafting Committee for *A Juvenile Court Act for Florida,* Explanation and Presentation, Jacksonville, Florida, 1950, p. 18.
14. Reported in Cantor, Nathaniel F.: *Crime Criminals and Criminal Justice,* New York, Henry Holt & Company, 1932, p. 209.
15. Beemsterboer, Matthew J.: The Juvenile Court–Benevolence in the Star Chamber, *The Journal of Criminal Law, Criminology and Police Science,* Vol. 50, January-February, 1960, p. 465.
16. Bogen, David: Justice Versus Individualized Treatment in the Juvenile Court, *The Journal of Criminal Law and Criminology,* Vol. XXXV, November-December, 1944, pp. 249–252.
17. Healy, M.D., William: Thoughts About Juvenile Courts, *Federal Probation,* Vol. XIII, September, 1949, pp. 16–19.
18. Dobbs, Harrison Allen: In Defense of Juvenile Courts, *Federal Probation,* Vol. XIII, September, 1949, pp. 24–29.
19. United States Children's Bureau, *Juvenile Court Statistics,* 1937; 1946–1949.
20. *Ibid.,* 1956, and Children's Bureau Statistical Series, 61 1960, p. 11.
21. Neumeyer, Martin H.: *Juvenile Delinquency in Modern Society,* Princeton, New Jersey, D. Van Nostrand Company, Inc, 1961, p. 64.
22. Smigel, Erwin O.: Public Attitudes Toward Stealing as Related to the Size of the Victim Organization, *American Sociological Review,* Vol. 21, June, 1956, p. 320.
23. Carr, Lowell J.: Most Courts Have to be Substandard, *Federal Probation,* Vol. XIII, September, 1949, pp. 29–33.
24. Lenroot, Katherine F.: The Juvenile Court Today, *Federal Probation,* Vol. XIII, September, 1949, pp. 1–5.

25. Braude, Jacob M.: Boys' Court: Individualized Justice for the Youthful Offender, *Federal Probation,* Vol. XII, June, 1948, pp. 9–14.
26. Perkins, John F.: Defect in the Youth Correction Authority, *The Journal of Criminal Law and Criminology,* Vol. XXXIII, July-August, 1942, pp. 111–118.
27. Reinemann, John Otto: The Expansion of the Juvenile Court Idea, *Federal Probation,* Vol. XIII, September, 1949, pp. 34–40.
28. Rubin, Sol: State Juvenile Court: A New Standard, *Focus,* Vol. 30, July, 1951, pp. 103–107.
29. Smyth, George W.: The Juvenile Court and Delinquent Parents, *Federal Probation,* Vol. XIII, March, 1949, pp. 12–17.
30. Tappan, Paul W.: *Juvenile Delinquency, op. cit.,* pp. 179, 180.
31. Chute, Charles L.: *op. cit.,* p. 8.

# 9

## PROBATION

PROBATION FOR THE juvenile offender is a form of court-disposition of the child following his adjudication. Although it is a non-punitive method of treating offenders, it should not be interpreted as leniency or mercy.

As recounted by John Otto Reinemann,[1] the beginnings of probation anteceded the creation of juvenile courts. In 1869, Massachusetts passed a law providing for the supervision of juvenile delinquents by a state agent. This was probably the direct outcome of the efforts and services of John Augustus, a Boston shoemaker, today recognized as the "first probation officer," who in the years 1841 to 1858 had befriended countless juvenile and other offenders. From a legal standpoint, adult probation is the suspension of the imposition or the execution of the sentence during a period of freedom, on condition of good behavior. With a delinquent child, the juvenile court uses probation as a form of case disposition which allows the child to live at liberty in his own home or in the custody of a suitable person, such as a relative, a friend of the family, or a foster home, under supervision of an agent of the court and upon such conditions as the court stipulates.

Charles L. Newman[2] in his *Sourcebook on Probation, Parole and Pardons,* traces the development of probation and notes that probation as it is known today has been derived from the practical extension of the English common law, hence analysis of the legal origins of probation must be principally concerned with England and America. In England and in the United States, probation developed out of the various methods for the conditional suspension of punishment, as attempts to avoid the cruel precepts of a rigorous criminal law. Among these Anglo-American judicial expedients, the direct precursors of probation, are the so-called benefit of clergy, the judicial reprieve, the release of an offender on his own recognizance, and the provisional "filing" of a case. However, probation is America's distinctive contribution to progressive penology, because the development of probation has been entirely statutory, insofar as the system is an expression of planned state policy.

The development of probation has been slow. Only six states had permissive probation legislation at the turn of the century. It still would be quite proper to say that probation is a "new" method of dealing with delinquency and crime. It assists in rehabilitation, education, and reeducation, as well as helping the probationer in every way possible make a satisfactory readjustment to family and community living.[3]

According to Teeters and Reinemann, the term "probation," derived from the Latin *probare* (meaning to test on approval) has been used in relation to criminal matters only since the middle of the 19th century. The term "probation" in connection with correctional treatment, was used for the first time by John Augustus, when he reported on his first case, in referring to a drunkard he reformed, Augustus wrote: "he signed the pledge and became a sober man; at the expiration of this period of *probation,* I accompanied him into the courtroom. . . ."[4] Interestingly enough, John Augustus seems to have taken the term "probation" from Puritan theology, that period of life before death as trial and training to qualify the candidate for heaven, according to Chutes and Bell, who cite this inscription:[5]

> In memory of Frederick, son of Mr. Thomas Jackson and Mrs. Lucy his wife, who died March 15, 1778, aged one year and five days. O Happy Probationer! accepted without being exercised, it is thy peculiar privilege not to feel the slightest of those Evils, which oppress thy surviving kindred.

Probation attempts to deal with offenders as individuals; its social principle is to keep these persons out of reformatories and with their families. It tries to prevent suffering—hence, it is not, in principle, punishment. And this, paradoxically, seems to be the basic reason why numerous officials, and even a large part of the public, oppose it. Probation is a humanitarian method of administering justice—not a gesture of leniency or mollycoddling.

It is, in large measure, a counseling service which emphasizes attitudes of friendship, helpfulness and sympathy. As Sanford Bates[6] expressed it, "Probation may be regarded as an investment in humanity . . . it encourages rather than embitters. It builds up rather than degrades. It is an investment in community protection." Today probation may be defined simply as the suspension of the sentence, conditioned upon good behavior, during a period of liberty in the community. It is generally considered a substitute for imprisonment.

In deciding a case involving a child or adolescent who is not insane or feebleminded, most juvenile or criminal courts will either: (1) return him to his home *on probation,* (2) refer him to such welfare services as exist in larger cities, (3) place him in a boarding or foster home, (4) send him to a correctional house, or (5) confine him to jail. For chance offenders and for first offenders, it is generally believed, the most sensible disposition of the case is to return the child to his home on probation, under court supervision. There are many advantages of probation as compared with commitment to an institution, and as listed by Reinemann, probation is an individualized form of treatment; it applies the methods of social casework; it leaves the child in his normal home surroundings; it enlists the help of community resources; it is not considered punitive and therefore is free of social stigma, and as in the case of probation for adults, it is much less expensive than incarceration.[7]

It has been estimated that it takes about three years to rehabilitate a serious child offender at a cost of several thousand dollars. But, it will cost society even more to retain the same child in a prison, from which he may emerge, not a reformed person, but an enemy of society, more eager than ever to "get even." Therefore few steps would be more economical—as well as beneficial on other grounds—in the improvement of the administration of criminal justice, than the wise extension of probation and the raising of the quality of probation services.

However, for many children and youths in trouble, probation does not appear to be an appropriate practice. To return to his home and neighborhood an individual of any age who has become habituated to criminal practices or who has deep-seated maladjustments, or whose delinquent behavior springs from brutality or immorality at home, or from the breakdown of satisfactory relationships in the family, or perhaps, from membership in a neighborhood gang, may involve, as one writer stresses, a disservice to the individual himself, to society, and to the cause of probation as well.[8] But it also should be remembered that if probation is undesirable for violators in these categories, the present-day principal alternative—confinement in jail or "reformatory" or prison—may result ultimately in even greater harm to society and its members.

David Crystal points out the significance of family casework in probation. Since all of our knowledge of behavior stems from family living, it is important that we address ourselves to problems individually, to determine where the distortion in family life took place, whether it is remediable, whether it is possible to treat an individual *invacuo;* i.e., without reference to past experience in a family constellation. Casework, whether in an authoritative or voluntary setting, involves the same basic elements; that is, that helping an individual involves consideration of relationships within the family setting.[9]

Probation and parole are not synonymous terms, although many people use them interchangeably, even law enforcement personnel and court officials. As William C. Nau relates, at a recent state probation and parole institute, a state judge spoke of "paroling" defendants throughout his address when what he really meant was placing them on probation. In similar vein, conference speakers may speak of prison inmates leaving the institution on probation, when parole is indicated. Parole is conditional release from a penal institution, and serving time is a prerequisite for parole consideration. The dissemination of more information to the public is strongly indicated.[10]

Probation has been thought of in negative fashion, as saving the offender from a worse fate, or teaching him not to do this again. As Elizabeth R. Glover indicates, probation has assumed a more positive function, that of introducing the probationer to a better way of life.[11] One woman in commenting on her reaction to a series of articles on probation in the newspaper wrote, "Probation is putting Christ to work in everyday living. The "better life" requires a definite program based on treatment planned for the individual, around his own situation, to redirect the offender's emotions with supportive therapy from parents, relatives and friends.

Unfortunately, the way probation is practiced differs in various courts and in different states; therefore it is impossible to estimate accurately the total number of children on probation in the United States. The number must be several times the number of correctional school graduates, which approximate thirty thousand a year. Lowell J. Carr calculates that if one were to guess, that sixty-five thousand to one hundred thousand children are placed on probation each year, it would not be an overstatement of the facts. In a summary analysis by Ralph England of probation and postprobation studies, it appears from the available research that probation is an effective correctional device, on both juvenile and adult levels.[12]

## THE PROBATION OFFICER

The care of these numerous probationers and the administration of the probation system today are in the hands of personnel generally lacking in numbers and often handicapped by limited facilities and inadequate training. In 1947, there were 3,711 probation officers working with children in 1,469 counties and many were lacking in either education, experience, or both. At least 70,000 "workers in the field" have little or no training and trying to fill 100,000 professional-level jobs. Only a small fraction of these "workers" have had graduate training. In 1957, there were about 4,000 juvenile probation workers in the United States, about half of whom work full time with juvenile cases, the other half dividing their time between juvenile and adult cases.[13] The majority of persons actually employed in this kind of work are not trained in any formal fashion.

Recent years have brought considerable improvement in the standards for probation officials, but the need for trained specialists in this area remains a serious problem. A committee of the Professional Council of the National Probation and Parole Association, consisting of leading authorities in the probation and parole field, in 1945 formulated "Standards for Selection of Probation and Parole Officers,[14] after consultation with many administrators in the correctional field throughout the county. These "Standards" suggest as minimum requirements or qualifications: a bachelor's degree from a college or university of recognized standing or its educational equivalent, with courses in the social sciences; one year of paid fulltime experience under competent supervision in an approved social agency or related field.

In addition, a probation officer must possess a good character and a balanced personality, with the following traits considered essential:

> Good health, physical endurance, intellectual maturity, emotional stability, integrity, tact, dependability, adaptability, resourcefulness, sincerity, humor, ability to work with others, tolerance, patience, objectivity, capacity to win confidence, respect for human personality, and genuine affection for people.

Many state laws are silent regarding qualifications for probation officers; others couch them in such general terms that they can be met by any untrained person as long as he is a "discreet person of reputable character." Political influences, which as a rule have been successfully banned in the teaching profession, are still operating in the field of probation. There is a difference of opinion whether case work training is a good preparation for probation work or not.

Reckless prefers that trained probation officers have a good foundation in criminology and the field of corrections, in preference to other professional disciplines. The "Standards" state that "the best training for probation and parole work is in a graduate school of social work." This division of opinion is further complicated by the fact that schools of social work are reluctant to include courses in penology and corrections, while on the other hand, many departments of sociology have frowned at the prospect of offering practical training. Some sociology departments offer no courses in criminology, penology or juvenile delinquency. Moreover, under the laws of various states—certainly in the public view—there is no general agreement concerning appropriate qualifications for the probation officer.

Burbank and Goldsborough[15] stress the importance of personality as the leading attribute of a competent probation officer. "All the probation officer has to offer, when you come down to brass tacks, is himself." The probation officer's personality and the use he makes of it in helping his clients is his most potent therapeutic tool. The demands on an officer are great, for he is working with persons who almost always are playing a dangerous game. The probation officer needs maturity and integrity which require the following abilities:

(1) The ability to form and sustain wholesome interpersonal relationships. He must identify with a wide range of people.
(2) The ability to accept responsibility for the authority he carries. Many an adult is unwilling to face his infantile attitudes toward authority.
(3) Ability to work with aggressive persons, with a high degree of objectivity and poise.
(4) Ability to work with other agencies and people. Probation work is too complicated and difficult to provide space for a prima donna.
(5) Ability to improve in performance. Who helps the helper and how is it done? Probation officers are not born with helping skill nor is it thrust upon them. It is acquired.

The well-trained probation officer may become a dedicated person in the service of others, and occasionally, such service is somewhat less than appreciated, especially if the probationer commits suicide, as reported by Robert L. Noble, Jr.[16] in the case previously discussed in Chapter Two.

The probation officer has two main assignments, first, prior to the court hearing, he makes social investigations covering the family and home environment, the school career and all other pertinent data concerning the child's personality. The role of the probation officer in securing such data may be a difficult one. Often the probation officer is seen in the role of executioner by both offender and family, and frequently the family is seen by the offender as having rejected him and virtually adopting the probation officer as the responsible son, or as the idealized projection of what a father, or husband should be.

The probation officer must realize that he is neither mother, father, brother or sister, but a person who has been either invited or required by law to work on a problem affecting the whole family. Unless the probation officer is on the alert, he becomes in a psychological sense, a member of the family and unless this mantle which is unsought is not patiently removed, a real danger exists that the family's distorted relationships will deteriorate into a ridiculous caricature. The second assignment concerns the probation officer supervising the child who has been placed on probation by the judge.[17]

Although probation officers are not necessarily salesmen, missionaries, or public relations experts, they should feel the urge not only to explain and interpret but to participate in all community activities affecting their work. William C. Nau quotes Dean Frank Luther Mott:

> Probation officers ought to make the best public relations men in the world. For the very qualities which they need most in their work are the qualities which make good public relations. First, common sense—there is nothing better for meeting the problems that come up in connection with press and public. Second, patience and an equable temper—anger enlarges a rift to a chasm irreparably. Third, a co-operative spirit. Getting the other fellow's point of view, understanding his problems, sympathizing with his efforts—these attitudes are essential to both the probation officer and the public relations man.[18]

According to Hyman S. Lippman, M.D. the major contribution of the probation officer will consist of forming a strong, friendly bond to the delinquent—a relationship that will let the delinquent know the probation officer is on his side. At best, it is difficult to get the aggressive delinquent to accept an adult as an ally. He has thought of the adult for too many years as an enemy who cannot be trusted. Many have been disillusioned repeatedly by adults, and though he may sense the probation officer is his friend, he prefers to withhold significant information for a long time. As a delinquent he has had to learn to spot his friends quickly, and he will detect by a frown or sudden quietness or tenseness that the probation officer cannot accept him completely.

A sensitive probation officer may have difficulty in retaining a feeling of warmth for a boy who struck his mother who had just returned from the hospital; for an adolescent girl who got in after midnight after repeated promises and assurances that this would never happen again; for an aggressive boy who tells in a convincing manner that his school work is satisfactory though the probation officer knows he has not been to school since the last interview. To complicate matters, these are delinquents who will have no respect for the probation officer if they can outwit him. The delinquent has been sent to the agency; he has not come to it for help. He would have preferred to go on his own way of delinquency. The probation officer must realize that he will fail with at least half his probationers through no particular fault of his own.[19]

When juvenile courts were first created a half-century ago, many of the persons connected with them still thought partly in the language of criminal law. Consequently, for many people the title "probation officer" has come to be tinged with the aura of the criminal court, and to such an extent that the term is now entirely unsuitable for use in juvenile courts. The word "probation" does not suggest the social casework done with children in juvenile courts.

Sometimes the title "probation officer" keeps good-intentioned individuals from bringing matters involving children before the juvenile court early enough to help the children. These individuals often do not want the child to have a "record." Although the juvenile court laws specifically state otherwise, many people are not convinced that a child under the supervision of a probation officer has not been convicted of some high crime or misdemeanor. This interpretation is especially likely to be made when the probation officer in charge is either named by statute or is self-described as "chief probation officer"—in the manner of "chief of police" or "chief deputy sheriff." Lately some states have changed the title of the juvenile court probation officer to "probation counselor." In Rhode Island he is "youth counselor; in Mississippi, "director" and "counselor"; in the cities of Toledo and Cleveland, Ohio, "supervisor"; and in the District of Columbia, "director of social work."

In comparing the literature of probation with actual practice in the field of probation officers, Professor Lewis Diana [20] discovered some significant discrepancies. Experienced probation officers do not have as well defined views of what probation is as do those who write articles about probation. Probation officers agree with the writers that treatment of the individual probationer is the principal function which probation ought to serve. The main difference between theory and practice lies in the fact that treatment is actually a very small part of the work of probation officers; administrative work, such as obtaining reports on the activities of the probationer, is the main job of the probation officer today. In one survey it was learned that 64 per cent of the probation staff had fewer than six contacts with a child over a period of one year. Yet the number of delinquents on probation who later became criminals was less among those who had the *fewest* contacts with their probation officers. This apparent adjustment must be attributed to factors other than treatment received on probation.

There is no consensus or standardization of opinion concerning probation among probation officers, and few are qualified case workers. From the personal experience of Professor Diana, a former probation officer himself, the image that many probation officers have of themselves is a picture of a warm and understanding though objective person, a kind of watered-down or embryonic clinician. Convention papers, the literature and supervisors are filled with this ideology, so that it is constantly before the probation officer. It is no wonder, then, if the probation officer feels whatever he does and however he does it, it *is* treatment. Diana suggests that it would be worthwhile to investigate to what extent the clinical professions attract people with a basic impulse to direct and control the lives of others. In many cases, the therapist or counselor gains a great deal more in ego support from the therapeutic situation than does the "client." This current "obsession" with psychodynamics might well be challenged, and some of the effort now expended on the offender himself, might better be utilized in giving more attention to social reform.

In theory, to be sure, but hardly in practice, the probation officer is a case worker who carefully studies each child, works out a definite plan of treatment, and, by utilizing every available community resource, helps the child to solve his problems. No doubt many, if not most, officials would like to live up to the theory of their profession. Even in some of the large cities where numerous social welfare agencies aid in probationary work, genuine case work of the ideal type is a rarity. In too many communities only general supervision service is available. In the smaller centers very little is accomplished which meets case-work standards.

The probation officers duties are manifold. In California, for example, it has been brought out that the probation officer may have to locate boarding homes, supervise a detention home, and operate the county's forestry campus. He is asked to collect money from parents and guardians for the care of the wards of the court and for restitutions, fines, and court costs. He must make full reports on every child investigated and keep records of the progress and discharge of the wards of the court. To make matters worse, most of the counties in the state have very few probation officers and limited staffs for the probation program. In one instance a single probation officer was expected to supervise 140 girls, to handle the intake of all new cases (boys as well as girls), and to investigate the new girl cases, preparing on each a detailed report and a recommendation for the court. In addition, this same woman was secretary to the probation committee and, on finishing her day's work, served as night matron at a detention home.

In another county in California, the probation officer carried a case load of one hundred boys and girls and an equal number of adults. The county schools frequently called upon him to act as attendance officer. He had no aides and no clerk or stenographer. Naturally, he kept no records. The National Probation Association has claimed, after years of experience studying conditions of this kind, that no officer can supervise successfully more than seventy-five cases and that to do the best work the officer should carry no more than fifty boys or forty girls! Girls' cases should always be assigned to women probation officers; cases of boys under twelve years of age may be handled by woman probation officers, but all cases of boys above that age should be assigned to men probation officers.

In some areas, use is being made of volunteer probation service, according to Reinemann.[21] In small towns and sparsely populated rural areas an interested lay citizen may take over the supervision of a youngster placed on probation, as a neighborly sponsor. This volunteer worker should be well selected by the probation department of the county juvenile court and should be responsible to this department. Such an arrangement makes it possible to give supervision to children living in remote parts of the county, who, due to the heavy case load and geographically extensive work area of the regular probation officer, would not receive the benefits of probation service. There is a danger, however, that volunteer probation service may be misused by protagonists of a false economy in preventing the employment of qualified, full-time probation officers, where their services are really needed. The volunteer can render valuable service in supplementing, rather than substituting for, the work of the regular probation officer, in both large and small communities.

In one Pennsylvania County, business men, clergymen and professionals have banded together for the purpose of giving supervision and counsel to boys assigned to them by the juvenile court upon the recommendation of the chief probation officer. Beyond the service in individual cases there is another important asset in the utilization of volunteers in probation work; it provides a good channel to the public at large for the interpretation of the meaning of probation, the problems presented by delinquent conduct of children, and the need for community facilities for youth conservation and crime prevention.

According to Harleigh B. Trecker, few probation officers make full or even adequate use of the community resources at their disposal. To the question, "Why don't social agencies co-operate?" the answer seems to be that social agencies are composed of people. Staff workers do not always co-operate or make better use of one another due to heavy work loads, lack of time, and specialization of agency function. As one probation worker trainee remarked: "I have lived in my community 30 years, but have never really known it." Planned study of this community had helped him get a clearer focus and a deeper understanding of available community resources. When professional probation officers accept the fact of their own limitations and begin to use community resources, they begin to build professional practice beyond the specialized level to the level of integration. It is increasingly evident that prevention, treatment, and eventual control of juvenile delinquency and criminality rests with the community.[22]

The well-trained and conscientious probation officer may be hampered by unwise and unprofessional application of probation theory and techniques in his community. In many instances, probation is not probation, according to Sanford Bates.[23] For example, in one midwestern state, the local judge held a "parole court," to determine, by popular vote of those in his courtroom whether or not a high school student, convicted of a morals charge, but a valuable player on the basketball team, should receive "parole" (probation). The spectators, reporters, school students, and athletes were overwhelmingly in favor of "parole!"

In the criminal court in another midwestern state a young boy had been placed on probation for drug addiction, upon condition he gave up narcotics. During probation, the parents confided to the probation officer that their son had become readdicted. When the probation officer presented these facts to the court, the judge ignored the recommendations of the probation officer, and ordered the parents placed on the stand, under oath, and required them to testify before him in open court what they knew about the case. In another instance, a young woman probation officer with a social work degree attempted to keep in touch with her probationers by correspondence, because she didn't want to "embarrass" her charges by seeing them in their own "humble dwellings." They would be more relaxed if they came to her quiet, clean and pleasant office. When a hopeless congestion developed in a criminal court of one of the large counties, the special judge given the task of "clearing it up," did so by the simple expedient of putting practically every defendant on probation.

According to Sanford Bates, in one large trial court, it is the practice to tax the defendant for the cost of probation! He gets out of it in one jurisdiction by paying a $3 "initiation fee" for membership in the A.O.P. (Anxious Order of Probationers). In another court, the cost to the prospective probationer is determined by the anticipated number of probation cases during the current year, which amounts to about fifty dollars. In many instances the first and only obligation of the probationer is that he pay his share of the fifty dollar cost. Often, the probationer is without funds, especially if he had a lawyer, so he is accepted for probation with the warning that he had "better pay up."

Mr. Bates suggests that the National Probation and Parole Association, now the National Council on Crime and Delinquency develop uniform and comparable statistical data on probation and also develop definitions as to what constitutes success, failure, and improvement. Humanitarian efforts which characterize probation are too essential a part of the system of criminal justice to be stigmatized and injured by hasty and improvident applications.

In too many communities, probation is farcial in application. In some western counties, there are so few detention facilities for youngsters that a juvenile probationer may get "lost" from the courthouse, and commit another delinquency before being recaptured. In a small town of one western county, the probation officer was kept informed of his probationer's progress by the townspeople. Probation function varies from almost pure police work to social responsibility. The probation officer and his supervision may not agree on recommendations made to the judge, who in turn may question their professional competence. Probation officers may have to investigate "charges" such as "mulish," "stubborn" and "unlawful processing of garbage." [24]

It has been suggested before that probation officers should make speeches to the various civic organizations, P.T.A. meetings and the like to better acquaint citizens about the importance of probation to juveniles and adults as well. Probation office files are crammed with stories which rival "Mr. District Attorney," and "This is Your FBI" in human interest and universal appeal, if not in excitement. It may be up to the probation officer to "take the stump" and let others know about the work, for few projects are more rewarding than community interpretation. Since supervision and follow-up of juveniles on probation is often conspicuous by its absence, the "probation-salesman" may develop more interest on the part of the public who pay the bills, and something approaching adequate supervision of juvenile probationers will become a reality.[25]

For one kind of delinquent, the fact that the court has no program for follow-up or for supervision probably does no harm. The court experience itself is a jolt enough for the individual concerned so that he is less likely to commit additional offenses. Case work for delinquents who fall into this group would be merely a waste of time and money. For the delinquent who is given another chance but who probably should have been committed to an institution (a matter that can be decided, in the last analysis, only *after* the whole record is complete), case work is also a waste of effort and dollars. Between these two extremes lies the group of delinquents who need case work and who would profit from it. One of the basic problems of every juvenile court is to select for case-work treatment delinquents from this middle group. Unfortunately, when a child faces a judge no one knows in advance whether the child can come through without case supervision. Each judge must make the wisest decision he can in the light of the information available, his own knowledge of children, and his philosophy of life.

## THE FEDERAL JUVENILE DELINQUENCY ACT

Juvenile offenders against federal law, though not numerous, have presented a special problem to federal probation officers, and correctional workers because there is no provision for their handling in the penal structure of the federal government. In 1932, an attempt was made to alleviate this peculiar situation by legislation authorizing United States Attorneys to divert persons under twenty-one years of age to state or local courts, if these particular courts would accept jurisdiction. However, if, for one reason or another, diversion could not be effected, these young people would have to be processed through the federal courts in the same fashion as adults. Moreover, federal judges were forced to confine them with adults because there were no facilities for the confinement of youthful offenders.

In recognition of a long-established juvenile court principle—

that the young offender needs specialized care and treatment—and in recognition of the fact that the federal government had not provided for the juvenile offender in its courts, the Federal Juvenile Delinquency Act became a law on June 16, 1938. This Act provides that a person under eighteen years of age can be prosecuted on information rather than indictment, if he so consents in writing. He can be heard by the federal court judge in private and without jury trial at any time or place within the district of the court; he can be placed on probation or committed to any public or private agency which will segregate him from adult offenders; and he can be paroled immediately or at any time following his sentence.

The key person in administering this Act is the probation officer. Immediately upon the arrest of a juvenile, he interviews the offender, investigates his family situation, and consults the United States Attorney about the possibility of diverting the case to a local juvenile court. The probation officer's findings are made available to the Attorney and the United States Commissioner, as well as to the Federal Court, the Bureau of Prisons, and the Parole Board; the officer notifies the United States Marshal of suitable places of detention for the particular offender and arranges an early court hearing. He does not permit the youth to be fingerprinted. Finally, the probation officer makes sure that the offender is intensively supervised from the time of his arrest until the completion of his term of surveillance. No doubt the probation officer's responsibility to the juvenile offender under the Federal Juvenile Delinquency Act places upon him important and exacting duties. The procedure, however, leaves the juvenile with a conviction record.

In January, 1946, an official attempt was made to circumvent a court record for juvenile offenders. The Attorney General authorized all United States Attorneys to make use of the "deferred prosecution" procedure whenever juvenile offenders were involved in court proceedings. This authorization is sometimes referred to as the "Brooklyn Plan" because the procedure was employed as early as 1936 by the federal prosecutor and probation officer of Brooklyn, New York.

Under this plan, the United States Attorney, on the basis of a report made by the probation officer, may defer prosecution for a definite period and request the probation officer, in writing, to exercise supervision over the youth—that is, treat the offender as if he were on probation. The probation officer must submit progress reports to the United States Attorney, as well as make an appropriate recommendation at the termination of the supervision. If the report is a favorable one, the original complaint against the offender is dropped. This procedure protects the youth against the stigma of an official criminal record. Of two hundred cases supervised in Brooklyn on this deferred prosecution plan, only two violators had to be referred to the court by due process of law.[26]

The success of the Brooklyn Plan and numerous other recent advances in the probation system in the United States are encouraging signs in the treatment of juvenile delinquency. As is seen, however, serious problems remain if this promising method of coping with the young offender is to match the hopes of its founders.

## REFERENCES

1. Reinemann, John Otto: Probation and the Juvenile Delinquent, *The Annals* of The American Academy of Political and Social Science, Vol. 216, January, 1949, pp. 109–119.
2. Newman, Charles L.: *Sourcebook on Probation, Parole, and Pardons,* Springfield, Thomas, 1958, pp. 60, 69.
3. York, James N.: Evaluating the Everyday Work of a Probation Office, *Federal Probation,* Vol. XII, September 1948, pp. 24–29.
4. Teeters, Negley K., and Reinemann, John Otto: *The Challenge of Delinquency,* New York, Prentice-Hall, Inc., 1950, pp. 384–385.
5. Chute, Charles Lionel: and Bell, Marjorie: *Crime, Courts and Probation,* New York, The MacMillan Company, 1956, p. 136.
6. Reported in McGrath, J. Howard: The Role of the Federal Probation Officer in Criminal Justice, *Federal Probation,* Vol. XIV, December, 1950, p. 5.
7. Reinemann, John Otto: Principles and Practices of Probation, *Federal Probation,* Vol. XIV, October-December, 1950, pp. 26–31.
8. Ellingston, John R.: *Protecting Our Children from Criminal Careers,* New York, Prentice-Hall, 1948, pp. 82, 83.
9. Crystal, David: Family Casework in Probation, *Federal Probation,* Vol. XIII, December, 1949, pp. 47–53.

10. Nau, William C.: Let Them Know About It, *Federal Probation,* Vol, XV, September, 1951, pp. 35–38.
11. Glover, Elizabeth R.: Probation: The Art of Introducing the Probationer to a Better Way of Life, *Federal Probation,* Vol. XV, September, 1951, pp. 8–12.
12. England, Ralph: What is Responsible for Satisfactory Probation and Post-Probation Outcome? *The Journal of Criminal Law, Criminology and Police Science,* Vol. 47, March-April, 1957, pp. 667–677.
13. Bloch, Herbert A., and Flynn, Frank T.: *Delinquency: The Juvenile Offender in America Today,* New York, Random House, Inc., 1956, p. 368.
14. Reinemann, John Otto: Probation and the Juvenile Delinquent, *op cit.,* p. 110.
15. Burbank, Edmund G., and Goldsborough, Ernest W.: The Probation Officer's Personality: A Key Factor in Rehabilitation, *Federal Probation,* Vol. 18, June, 1954, pp. 11–14.
16. Noble, Jr., Robert L.: What a Difference One Year Makes, *Federal Probation,* Vol. XIII, June, 1949, p. 49.
17. Crystal, David: *op. cit.,* p. 50.
18. Quoted by Nau, William C.: *op. cit.,* p. 36.
19. Lippman, M.D., Hyman S.: The Role of the Probation Officer in the Treatment of Delinquency in Children, *Federal Probation,* Vol. XII, June, 1948, pp. 36–39.
20. Diana, Lewis: What is Probation? *The Journal of Criminal Law, Criminology and Police Science,* Vol. 51, July-August, 1960, pp. 189–204.
21. Reinemann, John Otto: Probation and the Juvenile Delinquent, *op. cit.,* p. 112.
22. Trecker, Harleigh B.: The Use of Community Agencies in Probation Work, *Federal Probation,* Vol. XI, October-December, 1947, pp. 21–24.
23. Bates, Sanford: When is Probation not Probation? *Federal Probation,* Vol. XXIV, December, 1960, pp. 13–20.
24. As reported in the NPPA *News,* Vol. 36, July, 1957, p. 305.
25. Nau, William C., *op. cit.,* p. 37.
26. Meyer, Charles H. Z.: A Half Century of Federal Probation and Parole, *Journal of Criminal Law and Criminology,* Vol. XLII, March-April 1952, pp. 707–728.

# 10

## THE CORRECTIONAL INSTITUTION

Reform schools or their equivalents have a moderately long history. It begins with the opening of the New York House of Refuge on January 1, 1825. The founders of this House envisaged the institution as a "prison, manufactory, and school." The next year Boston inaugurated a similar type of institution, and Philadelphia followed in 1828. These three institutions for juvenile delinquents were the only ones of their kind until a municipal boys' reformatory was established in New Orleans in 1845. In 1847, the first state reform school for boys was founded in Westboro, Massachusetts, and later came to be known as the Lyman School for Boys. The first girls' industrial school in the United States was established in Lancaster, Massachusetts. At first, an institution of this type was called a "house of refuge." Later to remove all doubt about the purpose, the name was changed to "reform school"—a label carrying with it a definite stigma for the inmates of the institution. In an effort to remove the stigma of the name and since trade-training was often part of the school program, various authorities adopted the name "industrial school." However, this name also developed invidious overtones, and the later usage of "house of correction" did little to help the situation. Finally, these schools were named for persons or locations in an effort to avoid an unhappy connotation.

But name-changing has not greatly affected the "reform school" image commonly held by inside inmate and outside public alike. In fact, many people consider correctional institutions as places where dangerous offenders are kept out of circulation temporarily rather than as rehabilitative agencies. That there is some measure of justification for the former view is seen when the results of rehabilitative efforts are examined.

## DOES THE CORRECTIONAL INSTITUTION "CORRECT"?

The crucial test of the success of a reformatory, of course, is its ability to rehabilitate its charges. That this goal is not being met in any large degree is evidenced by the fact that there are between 65 and 85 per cent rehabilitative failures among the former inmates who have spent time in reformatories and industrial or "training" schools. An extensive survey of the situation, undertaken by the Gluecks in the 1930's, which reported the careers of inmates of the Massachusetts Reformatory for more than fifteen years after their discharge from the institution, revealed that only 22.6 per cent of these young people refrained from criminal activities during the post-institutional period.[1] Many studies of the 1930's and 1940's indicate success rates ranging from a low of 6 per cent to a high of 74 per cent, indicating a wide range of results from various investigators.

The findings of the Gluecks seems consistent with those concerning the crime careers of reformatory graduates in many states. For example, one authority relates the story of 250 boys discharged in 1929 from California's Preston School of Industry, whose after careers could be traced. By 1939, 60 per cent of these boys had been arrested one or more times and 47 per cent had been sentenced to state prisons. Moreover, the 250 were not the least promising, for the administration had granted them all either honorable discharges or the governor's diploma of honor.[2] In one survey at Leavenworth, out of seventy-seven boys who had been in reform school together, only thirteen were not in Leavenworth. These findings and the similar conclusions of many investigations may constitute, in part, an indictment of correctional institutions. More significantly, perhaps, they raise the question of the severe handicaps that reformatories and training schools face.

The training school may be defined as a specialized children's institution serving delinquent children committed to it by the courts. Forestry camps, detention homes, and psychiatric institutions are not training schools. Although residential training and treatment services for delinquent children are provided by a number of different types of facilities, the training school has been the traditional and most commonly used type of facility for most of the delinquent children in this country. There are approximately 200 public and 80 voluntary training schools in the United States, Puerto Rico, and the Virgin Islands.[3]

To the question, "Does the correctional institution 'correct,' the answer would seem to be in the negative. As Hertha Tarrasch has pointed out, the stigma of having been in a corrective institution cannot easily be removed. Training schools expend so much of their energy on custodial care that little opportunity is left for rehabilitative measures. Youngsters sent to a training school get physical care, regimentation and some vocational training, but little consideration is given the ailment which brought them there. Sending a child to an institution is the most expensive way of dealing with his problem.[4]

Tom Clark felt that at best training schools afford a poor disposition of a case. In the main, juvenile courts have grossly overestimated the contributions such institutions can make to delinquency prevention. Training schools are often best characterized as graduate schools to crime. The judge who commits a boy to a school to remove him from a bad gang of, say four, must realize the child may now have 400 such associates. It is a serious indictment of our school system if a boy must be sent to a training school to obtain vocational training. The discipline that is used in the training school seldom will be carried over into the community. The boy may continue to say "yes, sir" and "no, sir" long after he has left a training school, yet retain the motivations which prompted him to steal a car in the first place.[5]

Dobbs lists several shocking events that broke into the news which may indicate that correctional schools are "evil." Unruly boys have been killed by their caretakers . . . emotionally sick girls end their life to escape intolerable institutional living. The rape of cottage mothers has been attempted and other sex violations are said to be rampant. Aggressive gangs in institutions beat to death other boys they dislike. We still apparently place little value on the life and welfare of American children, delinquent ones particularly.[6]

There seems to be no way to avoid the admission that prisons for children, like those for adults, continue to be effective schools for crime. One reason, as Neumeyer has pointed out, why correctional (training) institutions often fail, is that they must accept whatever commitments the judges send them; the decision usually rests with the courts or state authorities. They get the cases after other attempts at rehabilitation have failed and the child has become habituated to antisocial behavior. Training schools frequently receive suspicious, hostile boys, slow learners, many of whom carry on a counter-adjustment program of their own, and they usually leave before the training school program is completed.[7]

Institutions must take first offenders and experienced gangsters, boys going through the emotional upheaval of adolescence, runaways, truants, disobedient children, and confine them with burglars, muggers, arsonists, rapists, and even killers. They must accept youths ranging from the feebleminded to the brilliant. They must take sex deviates, perverts, drug addicts, and alcoholics. They must take the highly intelligent though dangerous abnormal personalities, as well as the essentially normal youths; the innocent and immature along with the degenerate; the bully and the weakling. To complicate this situation, many institutions, though very large, are perennially overcrowded and forced to pack double-decker bunks into dormitories and two boys in a single room.

Unless care is exercised, almost any child can be sent to the reform school whether his offense is serious or not. The case is related of one unimaginative social worker and judge who assigned a child to the Illinois Geneva Training School for Girls because of truancy. Her history revealed that she had lost her hair following an influenza attack. Being poor, she had to accept a coarse flaxen wig, the type one sees in a hairdresser's window. She wore this when she returned to school and was ridiculed unmercifully by other schoolmates—the important reason for her truancy. Another unfortunate "delinquent" girl's "crime" was simply that her own mother had deserted her. Not knowing what to do with her, the local officials had solved their problem by sending her to a reform school.[8] These are extreme cases, no doubt, but they point up the need for cautious and wise policy in the assignment of youth to correctional institutions.

According to Sophia Robison, we are a nation of "faddists" on corrections and go by "fashions" in locking youngsters up. We used to lock up Irish children, two generations ago it was Italian youngsters, now its Negro and Puerto Rican children. It is difficult to make comparisons between the United States and other nations, as there are more girls locked up in Hudson, New York school for girls than in all the institutions in England. Today most children come from urban areas, yet in many institutions the emphasis is on "farming" which can have little or no carry-over value to the inmate after he is discharged or paroled. Extolling such "cliches" as "get close to the land," "fresh air and sunshine" are meaningless to city youth and farming and animal husbandry are probably sheer drudgery to most reformatory inmates. Despite the preponderance of urban youth in our training schools, at least 25 per cent of the youngsters are assigned permanently to farming activities, with the time-worn excuse of "making boys pay their way." Presumably, juvenile offenders were committed for corrective treatment, not committed to "pay their way."

Several recent studies have attempted to evaluate the effectiveness of the treatment offered by state training schools and similar institutions under private auspices as reported by a Children's Bureau publication, under the direction of Paul Schreiber.[9] Their findings indicate varying rates of success as measured by the proportion of non-recidivists. One large group reports success with 60 per cent to 70 per cent of cases; another group clusters closer to 50 per cent. A report on the experience of the British Borstals also shows results in this range. Judge Youngdahl, in his article in *Federal Probation,* March, 1956, quotes parole violation in Minnesota of 32 per cent, and in California of 24 per cent (76 per cent success.) Howland G. Shaw, in his testimony before the Senate Subcommittee, estimates a success rate for training schools of 60 per cent to 70 per cent.

The St. Anne Institute in New York State, a private institution under Catholic auspices, reports that 76 per cent of its former inmates have made an "excellent adjustment." Similar results are reported for Children's Village, New York State, with 73 per cent making adequate to "good adjustment." These figures suggest that the Chief of the Children's Bureau was on the conservative side when she indicated in her testimony to the Congress that at least 15 per cent of the 52,000 children admitted to public training schools within a single year are being returned there.

The most extensive recent evaluation of a training school program was published in 1958 by Lloyd W. McCorkle, Albert Ellis and F. Lowell Bixby (*The Highfields Story: An Experimental Treatment Project for Youthful Offenders* New York, Henry Holt) which reported the effect of the new short term program at Highfields, a public small-group facility in New Jersey. The study set out to compare the success of this experimental program with that of Annandale, a traditional State training school. The findings for each institution follow: Of the 229 boys sent to Highfields, 145 (63 per cent) completed their treatment and were in no further difficulty great enough to send them to another custodial facility after having been released for at least a year. Of the 116 boys sent to Annandale, 55 (47 per cent) completed their treatment program and were in no further difficulty severe enough to send them back to Annandale or to another custodial facility after having been released for at least eight months or more.

It would appear from these findings that Highfields was more successful than Annandale in the treatment and rehabilitation of juvenile delinquents, but such a conclusion may be open to question. The lower rate of recidivism of the boys from Highfields is a result not of their experience there but of the juvenile court judges' selection of boys most likely to reform to be sent to Highfields and of those less likely to reform to Annandale. There is some evidence that the juvenile court judges did in fact send boys to Highfield because they *thought* them better prospects for successful treatment.

It should be remembered there may be more doubt about success rates than about failure rates. Despite a certain number of misleading entries due to unjustified or purely formal arrests, and despite differences in classification, on the whole, the failure rates probably represent minimal figures. A considerable proportion of delinquencies go undetected. It may be assumed, therefore, that success rates based on official non-recidivism probably represent maximum figures. Hence, the effectiveness shown by such studies is more likely to be exaggerated than underplayed; and that results are likely to be worse than they are painted—not because of any effort to distort, but because "failure" is more likely than "success" to go unreported.

It seems reasonable to conclude, then, that more than 15 per cent "fail" during probation; more than 30 per cent "fail" after probation; and more than 40 per cent probably "fail" after a period in a training school. This suggests that successful coping with juvenile delinquency will require doing something about our treatment methods as well as doing something about our young people. Ideally, rehabilitation, retraining, and treatment services should be provided for the bulk of delinquent children in their own communities and homes, a more suitable environment than an institutional setting. When the on-going practices of the reformatories themselves are examined further reasons why they are often breeders of crime are revealed.

## REFORM SCHOOL PRACTICES

One predominant reason for the failure of these juvenile institutions to rehabilitate youth is the continuance of traditional punitive motives and methods, which seem to produce only more hostile and aggressive responses from most boys and girls. The *Saturday Evening Post,* May 27, 1950 stated that reform schools may be tougher than prisons. Some cells are too small for inmates to stand up at the same time, so they take turns washing and dressing. At 7 A.M. inmates must quickly jump through the iron doors, because the guard will quickly close them hoping to catch a late riser, thus smashing him in the door, then he can send him to solitary.[10]

Correctional incarceration, however elaborate and refined its program, can scarcely avoid a large admixture of punishment, children are still often subjected to severe disciplinary methods, even for petty infractions of the multiplicity of rules. At one institution, until recently, when retiring at inspection, boys had to raise arms, spread fingers, open mouth, stick out tongue and pass by on their toes. Also walk on toes at all times in the cottages. While in bed, the youthful inmates were not permitted to snore, and if they "talked in their sleep" were punished for "running off in the mouth," a serious offense. On Sundays inmates were allowed one minute to wash hands, or to use toilet facilities, and it was against the rules to breathe audibly. The consequence is a training in hate, bitterness, and vindictiveness.

In *Time* December 13, 1954, a police newspaper reporter found three emaciated teen-agers on a bread and water diet in a western state reformatory. One boy had been tied to a carpenter's sawhorse and whipped with a strap. Both paddles and belts were used on the boys. A teacher, reported: "Over and over again boys come to classes with deep cuts on their arms and faces . . . I try to teach the Constitution and American ideals, and I am laughed at, because these boys would prefer Communism to our system of handling youths." Because this teacher made the statement, he was fired and the governing Board stated that it was not interested in the truth or falsity of his statement, but only that he had made it. Still somewhat prevalent methods of corporal punishment may be found in most institutions for juvenile delinquents. Such punishments include, for example, the "bends," the "squats," and "standing on lines" which some inmates are forced to do for inordinate periods of time, and whippings and strappings administered by the custodial staff. There are still reformatories that employ bloodhounds and offer rewards for the capture of escapees.

Reform schools for boys have a black record of stupidity, gross brutality, and human tragedy, and largely because of the practice of sadistic punishments. Their attempts at "vocational rehabilitation" are sometimes accompanied by "tools of control" such as paddles, shaved heads, prolonged icy showers, whips, and blackjacks, and other such procedures which are supposed to inculcate in boys the principles of "democracy."

Bloch and Flynn document shocking conditions: at the Kansas State Industrial School for Boys, the disciplinarian carried a blackjack and all the officers were permitted to inflict corporal punishment, resulting in a "government by fists." At the Missouri Training School for Boys, the youngsters had shaved heads, prison uniforms were worn, and numbers were used instead of names. At that institution the chief occupation was quarry work, crushing stone for a commercial firm. The State Training and Agriculture School for Colored Boys (Tennessee) with an average daily population of about 300, had a library of exactly eight books, including Chaucer's *Prologue*. At the Washington State Training School for Boys, the youngsters were marched to and from the dining room with arms folded and strict silence was required throughout the meal hour. The leather strap was used for punishment because "boys must realize that the school is the authority." [11] At this institution, the boys "actually lift their chairs in slow motion so that . . . . hardly a sound can be heard in the diningroom." [12] Again these are extreme and, by no means, daily occurrences. But they do provide evidence of grave conditions and outmoded practices in correctional institutions.

In some reform schools a strong emphasis is given to *outward* cleanliness and neatness; the walks, lawn, windows, and trees are kept very well. But life inside the walls, marked by the monotonony characteristic of institutions for the care of segregated persons, reveals a wide range of unhappy practices. Gisela Knnopka found strict conformity in a Minnesota institution. Often the whole "company" had to stand "on line," if *one* of the boys had done something serious, such as running away.[13]

One journalist who investigated the institutional way of life, unhampered by governmental or private agencies, reported that monotony may be varied with hydrotherapy (playing a seventy-pound fire hose on the backs of nude boys trapped at the side of a brick wall), or "rag-sniffing" (the boys sink their noses into rags soaked in gasoline, kerosene or shoe polish, which makes them dizzy and causes them to vomit).[14]

According to other reporters, ingenious forms of punishment included brick-counting (the child stands erect with his eyes turned up to the ceiling); line toeing (the child stands erect and silent, with both hands upraised); rice-polishing (the boy crawls on his knees across a floor covered with rice grains, inducing bleeding); post-walking (the boy marches between or around posts for hours, sometimes carrying a forty-pound bag); and runaway-pills (the captured runaways are dosed with laxatives to "help them run").[15] Under such harsh and repressive discipline, inmates tend to develop negative self-concepts, including such nicknames as "pimples," "crip," or "scars." Most delinquents see themselves as worthless or bad individuals.[16]

The Jacksonville (Florida) *Times-Union* in its January 12, 1952, issue reported on an investigation of the Arizona Industrial School for Boys and revealed that an attendant kicked a boy in the face for not moving fast enough. The report also noted that boys were whipped with pieces of fanbelts, doubled ropes, and bicycle tires, or forced to walk barefooted across the desert from Wilcox, some thirty miles away.

Practices such as these are fairly prevalent in reformatories for boys. Some of them are found in institutions for the care of girls as well, along with the persistent conditions of monotony and enforced isolation. Bloch and Flynn mention The South Dakota Training School housing both boys and girls, which was described as an "old-time reform school, housed in shabby buildings, animated by a punitive spirit, and employing regimentation, fear and shame as the instruments of 'reformation.' "[17] Teeters and Reinemann list The Missouri Home for Girls as characterized by "ill-defined administrative policies, shameful overcrowding, dissension among staff members . . . and the housing of girls in delapidated fire-traps under physically and morally unhealthy conditions. Girls with unusually beautiful hair sometimes have their tresses shorn by an irate matron if they dare to run away or engage in incipient homosexual relationships. The cold bath is often used to "subdue" emotionally unstrung girls.[18]

In the Home of the Good Shepherd in a western state, in which are confined all delinquent girls, since the state has no other facilities for them, are found frustrating pressures. For example, the girls are forbidden to talk or communicate in any way while in the dormitory. This procedure is excessively restrictive and unnatural, and the "withdrawn" girls will tend to withdraw even more.

All the discipline is tied to a point system, stars given for so many points. Unusually good behavior can earn an extra star, insolence can lose a star, and running away can lose all stars. Two stars allow a monthly two hour visit with the girl's family. However, most families do not happen to be on any star system. Only the court should restrict family visits, not stars!

In one midwestern girls' school, a young male political appointee raped one of the girl inmates, who later had to be returned as a "parole violator," due to the pregnancy induced within the training school.[19]

However, there seems to have been considerable improvement in girls' reform schools in recent years. For example, the inmates at Ventura, California, no longer have shaved heads, neither are they forbidden to talk to one another, as was once the case. By way of punishment, spankings are not now permitted; solitary confinement is no longer prescribed at the least provocation; and the girls are not forced to parade naked before the inmates (a practice followed by at least one state reform school and reported in the press). Conditions have likewise improved at the Texas School for Girls at Gainesville. No longer have the girls shaved heads, shackles on their ankles, or forced to wear blue denim uniforms, or marching two by two from one building to another. Corporal punishment, meted out at Claremont, the Indiana girls' school up until 1954, it not nowadays officially permitted in most schools.

Large inroads are being made here and there to eliminate old-fashioned "remedies" in schools for boys as well as for girls. And conspicuous improvements in physical architecture, diet, recreational facilities, and in medical and educational provisions have been made. But big problems remain, most of them the inevitable consequence of enforced segregation. The feeling of incarceration —the more extreme among members of a society that accents individual freedom; the extended boredom; the constant contact with teachers of crime and the regrettable lessons learned thereby; the frustrated social and sexual life and the consequent ubiquitous homosexuality—practiced by both boys and girls; the persistent conflict between "keepers" and inmates—these remain chief marks of what are often thought of as "junior prisons."

## REFORM SCHOOL SUPERINTENDENTS

Reform school superintendents, to a very large extent, are "the law" in their own institutions. Sullivan describes one woman superintendent who bragged about her powers, and, with an all-embracing gesture of her hand, pointed to her institution and said: "Without so much as leaving my office, I can put any woman in my institution away for life. I just pick up the telephone, talk to the District Court judge, explain that "Nellie" is guilty of refractory conduct, send him down the papers which he always signs, and away goes "Nellie" for life![20] It is the unusual superintendent who escapes the "institutionalization" that seems inevitable to most of those identified with reform schools or prisons. As Miss Konopka has indicated, institutions lag far behind, with today's emphasis still on the punitive approach, even in the field of child welfare.[21]

The superintendent is faced with heavy responsibilities, and is judged, ironically enough not by the extent of rehabilitation accomplished, but to what extent he can keep his charges in custody. Runaways concern the administrator in several ways: (1) The public reacts in the same way they do to an escaped adult convict, (2) Runaways are apt to be desperate, and more prone to impulsive behavior, (3) Runaways are trying to solve problems by socially unacceptable means, and (4) "You can't treat 'em, if you haven't got 'em." White boys, returnees, and rural boys are far more likely to run away than Negro boys, boys committed for the first time, and city-bred boys.[22]

The public tends to ignore both the institution and the superintendent except in escapes, riots or scandals. Behind this protective cloak of "isolation," many of the juvenile institutions become little "Balkan dictatorships," with the superintendent answerable to almost no one. As a result, there is sometimes found a frequent abuse of power by the superintendent and some members of his staff. The conclusion should not be drawn, of course, that all reformatory officials are so lacking in an informed and professional viewpoint—a viewpoint increasingly found.

In the course of time, superintendents are apt to leave an indelible impression on the staff and on the structure of the institution itself. High type public service by the superintendent may go unappreciated and unacknowledged. Despite the national reputation built up by first-rate administrative skills of Florence Monahan at the Minnesota Reformatory for Women at Skakopee, when the history of the institution was published, her name was not even mentioned.

Resistance to change is brought about in part, by the supervising authorities. The authorities—superintendents and lesser officials—in turn often help to strengthen the frequently found "institutionalism" that constitutes such a high barrier to needed reforms. For as superintendents and their staffs become accustomed to procedures that "work" these tend to become routine. This typical mark of bureaucratization, which is found in all formal organizations, in some measure lessens the officials' capacity to see new situations realistically, to improvise, to experiment, to meet newcomers as distinctive personalities.

Institutional superintendents have their problems especially if their institution is subject to political control. Florence Monahan recounts some of her experiences at one School for Girls which can be duplicated in most state institutions, at one time or another. Due to an economy drive one winter, there was not enough heat in either her office or living quarters, so Miss Monahan was forced to make several trips to a nearby town to sit in warm movies or restaurants as long as she dared.

Donations to the "party" were mandatory, and after election time, the school became a political pie-counter with constant dismissals of employees, regardless of their knowledge or ability, to make room for "deserving" party members. When she consulted her superiors at the state capital, she was informed: "There are plenty of deserving party members and eventually we intend to change everyone from top to bottom." Hence, Miss Monahan, as superintendent, was obliged to accept every political appointee who arrived at the institution: a lame woman who couldn't move, but sat and rocked all day; a farmhand with only one arm, one leg; a woman so afraid of the inmates she locked herself in her room; another woman wrapped her hands in a handkerchief so she wouldn't get syphilis; a state senator sent his mistress to teach the inmates cosmetology and head the beauty shop. One political appointee was able to make expensive purchases, plus three long motor trips on a very modest salary, and was later discovered to have stolen money from the inmates by opening their letters.

The bonding company reimbursed the institution by a sum exceeding $2,000 and the whole matter was "hushed up." A fine, trained and devoted personnel can never be achieved under the domination of any political party.[23]

However, the superintendent's own personality often plays the dominant role in determining the practices and policies of the institution, regardless of political pressure. If he is susceptible—as so many people are—to the temptation of domination, his official situation gives him almost free reign. For he has very large powers, usually supported by wide official authority, over the human beings committed to the institution in his charge. To all the sundry, he becomes "the man," to whom all obey without question, in most instances. It may be argued, as Ellingston puts it, that the less competent the superintendent, the more likely he is to find compensation in the abuse of his power and to build up his own ego at the expense of the inmates who are not in a position to resist effectively.

There is always danger in power, to be sure. But the professionally qualified, emotionally stable, and imaginative superintendent will strive to avoid the temptations of his office and work to enhance the lives of the members of the segregated world that he supervises.

## INSTITUTIONAL REFORMATION AND RESEARCH

As stated previously, there are approximately 200 public and 80 voluntary training schools in the United States, Puerto Rico, and the Virgin Islands, serving about 40,000 children who have been adjudged delinquent. Of the 200 schools under public auspices, approximately 140 are state and national schools and the balance are county and municipal institutions. Despite the magnitude of the situation, the public is generally unfamiliar with the nature of correctional institutions. What about the views of informed authorities?

Florence Monahan, a competent and successful administrator of more than twenty years experience with girls' reform schools, sums up the situation in these words:

> The longer I live in one, the more I am impressed with the

abnormal atmosphere of an institution. It is an unnatural existence. No institutional-life can take the place of family-life where the child has a chance to develop as an individual. I would rather place a child in an average dirty home, if there is love and affection there, than in the finest, cleanest institution in the country.[24]

Some support for Miss Monahan's conclusion is found in the words of Howard McGrath, former Attorney General of the United States:

> Imprisonment as a punishment for a juvenile delinquent has been an unequivocal failure. Reform schools are not reform schools, but crucibles wherein boil the worst instincts of humanity and where innocence vanishes and insolence takes its place. The general course is from a reform school to a reformatory, then to a prison.[25]

There is no shortage of well-meaning plans for institutional reform. If they could be put into effect, rehabilitative training might become truly rehabilitative. As Hertha Tarrasch, a physician, expresses it, "I am not advocating the elimination of correctional institutions. If they could be made into havens of treatment and cure of the more severe emotional illnesses of children they could become of inestimable value. Like the legislators, the members of governing boards of the training schools need education in the dynamics of behavior for it is in their power to make of these correctional schools institutions of rehabilitation which in time would cease to stigmatize the children committed there."[26]

As Harrison Allen Dobbs has pointed out, correctional schools have helped some needy children. What the school has helped the child to accomplish is little appreciated by the public. The failures receive the publicity. The attainment of many rehabilitative goals is seriously hampered by lack of funds, lack of personnel, little sustained public interest—except in jailbreaks and tabloid publicity and "politics" both inside and out. Some institutions experience a change of supervision with every switch in elections (as if it makes any difference to children whether they are neglected or helped by Democrats or Republicans).

On the whole there is an encouraging tendency away from punitive and toward correctional policy. Today's superintendents and staffs, although they cannot do much about the situation, are increasingly aware that children in trouble need the most expert psychological handling by specialists trained in modern techniques of case and group work. However, the "staffs" mentioned above have reference to the professional, and not the custodial staffs. By and large, custodial staffs take a dim view of the modern techniques of case and group work. There is much conflict between the "professionals" and the "non-professionals."

Non-professionals regard the professional as a "crystal-gazer," as pseudo-intellectual, too theoretical, one who over-values material wealth and education, one who is "so busy he doesn't know the rest of the world the kid lives in," and professionals put their "findings" in "language nobody can understand." Custodial staff tend to regard the social worker as a glorified bill collector, or a cross between the cash girl in a department store and the telephone clerk at the information desk. The professionals tend to regard those in custody as hard-working, simple, generous, kind, good-hearted, strict disciplinarians, reluctant to take suggestions, practical, and the "get-something-done" type. As a result of this schism in juvenile correctional institutions, both groups try hard to avoid each other and the more sophisticated inmates often play one group against the other.[27] This basic conflict between custodial and professional ideology is widespread and may be found in nearly all correctional training schools, on both the juvenile and adult level.

Training schools and prisons, like detention homes, seem to be noted for their capacity to withstand improvement and what may be the fundamental problem in institutional reformation is pointed out by Robert Lindner, one of the more articulate critics:

> There is utter futility, sheer waste in confining individuals in barren and turreted zoos for humans without trying to recover men. We point the finger of ridicule at the sterile corridors of modern prisons, the gleaming shops and factories, the bright young social workers, the custodial hierarchy, in brief the whole hollow structure of rehabilitation that is based on expediency,

> untested hypotheses, unwarranted conclusions, from a pseudo-scientific empiricism. In spite of the self-flattery in which criminologists, penologists and the assorted professional and warder complement of the modern prison indulge, we are not today treating criminals, and what is worse are not even learning anything about them. We are doing nothing fundamental about crime or the criminal.[28]

While the provocative criticisms of correctional institutions and correctional research seem directed at adult institutions of confinement, much of the criticism and suggestions could well apply to juvenile institutions of corrections, since in many ways, juvenile training schools may be aptly described as being "junior prisons." Howard B. Gill makes a penetrating criticism of institutional research itself in the correctional process, as well as listing some of the current research in corrections.

> For years, research was conducted by white-jacketed students in laboratories or by bespectacled professors in ivory towers. Then Kurt Lewin introduced Action Research in the field of youthful behavior at both the Massachusetts Institute of Technology and the University of Michigan, and thus began a whole new concept of correctional research. Today, the three main types of research are operational, laboratory, and statistical.
>
> Operational research, or research in action, may be of two kinds: *exploratory* or *evaluative*. The first seeks to solve a problem by random observations, hunches, systematic observations, working hypotheses, and trial-and-error projects—all aimed at developing a hypothesis; the second seeks to prove or disprove the hypothesis that has grown up out of a controlled experiment.
>
> A second type of research, which may be either exploratory or evaluative, is laboratory research. From it have come the science of criminalistics, crime laboratory techniques, and psychological and other clinical tests proving so valuable to twentieth century correction.
>
> In vogue for a long time, statistical research simply starts with a hypothesis or an assumption and then discovers whether it correlates with past statistical studies or records. If this type of research, degree of recidivism is often used as the criterion of success for any correctional program; and so base expectancy

analyses are developed which differentiate offenders given "average treatment" according to risk. Thus a false assumption regarding recidivism is accepted and the assumption of "average treatment" as being "fixed" leaves the correctional process in a perpetual rut. More than anything else, this preoccupation with prediction has kept criminological research on an academic level and blocked out more useful operational research.

Some of the more important projects being undertaken in these three areas of research include "Team Treatment Aftercare in a Community Hostel," the basic hypothesis that "a man needs some support while he is adjusting to free society," and has found expression through establishment of a "halfway house" for men released from Delaware's prisons. The University of Illinois is trying to determine which elements of the programs currently operated by the Federal Bureau of Prisons contribute to postrelease success or failure, and is studying the programs of Leavenworth, Terre Haute, Milan, Chillicothe, and Ashland, and of five federal probation and parole areas in the midwest. The Rockefeller Brothers Fund granted the NCCD $41,900 for ten months for a National Research and Information Center on Crime and Delinquency, a central clearing house. The University of Pennsylvaina has for many years operated a somewhat similar center under the direction of Thorsten Sellin. The Chicago Boys Clubs received a Ford Foundation grant of $875,000 for a six-years delinquency prevention program in three deprived Chicago neighborhoods. Other Ford Foundation grants for delinquency research totaled over $700,000. Perhaps the most ambitious research program is that undertaken by the California Department of Corrections. Over 100 staff members of various correctional agencies are engaged in full-time or part-time research. (Other significant research projects are currently being carried on in Massachusetts, Connecticut, Rhode Island, and the District of Columbia.)

## CONCLUSIONS

The combination of operational and research personnel is a welcome one. Too often those who are competent in research are woefully ignorant of operational problems and needs, and those competent in the operational field are utterly untrained in methods of research. The professional researchers prevail in

> academic studies because they are more articulate; but their work is ignored by operational personnel because it is either misunderstood or not applicable. Correction could stand a moratorium on those studies seeking a quick and easy method of prediction in order to avoid the risk of possible failure. Screening tests and prediction tables are poor substitutes for the courage of exploration and new discovery.
>
> . . . research often begins with a problem and not with a hypothesis. . . . Chi-squares and correlations are all right in their place; but they can never replace the spirit and the vitality essential for finding new intellectual frontiers.
>
> What is sorely needed in correctional research today is as much emphasis on *search* as on the *re* (the "back" look). What is needed is more of the dynamic pioneering of Norfolk Island, Norfolk, England; . . . of Highfields . . . of Judge Baker Foundation . . . of John Howard . . . of Elam Lynds, Alexander Maconochie, Enoch Wines, Zebulon Brockway . . . Thomas Mott Osbourne, Austin McCormick, Mary Harris, Kenyon Scudder, Norman Fenton and Reed Cozart. These projects and men represent operational research of the highest order. And their results were achieved mainly through "hunch," "intuition," and "experience." As Truman Kelly, a truly great statistician, has pointed out, "In markings near about we discern the contour of the land and glimpse the portal of the future."[29]

Another astute observer of the correctional scene, who has written under the pseudonym of the "Cockleburr" for many years for the *American Journal of Correction* voiced his dissatisfaction with "research" and some types of research discussed by Howard Gill in his comment that appeared a few years ago:

> We have enough research, enough methods, enough experiments and enough convicts. How about some action? No more committees, no more experts, no more meetings, no more conferences, and Please God, no more research; just let's use what we know.[30]

As the current research projects mentioned above suggest, modern methods of reconditioning offenders are being introduced, as well as among a few denominational and private welfare projects which operate training schools in various states. Massachuetts,

New York, California, New Jersey, Wisconsin and Ohio, among other states, have been emulating the experience of these private but quasi-official youth centers and setting up bungalow or residence schools rather than large institutions. Unlike the latter, these schools eliminate walls and bars and other symbols of the prison. Simulating home conditions, these agencies provide a background generally more suitable to rehabilitation. With girls especially the small residence arrangement is often successful, for it provides training in domestic affairs of the very kind which may engage them in the outside world.

Approaching the conditions of the outside world is, indeed, the direction of these hopeful trends. Generally we are learning, perhaps, that one requirement of effective rehabilitation lies in making the institutional setting of correction something other than a "junior prison."

## REFERENCES

1. Glueck, Sheldon and Eleanor: *Later Criminal Careers,* New York, The Commonwealth Fund, 1937, pp. 75, 76.
2. Ellingston, John R.: *Protecting Our Children From Criminal Careers,* New York, Prentice-Hall, Inc., 1948, pp. 84, 86, 87.
3. *Comparison of Expenditures and Estimated Standard Costs For Selected Juvenile Delinquency Services,* Children's Bureau, Publication No. 10, Washington, D. C. p. 18. (1960).
4. Tarrasch, M.D., Hertha: Delinquency is Normal Behavior, *Focus,* Vol. 29, July, 1950, p. 100.
5. Clark, Tom C.: If You Make the Boy Right, You Make the World Right, *Federal Probation,* Vol. XIV, December, 1950, pp. 10-12.
6. Dobbs, Harrison Allen: Are Correctional Schools Evil or are We? *Federal Probation,* Vol. XIV, December, 1950, pp. 35–41.
7. Neumeyer, Martin H.: *Juvenile Delinquency in Modern Society,* Princeton, N. J. (third edition), D. Van Nostrand Company, Inc., 1961, p. 353.
8. Monahan, Florence: *Women in Crime,* New York, Ives Washburn, 1941, pp. 111–113.
9. Schreiber, Paul: *How Effective are Services for the Treatment of Delinquents,* Children's Bureau Publication, No. 9, Washington, D. C. 1960, pp. 9–13.
10. Martin, John Bartlow: Criminal at Large, *Saturday Evening Post,* Volume 222, May 27, 1950, p. 20.

11. Bloch, Herbert A. and Flynn, Frank T.: *Delinquency: The Juvenile Offender in America Today,* New York, Random House, Inc., 1956, pp. 428–429.
12. Teeters, Negley K. and Reinemann, John Otto: *The Challenge of Delinquency,* New York, Prentice-Hall, Inc., 1950, p. 457.
13. Konopka, Gisela: The Group Worker's Role in an Institution for Juvenile Delinquents, *Federal Probation,* Vol. XV, June, 1951, pp. 15–23.
14. Deutsch, Albert: Is This Reform? *Woman's Home Companion,* March, 1948, p. 30.
15. Teeters, Negley K. and Reinemann, John Otto: *op. cit.,* p. 461.
16. Barker, Gordan H. and Adams, Thomas W.: The Social Structure of a Correctional Institution, *The Journal of Criminal Law, Criminology and Police Science,* Vol. 49, January-February, 1959, p. 422.
17. Bloch, Herbert A. and Flynn, Frank T.: *op. cit.,* p. 429.
18. Tetters, Negley K. and Reinemann, John Otto: *op. cit.,* pp. 457, 462.
19. Monahan, Florence: *op. cit.,* p. 144.
20. Sullivan, Kate: *Girls on Parole,* Boston, Houghton, Mifflin Company, 1956, p. 159.
21. Konopka, Gisela: Institutional Treatment of Emotionally Disturbed Children, *Crime and Delinquency,* Vol. 8, January, 1962, pp. 52–57.
22. Levine, Stanley: Runaways and Research in the Training School, *Crime and Delinquency,* Vol. 8, January, 1962, pp. 40–45.
23. Monahan, Florence: *op. cit.,* pp. 138–142.
24. *Ibid:* p. 173.
25. McGrath, Howard: The Role of the Federal Probation Officer in Criminal Justice, *Federal Probation,* Vol. XVI, December, 1950, p. 4.
26. Tarrasch, M.D., Hertha: *op. cit.,* p. 101.
27. Weber, George H.: Conflicts Between Professional and Non-professional Personnel in Institutional Delinquency, *Journal of Criminal Law, Criminology and Police Science,* Vol. 48, May-June, 1957, pp. 26–43.
28. Lindner, Robert M.: *Rebel Without A Cause,* New York, Grune and Stratton, 1944, p. 288.
29. Gill, Howard B.: Developments in Correction—1960, Crime and Delinquency, Volume 7, July, 1961, pp. 263–273.
30. The Cockleburr Speaks, *American Journal of Correction,* Vol. 17, November-December, 1955, p. 19.

# 11

## PAROLE SUPERVISION AND SPONSORSHIP

IT HAS BEEN reported that the first modern usage of the word "parole" in the United States was initiated by Dr. S. G. Howe of Boston who, in a letter to the Prison Association of New York in 1846, wrote: "I believe there are many prisoners who might be so trained as to be left upon their parole during the last period of their imprisonment with safety." The word is derived from the French word *parole* and is used in the sense of "word of honor,"—*parole d'honneur*. Although the initial parole legislation was enacted in Massachusetts in 1837, New York in 1877 was the first state to include the word "parole" in the statute.

Parole is an administrative act—a form of release granted to an inmate after he has served a portion of his sentence in a penal institution. When he is paroled he finishes serving his "time" outside prison or reformatory walls. Parole, in principle, is neither mercy nor leniency. Parole is an extension of punishment. It does not imply forgiveness and is not designed as a reward for good conduct in the institution. No inmate has the *right* to parole, and the public does not have the *right* to parole him. Obviously, parole is less expensive than incarceration, since the parolee is able to earn some money and in many cases contribute to the support of his family, thus, removing both himself and family from public support.

One of the fallacies concerning parole is the view that the individual inmate achieves eligibility by his own efforts. Some judges will tell the convicted or his family that if he maintains a "good work record and good conduct record" while he is in prison, he will be eligible for parole. The fact of the matter is that all inmates become eligible for parole consideration regardless of their records. At least ninety per cent of all prisoners make "good" records, but only approximately thirty per cent are paroled. However, in recent years, an increasing rate of institutional parole for juveniles has been noted.

## PAROLE AND THE YOUNG OFFENDER

Oddly enough, the first elements of parole began in the United States in colonial times as a system of indenture for juvenile delinquents. Under this early practice, young prisoners were released and placed in the employment of private citizens to whom such prisoners were legally bound. While these juveniles were not subject to supervision by the state, they were permitted to earn their final discharge from their employers. A further development occurred when state visiting agents were appointed to supervise the children and to prevent their exploitation by employers while on indenture. This system was adopted by the New York House of Refuge, founded in 1825.

Juvenile parole, sometimes referred to as "after care" has for many years constituted a neglected field in the child welfare program. Little uniformity is to be found in its administration. This unevenness reflects the great differences in the regulations governing state institutions and is also partly the result of the fact that many schools and institutions for juvenile delinquents are private or semiprivate, and only in a measure subject to state regulation and supervision. The growing policy governing adult parole, a policy leading toward greater centralization in the granting and supervising of parolees on the state level, has not been adopted in the juvenile field. In view of the fact that one of the most important phases of the training program involved in institutional experience is the inmate's parole into the community and the facilitation of the offender's adjustment there, the need to improve parole procedures is evident.

## WHAT DETERMINES THE USE OF PAROLE?

In the case of adults, the two prerequisites for parole, outside of an acceptable institutional record, are the absence of detainers (that is, legal "hold orders" for other authorities) and guaranteed employment. In some states the applicant for parole must have a home, a sponsor, and a job, and these must be *bona fide*. However, many factors affect the probable fitness of a child or youth for parole or conditional liberation.

Parole boards, institutional heads, and juvenile courts are interested to receive information that will help them in arriving at a correct and intelligent decision concerning who shall be paroled. It must be determined if the applicant is capable of living in the community and remaining at liberty without violating laws. In considering an inmate's release on parole, both negative and positive considerations in each case shall be appraised. References are made, if available, to the psychiatric and psychological reports worked up by the professional staffs within the institution of commitment. An analysis is made of the inmate's educational progress within the institution, his plans for the future, his maturation, his seriousness of purpose. In addition, the parole applicant's conduct, during incarceration, previous offense record, military experience, past occupational history, and present attitude toward life in general are studied.

The California Authority believes the wisest course is to give selected youthful inmates a trial on parole, a procedure followed only after inmates have been in a training school for a period of time that has proved sufficient to effect a measurable change of habits in other persons with similar difficulties. Should the youth fail on parole, the Authority can return him to the reform school for additional or perhaps different training. It is true that some youths who seem least favorably influenced in a training unit show, as soon as they are on parole, that they have acquired a new attitude and are now able to adjust well in the community. The California Authority has encountered difficulties in removing the idea of "doing time" from the minds of its charges, especially the older boys. Courts find them delinquent or guilty and commit them to the Youth Authority; the boys are apt to look upon the parole procedure itself as regular court sentence. At the diagnostic clinic often their first question is: "How much time will I have to do?"

Progress has been made in some institutions in their ability to make wise selections of parolees. Improved training and treatment methods within the institution, as well as the utilization of modern methods of classification and analysis of the inmates assist the paroling authority to base its selection upon facts and performance, instead of upon whim, fancy, or "intuition."

## PAROLE SYSTEMS AND PROBLEMS

The rapid growth of parole legislation necessitated a corresponding spread of parole systems to administer this new social technique. By 1900, parole systems of a sort had been introduced into twenty states; by 1910, thirty-two states and the federal government had adopted parole systems; and by 1922, parole was in operation in forty-four states, the Territory of Hawaii, and the federal government. Today all states have parole laws of some type.

In large part, because of this rapid development of the philosophy of parole among the fifty states, the various administrative parole systems present a somewhat kaleidoscopic view. According to one specialist in this field, organizations and agencies granting parole within the various states are of three types: central board, governors, and institution boards. In twenty-nine jurisdictions, central boards are vested with the power to grant paroles, or so-called paroles, to inmates of state prisons and reformatories. In seventeen states the sole power to grant parole is vested in the governor, acting independently or assisted by an advisor or an advisory board. Seven states utilize institutional parole agencies.[1] Where institutions serve a rather large territory and cannot let their staff members travel to outlying counties for purposes of investigation, the granting of parole and the supervision on parole may be in the hands of the committing juvenile court. State agencies such as the Youth Authority in California, the Youth Service Commission in Wisconsin, the Youth Service Board in Massachusetts, and the Division of Field Services of the Illinois Youth Commission are charged with the preparation and the supervision of parole of those committed to institutions in these states.

There is no one parole system, but rather fifty state systems of parole, plus the federal system of parole. The National Probation and Parole Association[2] has listed the conflicting and overlapping "regulations" imposed upon the parolee in the various states, and suggests that parole regulations need re-examination. Lack of uniformity is the most obvious defect, and not a single one of the twenty-four parole regulations appears in every one of the fifty state documents. For example, liquor is completely prohibited in forty-one states, but no restrictions in Missouri, Virginia or West Virginia. In thirty-eight states, no association or correspondence is permitted by the parolee with persons of poor reputation, but six states ignore this matter entirely. The parolee agrees to waive extradition as a condition of parole in nineteen states, but no mention is made of it in twenty-three states. There may be a real question about the legality of the regulation which requires the prospective parolee to agree to waive his right to extradition.

In only two states, Florida and Pennsylvania is the parolee compelled to take treatment for venereal disease as a condition for remaining on parole, but this "regulation" is not even mentioned in the remaining states. Church attendance is mandatory in Kansas and Nebraska, the parolee is required to attend church regularly as a condition of remaining on parole, while this subject is not mentioned in the other states. In one state, the official title is probation officer, but he supervises parolees and has nothing to do with probation. In a few states the number of stipulations about behavior exceed twenty. One of these states even requires the parolee to read the regulations periodically during the entire parole period. Parole regulations among the various states are characterized by impracticality, multiplicity, redundancy, complexity, inconsistency and irrelevancy. The application of the "Ten Commandments" would be more functional.

The administration of parole is beset with many problems, one of the most important of which center in the violation of parole by the youthful offender. When a state training school paroles a juvenile offender, it is expected that the boy or girl will adjust satisfactorily under the supervision of the parole officer and not return to the training school. In a report prepared for the Governor's Committee a Penal Affairs for Iowa (1960), Professor Walter A. Lunden[3] of Iowa State University submits a tentative list of the factors to account for the various reasons why the juvenile failed "to make good" on his parole:

(1) The conditions surrounding the parole placement were not

satisfactory and had not been well investigated prior to parole.

(2) The child was not prepared for parole because the program within the training school had not affected an adequate rehabilitation of the child.

(3) The parole officer failed to give adequate supervision to the child while on parole.

(4) The training school may have been overcrowded to the point where the child "had to be paroled" to make room for others coming into the school.

(5) The child may have been of such a nature that he or she was impervious to retraining programs.

(6) The child may have been returned to the same conditions which brought about the delinquency.

Professor Lunden further comments that whatever may be the situation a parole violation is a serious *break* in the whole chain of circumstances created to rehabilitate the child. It is normal to expect that a certain percentage of those paroled from a state training school will violate under the best conditions. Furthermore, it may be better to recognize a certain number of violations as a matter of "profit and loss," as a calculated risk, that it may be better to have some failures on parole, rather than keep the youngsters in a state institution. It may be that under the best conditions, parole as a method of treatment, is superior to institutional care. When a training school paroles a juvenile to a home community, the school extends the process of rehabilitation from the institution to the place the parolee goes. The transition from training school to release on parole is a crucial period for the juvenile and to those to whom the child goes.

Professor Lunden made an analysis of parole violations in seventeen state training schools in the North Central Region of the United States, from 1956 to 1959. Considerable "turnover" of juvenile inmates was revealed. Within twelve months, 13,270 entered, and 13,169 left the various institutions, while the institutional population remained at 6,530 juvenile inmates. The average stay in the training schools amounted to 11.6 months.

Illinois, Minnesota and Wisconsin make the most extensive use of parole, in contrast to Nebraska, Kansas, and Missouri who do not use as much parole. With few exceptions, wide use of parole is associated with higher rates of parole violations, and low violation rates are related to schools making little use of parole. In the training school for girls the lowest number paroled in relation to the average inmate population appeared in South Dakota where thirty-two were paroled for every 100 inmates present. In contrast to these, Iowa ranked highest with 124 paroled for every 100 inmates. When parole violations for boys are compared with rates for girls on a state by state basis, it appears that where the rates are high for boys, the rates for girls are also high. With few exceptions, violation rates for boys are higher than parole violation rates for girls.

Lunden's data revealed what is already known about parole violation among adults; i.e., the first three months constitute the crucial period for parole violations. If the juvenile does break parole, the boy or girl is most apt to do so within the first three months after the date of parole from the institution. A parole agent needs to give extra attention to the "new cases" during the first few weeks after the time of release from the training school.[4]

Problems of parole systems are often complicated by inefficient administrative planning and inadequate staffing (some parole systems exist largely on paper). Again, many parole officers are burdened by very large case loads. And both officers and parolees are sometimes handicapped by detailed legal and administrative rules that restrict needed flexibility of operation.

Parole staffs are often of low quality because of unattractive salary scales. Competent men may not stay in parole service long for that reason, or are they always obtainable through Civil Service examinations. As one author stresses, tests do not always measure what they set out to measure; it is not possible to determine from a written test whether an applicant has the temperament, the ability, and the personal integrity demanded in an efficient parole officer. Candidates may place high on the competitive lists and yet be very poor material, even emotionally unstable. For example, in one Civil Service examination, an applicant passed the test with flying colors only to go to prison later for dishonesty; another, at the bottom of the list, barely managed to be appointed but became one of the most valuable members of the parole staff.[5]

There are, then, serious problems in on-going parole systems; problems of personnel selection and quality, of inadequate facilities and funds, of administrative policy and practice. But these problems are by no means insurmountable. Nor should they overshadow the positive accomplishments of parole itself. However, of all problems that beset the administration of parole, the most important of which center in the supervisory process—the crux of the parole system.

## PAROLE SUPERVISION

It was pointed out above that one of the most important phases of the whole rehabilitative process is intelligent and efficient parole supervision. And some of the handicaps facing supervisors today are noted, including inadequate staffing, large case loads, and administrative inflexibility. A more detailed consideration of supervision and its problems should form part of any serious discussion of parole.

Releasing the youth from the correctional institution and his subsequent adjustment under parole supervision should be a gradual process. A weak link in the chain of rehabilitation at the present time is the supervision of youth while on parole. In one instance, only postcard supervision was used because of a huge case load, and the parole officer received about the same report from the parolee as "Everything OK. Nothing new" for several dozen times. The final entry in the officer's file, via newsclipping was "Parolee killed when opium still explodes."

There are few parole staffs which are sufficiently large or well enough trained to cope readily with the problems of the post-institutional training period. In some states parole services for children are conspicuous by their absence; upon release from the institution children must get along as best they can unsupervised. Yet the program demanded in training children while on parole, in principle, involves extensive and professional case work. As Dean Arthur E. Fink indicates, it makes a difference whether the helping person—the parole officer—lectures and directs the parolee, or whether he is understanding . . . and affords the parolee opportunity to participate in the planning and thinking. What the parole officer says, and how he says it is very important.[6]

Dean Fink lists some general principles to guide supervision of parolees:

(1) One should have a full knowledge of community resources.
(2) A delinquent, like any other person, does not live in a vacuum. During the period of confinement, for those delinquents who are institutionalized, some prerelease work should be directed toward treatment of faulty attitudes and habits of parents.
(3) The selection of a parole adviser is of great importance, especially where the parolee lives in a town or city quite a little distant from the parole office.
(4) Study a case thoroughly before release as well as during supervision. So far as possible, prevent problems before they occur. At least, work for a solution before they become serious. It is important to make frequent contacts in the early phases of supervision.[7]

Short of these principles and of the needed personnel to carry them out, alternative methods have been devised, including sponsorship.

Authorities often require a sponsor if the youth is to be released on parole. The sponsor may be a family friend, a clergyman, or other interested citizen, but he should be selected by the paroling officials with utmost care. The sponsor is no substitute for the parole officer who officially supervises the boy. In some states, in the case of adult parole, the sponsor may be accepted by the parole authorities as a substitute for the parole officer for all practical intent and purposes. In juvenile parole, the sponsor cooperates with the parole officer and seeks his advice. Since the sponsor is responsible for one individual only, he can more readily concentrate his efforts and available time than an over-burdened parole officer.

Brager and Chappell suggest a few qualifications the sponsor should possess in order to measure up to the opportunity and challenge of acting as a sponsor to a juvenile offender on parole. The following points are recommended by the authors. "Pick men who will be able to give of their time. Try to match the right sponsor with the right boy. Find men with an understanding of human behavior. Lay off the perfectionist. Select the man who doesn't moralize. Find cheerful men—the "optimistic type. Avoid the Casper Milquetoast type. Pass over the lonely soul. Select men with a reputation for following through. Select men who will stay with it when the going gets tough. Look for men who will accept a boy right from the start."[8]

Brager and Chappell further suggest that after the sponsor has known the parolee for a while, the sponsor should ask the parolee's advice about things, even trivial matters. One of the important needs of the juvenile is to feel important and being asked about something will help him develop that feeling. Also encourage the juvenile to participate in sports, begin a hobby. The authors caution the sponsor that it is a bad policy to criticize the training school or the parole officer in the boy's presence.

Never forget that friendship is the thing the boy needs most. All else is secondary. Real friendship demands that as a sponsor, one can't be a "fair weather" friend. A real test of friendship is to stick to a boy through *any* kind of difficulty. Remember, many people have deserted him when he's failed in the past. Friendship can't be bought, so don't be a "good time Charlie." Always keep any promise you make. If you want the parolee's respect, it must be earned. And above all, do not become discouraged if you don't seem to be getting anywhere. There are bound to be failures. Sponsorship is an activity for men of good will that pays off in a special kind of gratification. There are really no hard and fast rules. One part good heart and one part good mind is the perfect recipe for the successful sponsor.[9]

G. Howland Shaw,[10] one-time Chairman, Continuing Committee, National Conference on Prevention and Control of Juvenile Delinquency, Washington, D. C. adds some pertinent observations and suggestions about sponsoring a delinquent. Sponsorship is simply the art by which an adult works out a constructive relationship with a youngster who has been or who is in trouble, to the mutual benefit of both the youngster and the adult. It has been called "the art of disinterested friendship." Echoing Brager and Chappell, Shaw stresses three basic requirements of a sponsorship program:

(1) *The sponsor must be selected with the utmost care.* By no means should everybody who would like to be a sponsor be allowed to be one. Beware of those always wanting to "do good," and who wander around seeking victims for their predatory kind of altruism. Avoid the "gentleman and lady bountiful type" who lavish upon their victims entertainment which is as inappropriate as it is bewildering and destructive to those who have to receive it and seem to be grateful.

(2) *The sponsor should be selected to match the boy.* We are not on terms of close friendship with everyone we meet and there is no more reason why a man chosen at random should be the proper sponsor for a boy chosen with an equal lack of discrimination.

(3) *The sponsor must seek professional guidance.* The sponsor is a lawyer, a businessman, a physician—in a word, from the point of view of the several disciplines which deal scientifically with human behavior, he is a layman. The success of the relationship depends upon his constant awareness of that fact. The sponsor remains a layman and any illusions to the contrary are certain to lead to serious consequences.

Mr. Shaw comments further on the major problems facing a sponsor. There is the very real and very difficult problem of bridging the gap between the sponsor and the boy sponsored. That is not a problem which can be easily solved by taking the boy to a baseball game which you both enjoy and it may be intensified by having the boy to supper at your house. The fact remains that you have lived all your life under circumstances which seem to the boy luxuriously comfortable. You're "good," you're a prominent citizen. The boy you are sponsoring is none of these things and he may start out by hating you or at least distrusting you. It may take months of patient, thoughtful effort to overcome that hatred and suspicion.

Talk about your own blunders, disappointments and discouragements. And don't be disturbed if your boy thinks at first that your success has been achieved by crooked means and inquires as to what your "racket" may be. Another hard problem facing the sponsor is to picture just how it feels to get out of training school or reformatory and start life again on the outside. Finally, there is the problem which is the acid test of the sponsor and often his Waterloo. Your youthful parolee commits some new offense in spite of all your time and effort to change his attitudes and become a good citizen. If you are a real sponsor, never give up. Don't say: "That impossible boy; he's headed straight for the penitentiary or the electric chair." Instead, ask yourself first of all: "Where did I fail?" And then in the light of the answer to that question make a fresh start.[11]

Civic organizations have in recent years volunteered as sponsors of delinquent youth. In Philadelphia, Junior Chamber of Commerce members have successfully sponsored boys released from the Pennsylvania Industrial School. The National Exchange Club has undertaken a nation-wide program of supplying sponsors for boys returning home from the National Training School. One of the most recent manifestations of a service club's work in this field is that of the Kiwanis Club of Pueblo, Colorado, which reports about ninety per cent success in their sponsorship program.

Parolees fortunate enough to have officially approved sponsors are not infrequently enabled to make a satisfactory adjustment to their community. They are not only freed from the "professional-client" relationship but also removed from the multiplicity of restrictions which are imposed upon them by the parole office, where all too often the standards for the worst parolee are extended to all. With this system in full operation the authoritarian pressures inherent in formalized systems of parole would be very likely to disappear.

Much still remains to be accomplished in the parole area. At the present time, a majority of the institutions are without psychiatric counsel, a lack that increases the work and responsibility of the parole authorities in selecting those inmates eligible for parole. Parole authorities are especially handicapped in dealing with psychopathic delinquents, the mentally retarded, and habitual "sex" cases without psychiatric aid.

Parole is also an area in need of the help of scientific knowledge. A long-range program of research could be initiated, for example, to study the behavior of released inmates over a prolonged period of time. Very little is known about the details of parole violations. Such research might form the basis of valid prediction instruments which could serve as a source of guidance in selecting parolees. On a broader scale, research would shed light on a field about which too little is known.

## REFERENCES

1. Killinger, George G. in Tappan, Paul W. (ed.): *Contemporary Correction,* New York, McGraw-Hill Book Co., 1951, p. 362.
2. Arluke, Nat R.: Summary of Parole Rules, *National Probation and Parole Association Journal,* Volume 2, January, 1956, pp. 10–13.
3. Lunden, Walter A.: Juvenile Parole Violators, in *Statistics on Delinquents and Delinquency,* Ames, Iowa, Art Press, 1961, pp. 137–144.
4. *Ibid:* p. 23.
5. Dressler, David: *Parole Chief,* New York, The Viking Press, 1951, p. 309.
6. Fink, Arthur E.: Parole Supervision: A Case Analysis, *Federal Probation,* Vol. XV, September, 1951, pp. 39–42.
7. *Ibid:* pp. 44–45.
8. Brager, Harry E. and Chappell, Richard A.: Jim, Mr. Brown, and You, *Federal Probation,* Vol. XIII, June, 1949, p. 46.
9. *Ibid:* pp. 47–48.
10. Shaw, Howland G.: Sponsoring a Delinquent, *Federal Probation* Vol. XII, December, 1948, pp. 13–14.
11. *Ibid:* p. 15.

# 12

## COMMUNITY RESPONSIBILITY

IN THE FINAL analysis, everyone must share part of the responsibility for the high incidence of juvenile delinquency and criminality. Delinquency cannot be effectively prevented or controlled without community action. In other words, members of the community themselves—and this includes everyone—should support agencies and programs designed to reduce or control delinquent behavior.

But "community," one may protest (and correctly), includes so much and so many: towns, villages neighborhoods, huge cities, the nation itself. According to Lowell J. Carr,[1] the problem of crime-proofing a community seems to run all the way from the family to the state and the national government. It may be answered that the community of crucial importance in this context is the *local* living area—the community the child first meets and of which he is usually an active member. Perhaps the final solution to the problem of delinquency, must be sought in the local community. As Paul G. Cressey[2] indicates, efforts to prevent juvenile delinquency can be most effective as they come to grips with the child's *own* immediate social world in his *own* community. Any planning of programs for delinquency prevention can best be done in the local community—and best of all in the neighborhood itself. The primacy of the local situation arises from the fact that conditions contributing to delinquency in an individual case are always found on close inspection to be unique. A local community solution, however, if it is to be achieved in any substantial measure, calls for an all-out effort to promote and to use techniques and facilities capable of being developed in the community in which the delinquent and potentially delinquent child himself lives.

This approach is supported by a growing number of professional workers in the field. The fruitfulness of the approach requires realistic understanding of the vast changes that have taken place in the social environment of children. The local community, especially in urban areas, is no longer firmly integrated by the interlocking primary groups of family and neighborhood. The latter once constituted the principal context of social control and of "living" in general for most people—particularly for children. To be sure, these primary groups continue to play an important role in the life of the young, and of the young delinquent; but more and more they compete with other groups, for example, the gang and school group, and with the pressures and appeals and cultural contradictions of modern urban society. Understanding the community, then, and exploiting its resources in the fight against delinquency demand knowledge of social changes and realization of their growing influence in the lives of young people.

Delinquent and criminal behavior, as brought out in earlier chapters, is especially prevalent in neighborhoods and urban residential areas where traditional social controls are weak and where conflicts between control agencies, such as the family and school and gang, are widespread. Community institutions in these areas are limited in their capacity to meet individual and group needs. Here, too, the temptations of the "shady world" are strong. These are the local communities, therefore, that require the greatest efforts and pose the largest problems for all concerned with delinquency.

Attitudes of the "modern" community still pose serious problems, in relation to juvenile delinquency and criminality. The public attitude and understanding of crime is about at the state that medicine was at the beginning of the 19th century. People still deny it in themselves, turn away from anyone accused or suspected of such misbehavior, are woefully ignorant of its varieties and treatment, and prefer to believe that it does not exist. The community's attitude toward youthful offenders, like its treatment of youth generally, is a mixture of soft-heartedness, exasperation, wounded resignation, and sadistic pleasure in punishment. We act first and think afterward. No responsible authority operates in this field.[3]

According to Lauretta Bender many youngsters show amazing capacity to tolerate bad parents, poor teachers, dreadful homes and worse communities. Public effort is colored with political considerations and individuals make personal capital out of waves of hysteria stirred up by parental and community, concern. Juvenile delinquency and criminality deserve serious study. One cannot help but be skeptical of the random, sporadic, superficial and opportunistic manner in which it is being diagnosed and countered; hence delinquency is apt to remain a nebulous question, rather than a field for effective remedy.[4] As Lowell J. Carr has indicated, hundreds of communities permit politically-minded sheriffs and prison wardens, underpaid staffs and utterly prescientific correctional programs to "jam-pac" youthful offenders into jails, reformatories, and prisons, already over-crowded with longtime seasoned offenders.[5]

As offenders are released and return to the community, how are they reabsorbed into the general social life from which they have been separated? This question with its many ramifications has been partially answered by Professor Richard A. Cloward in his address to the 1961 30th Annual Illinois Governor's Conference on Youth.

> Consider . . . . the situation of a person being released from an institution. He may be well motivated to adjust upon release, and he may possess a number of personal attributes conducive to success. . . . . . . . As the individual moves back into the community, changes in his values, personality, and skills are not necessarily acknowledged by those who control access to these resources. Thus his family may continue to reject him, teachers may respond to him in such a way as to bring about the very behavior they have imputed to him, since he is a deviant. Employers may not wish to run the risk of hiring him for fear that he will engage in behavior that will be troublesome . . . . . . his old gang may be reluctant to accept him back because he is "hot" . . . and an object of police surveillance. . . .
>
> The problem of the released boy is, in short, one of gaining reentry to the society which only recently expelled him. This is a problem common to many categories of institutionalized persons, including the physically handicapped, the mentally ill, as

well as the prisoner. In the case of the prisoner, the problem of reentry begins with arrest. Once apprehended, the individual is forced to participate in the rituals of being charged, prosecuted, sentenced and confined.

Throughout these "status degradation ceremonies" what is actually taking place is the destruction of the individual's public identity, he is being progressively assigned a new public identity—that of a delinquent or criminal, which operates as a major obstacle to subsequent conformity in the community following release. . . . . . . A boy who is released and seeks to conform . . . . quickly finds he cannot succeed in persuading society that he has become eligible for readmission to it. There are no status-restoration ceremonies to proclaim and legitimize his eligibility. Hence he is prevented from conforming, and recidivism is the consequence.

During World War II, the State of Illinois arranged to parole a number of felons to the military. The rate of recidivism among those paroled to the military was much lower than among a comparable group released in the traditional way to their home communities. What accounts for the difference? . . . . Men paroled to military service, if they served honorably were permitted to earn an Honorable Discharge. Having received this symbol of honor, they then could return to their home communities as patriots, rather than pariahs . . . . they had little difficulty explaining to employers where they had spent the last several years. The difference, in short, is that the military service performed a kind of status-restoring function for the prisoner, while among those paroled directly to the community no such legitimizing of status shifts occurred. Without some way of legitimizing one's eligibility for readmission to the society, the likelihood is that the social resources for conformity will be withheld.

Socially-structured barriers to reentry to society encountered upon release from confinement cannot be ignored . . . . . . . . internal institutional changes do little to open channels to the community . . . . they do little to provide youngsters with "a way back." [6]

Public reaction to juvenile delinquency and criminality remains laden with emotional hysteria and misunderstanding. The public must be educated to appraise unemotionally antisocial individual delinquents. Until this comes to pass, problems in local community programs will be conspicuous by their presence.

## PROBLEMS AND PROGRAMS IN THE LOCAL COMMUNITY

Almost any type of effective remedial program in delinquency requires the active interest and support of community leaders and leadership groups. Their enlistment is essential, both as opinion leaders in the community itself and as avenues leading directly to the existing law enforcement, correctional, educational, recreational, and readjustment services. As has been seen in earlier chapters of this book, the strengthening of these services should be one of the basic objectives of a realistic delinquency control movement.

The enlistment of helpful leadership and the strengthening of community agencies, however, are not easy accomplishments. Business and professional groups in local communities, possessing leadership capable of understanding and controlling juvenile delinquency and motivated to undertake extensive programs in this direction, frequently encounter apathy and even hostility from others. Consider the case of Fayette County, Pennsylvania, the home of over two hundred thousand people drawn from many parts of the world, where a few years ago delinquency became a grave problem. The obstacles confronted by the committee of professional and business leaders created to cope with this problem are described by Ruth W. Love:

> Citizens read newspaper stories of teen-age criminals, of the activities in which it operated, of car-stripping gangs heckling automobile owners whose private garages were not excluded from the organized depredations of youth. By 1936, a group of professional and business men decided to move into action in Redstone Township where the heaviest taxes were paid by coal companies and the offenders came from homes of families that were one, never more than two, generations removed from "the old country."
>
> These men—teachers, storekeepers, salesmen—met, discussed the problem facing them and mapped a plan for making personal contacts with juvenile delinquents. Their efforts received a cool reception from parents, many of whom spoke only suffi-

> cient English to brand the well-meaning citizens as "meddlers" and "busy-bodies" stirring up trouble for the children of the foreign-born. Snubbed, rebuffed, cursed were the Redstone Township men as they began their program so quietly that few outside their own district knew of the efforts to correct existing evils spawning delinquency. Discouraged, they continued to wage battle, convinced that they were "doing good" but with meager results indicating merely wishful thinking.[7]

This case illustrated the difficulties sometimes encountered which are rooted in the economic and ethnic composition of the local community—difficulties enhanced by contrasting group ways and cultural values, the significance of which, incidentally, may not have been clearly understood by the local committee itself.

Some juveniles turn to delinquent and criminal behavior when they feel "left out" of community activities, as during war years. This feeling of "not belonging," according to Milton Lessner, is the most salient, contributing factor motivating juvenile delinquency. Delinquency increases noticeably during war time. Generally the sphere of interest of children during peace times were focused on the family, the school, the neighborhood, and the hometown. War extends this interest to the nation at large, and its relationship with other nations; members of the family enter the armed forces, there is regrouping of populations to meet industrial war needs, and there is a change of women's status as active participants in the war effort. These immediate and spontaneous changes tend to leave children with a feeling of insecurity, instability, and bewilderment. Their difficulties in adjusting to such changes have been intensified by the fact that they were *not included as a vital auxiliary in the war effort.*

The Boy Scouts of America, the Girl Scouts of America, and the Camp Fire Girls established programs based on war service as they gathered paper, knitted sweaters, and rolled bandages. However, the vast majority of juvenile delinquents are not members of there or similar organizations. In the event of future wars, the threat of increasing juvenile delinquency must be thought of as essentially a community problem which demands community planning and action. Youth must be organized in a program based on war service so that they can assume the role of junior citizens.[8]

Fred A. Romano[9] relates experiences in organizing a community for delinquency prevention that had had consistently high rates of delinquency. Since 1850, the neighborhood had been one of the low rent districts in Chicago. It had been a place of first immigrant settlement, successively occupied by Irish, German, Swedish, and Italian immigrants and Negroes from the South. The Italian community found some solace in the fact that Irish, Germans, and Swedes before them experienced the problem of delinquency and crime among their children and young adults while they lived in the neighborhood. Rates of delinquency remained relatively constant despite successive changes in the nationality composition of the community's population. Throughout the years traditions and patterns of delinquency and crime became established in the life of the community, and were transmitted by older boys to younger boys growing up in the district. They learned delinquency in the same fashion that children in more fortunate circumstances learn conventional forms of conduct.

Romano found that the large majority of delinquent boys in that neighborhood were normal children. An effort was made to organize a community council of *local* adult leaders, and the first undertaking was an attempt to create play facilities for the community children. Scouting was "sold" to community families, since it had been regarded as a "sissy" activity, and some parents were afraid it was a military program. Other community committees, such as the vocational guidance committee, the educational committee, the civic improvement committee all reflected community effort to improve the situation. A special effort was made to give supervision to all of the delinquents and potential delinquents in the community.

The juvenile police officers and the probation officers from the juvenile courts cooperated to the extent of referring official cases to community committees for supervision. Through community committee sponsorship of a camp for boys, one juvenile police officer reported that he had been able, while visiting this camp to establish a kind of relationship with the boys which he had been unable to achieve in years of police work. It was extremely helpful to have *local* persons in the positions of truant officer and parole agent because the parolees and truants themselves feel that these persons understand their problems and are working to help them. The community can do much, even in areas of high delinquency, in "helping their own."

One of the earlier attempts to provide another community resource was made by a former Salvation Army worker at the turn of the century, when he cleared two rooms of his west side flat, and installed some recreational equipment. Then he tacked a sign over the front door which read: "Do not wait to be an adult to be great. Be a great kid now." From this humble beginning sprang the boys' club movement, and in the Chicago area of today, nearly 25,000 youngsters enjoy the facilities provided at 25 permanent boys' club locations. Most Boys' Clubs receive community funds. However, results from Boys' Clubs are inconclusive. In a study made by Frederick M. Thrasher in the 1930's, it was found that a new and expensive Boys' Club in New York City did not help prevent delinquency. The members of the club showed a tendency to be even more delinquent during their membership than either before or after.[10]

Harrison Allen Dobbs asks for more substantial thinking and acting about community aspects of juvenile delinquency, stressing the principle of *synthesis.* Costly failures, countrywide, characterize a major part of the effort that communities put forth in trying to prevent and treat juvenile delinquency, perhaps due to persistent juvenile delinquency, perhaps due to persistent cultural patterns that adhere too closely to a microscopic rather than macroscopic penetration of such situations. Are we losing sight of the forest in this social endeavor, because trees or their lives get too much of our attention? The whole is something fundamentally different and greater than the sum of the parts.

Professor Dobbs formulates seven generic hypotheses that form a distinctive mosaic: (1) be dynamic and experimental in attitudes and methods, not controlled by traditional heritage and practice; (2) guide boys and girls with delinquency problems as being integers of a large human whole, not isolated segments; (3) make sincere effort to re-educate so-called "delinquents" for moral, thoughtful social living, rather than to some arbitrary pre-determined "social adjustments." (4) Prevent delimiting mental, physical, and social characteristics; (5) Recognize and utilize the undeveloped potentialities of the total individual, not stress his inherent or acquired limitations; (6) satisfy the growth and adjustment demands of needy children by an intelligent, co-ordinated effort of the whole community, not through isolated programs; (7) establish and nurture in the local community suitable welfare and educational services for children with problems, don't relinquish too much of this social responsibility to some far-away person or place. Changing over to such a unified front seems a sensible way out of part of our juvenile delinquency dilemma.[11]

Local committees, when they are formed, and professional workers in the field, must confront with regularity, problems which stem from the cultural complexity, the transitional growth, and, as it is sometimes stated, the "social disorganization" of the local community. They must realize, for example, that social disorganization of the local living area may severely handicap the very best remedial efforts. This situation is brought into sharp focus by cases involving young people, who, after having spent time in correctional institutions, return to their "home" neighborhoods only to find themselves once more living in a world of instability, temptation, and perhaps, corruption. Under such conditions, the task of encouraging such youngsters to be respected and useful junior citizens may well imply the larger but crucial requirement of transforming delinquency areas into socially healthful communities.

Campaigns against delinquency that promise some success require the enlistment of many specialists and many groups, including both policy-making officials and their junior colleagues in schools, police departments, courts of law, recreational agencies, public welfare departments and private welfare agencies, and churches. Delinquency is a many-sided problem requiring a many-sided attack by the several specialized forces of the local community if gains are to be made.

As Professor Carr indicates, it is impossible to find a community in the United States in which all that we know for the control of crime is being applied at anything approaching best practice. There are many communities which have outstanding school systems, but only mediocre police departments and the juvenile courts may be second or third class. Recreation programs will be below par or there will be no family case work agencies. If the police department happens to be good, the schools may be way below par. Nowhere is there any community that has brought all of its agencies and services to anywhere near the level of best practice; most communities function at about 30 per cent of best practice in the various fields.[12] Despite these "deficiencies," as in all effective campaigns of peace or war, there must be coordination of the various specialists and careful consideration of the tactical weapons at their disposal.

Specific plans for community-wide programs of an informed and potentially effective type, as Professor Carr has stressed, often meet resistance because of misconceptions about delinquency itself, and from real or assumed threats to special interests. Proposals for improving delinquency control in the local community may arouse opposition of taxpayers and here the interest involved is clear; of influential citizens for various reasons, often obscure; and even of social workers and other participants in the corrections field itself—if they feel slighted or left out. The latter reaction seems to be fairly common: coordination of efforts being hampered by the presumed "freezing out" of some official, say the juvenile court judge, the chief of police, or the school superintendent. On the other hand, sometimes individuals proffer assistance to programs in the interest of personal publicity and self-aggrandizement or for partisan reasons, a situation that may handicap the larger effort.[13]

Partisanship among professional workers themselves in the delinquency field is by no means unknown, reflected in the zealous advocacy of this or that remedial program. Such a situation not only lessens essential cooperation but creates uneasiness and confusion among the nonprofessional lay participants, whose assistance is a requirement for an effective broad-gauge program.

These several obstacles to coordinated effort are prevalent, to be sure, but they are not insurmountable. In various communities throughout the country numerous individuals and agencies have been enrolled in anti-delinquency campaigns, and their efforts and facilities have been brought together in integrated programs. One of the outstanding efforts of this kind has developed in recent years in California, suggestively referred to as the "community co-ordinating council program." This plan originated with the Berkeley Coordinating Council, organized in 1919, which established a rough model for other communities in the state. The Los Angeles program, which involved eighty-eight local councils in 1948, receives its sponsorship and overall coordination from the Los Angeles County Probation Department, Delinquency Control Division. The councils promote cooperation among agencies and institutions concerned with child welfare, study social conditions and community resources, sponsor educational programs for the public, and stimulate "social action."

More recently California has attempted to revive the Town Meeting idea to combat delinquency, and at such local level meetings concerned with the problems of juveniles, it was found that the greatest need was not a swimming pool, or a youth center, or a large allowance, or freer use of the family car. The greatest expressed need was for a job. The youngsters wanted to earn their own money and pay their own way. The "Big Town Meetings" in California attracted over four thousand delegates. One delegate pointed out that a girl in her community tried for weeks to get psychiatric help but to no avail. She then turned to alcohol, later to narcotics, and as soon as a petition was filed on her in the juvenile court, psychiatric treatment was made available to her. The delegate raised the question: "Do you have to steal, or otherwise misbehave, in order to get help with your problems?" One juvenile at the meeting summed it up, "the cure for juvenile delinquency is adult decency." [14]

The results of these efforts are sufficiently impressive to convince officials and observers in California that the most powerful deterrent to delinquency is to be found in coordinated programs of these types. While this conclusion may reflect, in part (justifiable), pride in local efforts, most authorities would agree that large-scale efforts to harness the resources of the local community are of basic importance in delinquency control.

Mary B. Novick, Consultant, Division of Research, Children's Bureau reports the results of a recent survey (1960) made of 258 "community welfare planning councils" that employ a paid executive, to find out what communities across the Nation were doing with the resources available to them. Questionnaires were sent to these planning councils in 2444 communities of 14,000 or more. All states except Alaska, Montana, Nevada, Vermont and the Commonwealth of Puerto Rico were represented in the survey. The findings are listed in the following Summary:

(1) All but one of the cities of 500,000 population have or have had (within the last five years) one or more projects specifically designed to prevent delinquency.
(2) Very few cities with less than 500,000 population have or have had such projects.
(3) All project directors believed that their program was moving toward its goal, but almost none of the programs were being scientifically evaluated.
(4) With few exceptions, the projects were largely financed from private funds.
(5) Although many projects were labeled "experimental," few of the methods used were new; most had long since been tried in other cities ...... it appears that many communities need help, advice, and consultation in adapting a proven method to meet the city's particular problems.
(6) From the evidence available, the expansion of many projects seems desirable, but there is a shortage of the qualified personnel needed to make this expansion possible.
(7) The concept of "primary prevention" is apparently a baffling one to put into practice, and many projects seem to include in it treating the known delinquency and so reducing recidivism.
(8) There seems to be a need to bring schools more directly into programs designed to prevent delinquency.

The report concludes with the observation that funds are needed for the continuance of worthwhile programs. If these projects are of value in helping reduce delinquency . . . their value is not being capitalized upon, for most of them are minimally staffed, provide service for relatively few children, and depend on ephemeral sources for their financial support.[15]

As Horace S. Volz has pointed out, probably most of the efforts expended to curb juvenile delinquency and criminality have been characterized by the "Hit-or-Miss," trial and error, and unorganized approach.

In this, the age of the studious, planned scientific approach to all kinds of problems—military, medical, legal, industrial, educational—in the field of behavior we continue to attack with panaceas, hunches, plans of cranks, and suggestions of well-meaning but unenlightened persons.

We repeat what has failed over and over again. We accept unproved reports of "successful" programs. We swallow prescriptions written by unqualified "social physicians" . . . . . . and we even disregard the suggestions of qualified social physicians.

When someone riding a hobby shouts that what we need is more recreational facilities, communities rush to build more playgrounds, gyms, swimming pools, tennis courts, and baseball fields, and juvenile delinquency continues! When another panaceist yells "better housing," communities rush to construct beautiful, low-rent housing projects, with abundant recreational facilities, and juvenile delinquency continues! When another insists that youth canteens will control delinquency, public-spirited citizens get on the job, but youth still comes before the bar, even canteen members. . . . . . . Quite naturally then, we continue to have the delinquents we deserve.

The problems facing America in respect to youth are immediate, vast, and complicated . . . . . and there is much activity at cross purposes. This condition is due to the failure of the trained and experienced to furnish leadership for the general public . . . . we find the old gap caused by the lag of practice behind theory. Certainly our social scientists are far ahead of our practitioners.

There is need for tested knowledge. Let us first of all gather all of the sound, scientific findings available and accept what seems to be the best diagnoses, plans of treatment, and prevention programs . . . . . . Let us take the findings of Healy and Bronner, the Gluecks, Shaw and others, and use them rather than the musings of Joe Doakes, Elmer Twitchell, and Mike McGee. Yes, there will be disagreement. Perhaps we shall have three or four schools of thought just as there is more than one school of thought in other sciences and disciplines. . . . The sociologists doubtless would differ with the psychiatrists in emphasis. They may differ with the religionists, the recreationists, and the educationists.

> One of the greatest needs is a set of guiding principles . . . . . a series of guideposts by which local communities may travel on the road to an effective plan. . . . . . . . At long last, then, we will be in a position to make an intelligent beginning and to terminate our promiscuous stabs in the dark.[16]

Although more than a decade has elapsed since Volz made his observations, there is little evidence to indicate that a "set of guiding principles" and a "series of guideposts" are yet available to those concerned with the problem posed by juvenile delinquency and criminality. As Professor Alfred J. Kahn of the New York School of Social Work, Columbia University has observed:

> Analysis of a group of court or institution cases reveals almost at once that something is wrong with our planning, with the values built into our programs, or with both. Children in trouble are 'found" briefly, only to be lost again until the trouble is severe. Agencies work with one child in a family and ignore the others, or concern themselves with parents to the exclusion of children. . . . The immediately relevant point is that, despite the positives that are present in many specific programs, the evidence is overwhelming that something must be done about overall community strategy and integration of services.[17]

As Cuber and Harper [18] point out, in many "problem" aspects of everyday life, we follow the dictates of expert rather than public opinion. If the physician diagnoses the patient's "problem" as diabetes, the patient accepts this "expert opinion" without insisting on a public-opinion poll in regard to the matter, but in the trouble areas of our society, we have no such popularly approved experts. For problems relating to crime and juvenile delinquency, who are to be regarded as "experts" with public recognition comparable to the acceptance that is accorded physicians, engineers, physicists, and chemists? "Expert opinion" rests ultimately upon public acceptance of the "expert." Society fails fully and consistently to accept "experts" on societal phenomena. Society simply does not hear sociological voices in regard to juvenile delinquency and criminality. There is considerable justification for lack of public acceptance. Social scientists are not in complete agreement, and as they communicate with one another use an intellectual jargon which the public does not understand. Such contributors seem more interested in impressing each other than in making information meaningful at all. As a result of this stricture in the communicative processes, it has been estimated that society utilizes about ten per cent of our sociological knowledge. Social scientists may get discouraged over the slowness of the public to accept their findings, but some progress is being made in the field of mental illness and its treatment.[19]

The need for the Federal Program to control and prevent juvenile delinquency was recognized on May 11, 1961 when President Kennedy established the President's Committee on Juvenile Delinquency and Youth Crime, naming the Attorney General as Chairman and the Secretary of Labor and the Secretary of Health, Education, and Welfare as the other two members. To assist in this task the committee has the services of a Citizens Advisory Council composed of twenty-one members representing both public and voluntary organizations.[20]

The same day that the President established the President's Committee, he sent Congress legislation that would allow the Federal Government to (1) undertake demonstration projects in the field of youth services, (2) train personnel to work with young people in trouble and (3) evaluate and disseminate the most effective ways of using total resources to combat juvenile delinquency in local communities. In transmitting his message, the President stated "Juvenile delinquency and youth offenses diminish the strength and vitality of our Nation; they present serious problems to all the communities affected; and they leave indelible impressions upon people involved which often causes continuing problems." [21]

The Administration bill was passed and signed by the President on September 22, 1961. Responsibility for carrying out the provisions of the Act is vested in the Secretary of Health, Education and Welfare. The President's Committee is charged with coordinating the activities of the various Departments concerned with programs for prevention and control of juvenile delinquency and youth crime.

Through the authorization of ten million dollars for each of three fiscal years ending June 30, 1964 Congress has now made it possible for the Federal Government to become a partner with the States and local communities in finding solutions to the spread of delinquency. There is a public responsibility to provide assistance and to protect society as a whole. The role of current Federal legislation is not to shift responsibility away from families and local communities, but to make it possible for the Nation as a whole to benefit from the fresh thinking and creative action of communities working on the problem.[22]

If the Federal Government can (1) stimulate new programs to deal with the underlying causes of delinquency, (2) spotlight a successful project in one community and encourage similar programs elsewhere, and (3) provide the opportunity to experiment with the best ideas available, invaluable contributions will be made.[23]

Juvenile delinquency and criminality is a frustrating social problem. For the most part the public is rather complacent and is apt to assume that the community is doing all it can for the problem of delinquency. Furthermore, any effort today must be made in local communities increasingly marked by characteristics of urbanism: functional interdependence but psychological impersonality; class and ethnic complexity and resulting barriers of social distance; ubiquitous apathy and frequent social blindness; and an ever-growing dependence on specialized agencies. All of these features of the modern urban world must be taken into account in formulating strategy against delinquency. Communities do not act unless they are stimulated and mobilized to act. The community becomes a new frame of reference, displacing former primary groupings. No type of human behavior is more important in times of stress and uncertainty than community leadership. Yet the men who manage groups best seldom write books about it, and the men who write the books seldom manage groups. Community organization and planning are matters of relatively recent developments, but they represent tremendously significant possibilities for the development of delinquency-deterring measures.

The sociologist is, of course, the scientist who is most familiar with the ills of the community. Much knowledge has been made available by Sociologists as well as other social scientists which needs to be synthesized and implemented into practice.

## REFERENCES


1. Carr, Lowell J.: Organized Efforts in Crime Prevention, *Federal Probation,* Vol. VI, July-September, 1942, pp. 49–52.
2. Cressey, Paul G.: Delinquency Prevention Begins at Home, *Focus,* Vol. 28, May, 1949, p. 78.
3. Cooper, Irving Ben: The Drama of Youth in our Criminal Court, *Federal Probation,* Vol. XIX, January-March, 1955, p. 38.
4. Bender, Lauretta: How Bad is Juvenile Delinquency, Point of View *The Journal of Social Therapy,* Vol. II, October, 1955, p. 212.
5. Carr, Lowell J.: Commitment of the Youthful Offender, Vol. 2, *National Probation and Parole Journal,* April, 1956, p. 152.
6. Cloward, Richard A.: Finding and Testing New Ideas, 30th Annual *Governor's Conference on Youth,* (Illinois) Sherman House, Chicago, April 13, 1961.
7. Love, Ruth W.: Boys of Today—Citizens of Tomorrow, *Federal Probation,* Vol. XI, October-December, 1947, p. 43.
8. Lessner, Milton: Controlling War-Time Juvenile Delinquency, *The Journal of Criminal Law and Criminology,* Vol. XXXV, November-December, 1944, pp. 242–248.
9. Romano, Fred A.: Organizing a Community for Delinquency Prevention, 1940 *Yearbook,* National Probation and Parole Association, pp. 1–12.
10. Thrasher, Frederick M.: The Boys' Clubs and Juvenile Delinquency, *American Journal of Sociology,* Vol. 42, July, 1936, pp. 66–80.
11. Dobbs, Harrison Allen: A New Viewpoint to the Juvenile Delinquency Problem, *Federal Probation,* Vol. XI, October-December, 1947, pp. 18–21.
12. Carr, Lowell J.: Organized Efforts in Crime Prevention, *op. cit.,* p. 49.
13. Carr, Lowell J.: *Delinquency Control,* New York, Harper & Brothers, 1950, pp. 419–421.
14. Stark, Heman G.: California Revives Town Meeting Idea to Combat Delinquency, *Federal Probation,* Vol. XX, September, 1956, pp. 59–62.
15. Novick, Mary B.: Community Programs and Projects for the Prevention of Juvenile Delinquency, *Children's Bureau* Publication No. 14, Washington, D.C. 1960, pp. 11–12.

16. Volz, Horace S.: Let's Stop Fooling Around, *Federal Probation,* Vol. XII, September, 1948, pp. 18–20.
17. Kahn, Alfred J.: First Principles in Planning Community Services to Deal with Children in Trouble, *Social Service Review,* Vol. 30, December, 1956, p. 421.
18. Cuber, John F., and Harper, Robert A.: *Problems of American Society,* New York, Prentice-Hall, Inc., 1951, p. 27.
19. Woodward, Julian L.: Changing Ideas on Mental Illiness and Its Treatment, *American Sociological Review,* Vol. 16, August, 1951, p. 443.
20. Pamphlet, The Federal Delinquency Program Objectives and Operation under the President's Committee on Juvenile Delinquency and Youth Crime, and the Juvenile Delinquency and Youth Offenses Control Act of 1961 (Public Law 87–274) *Department of Health, Education and Welfare,* Office of the Secretary, Office of Special Assistant for Juvenile Delinquency, Washington, D.C., U.S. Government Printing Office, (O-624264) 1962, pp. 1–9.
21. *Ibid:* p. 1.
22. *Loc cit.:* p. 1.
23. *Ibid:* p. 2.

# NAME INDEX

# SUBJECT INDEX